CONTENTS

Dornier Do 335

In its intended role as a bomber destroyer the Dornier Do 335 Pfeil could have spelt disaster for the Allies. Very fast and well armed, it was another example of the innovative approach of German aircraft designers. It was also an example of one of the Luftwaffe's greatest problems in the closing stages of the war: fielding important new aircraft, too little and too late.

No-one can accuse the World War II German aircraft designers of conservatism, and while the majority of combat aircraft were of conventional design, there were many others which pushed the forefront of aeronautics. Unhampered by tradition, German designers sought fresh means to solve old problems, and in so doing provided the Allies in both East and West with a wealth of advanced research material following the end of hostilities. One of the most famous of the bizarre shapes which took to the air over Germany was the Dornier Do 335 Pfeil, a brave attempt to provide the Luftwaffe with a potent fighter-bomber, night fighter and reconnaissance platform.

Prof.-Dr. Claudius Dornier was the genius behind the famous company of Dornier-Werke GmbH, and he had established a long line of successful aircraft, notably in the field of flying boats. For most of the late 1930s and World War II, Dornier was primarily concerned with the production of bombers for the Luftwaffe. Since the end of World War I, Claudius Dornier had been interested in the field of centre-line thrust, whereby two engines shared the same thrust line – one pulling and one pushing. Benefits of this system were obvious over a conventional twin layout, with only the same frontal area as a single-engined aircraft, the wing left clean of engine nacelles and attendant structures, and no asymmetric pull if one engine cut out. However, problems did exist in the area of the drive shaft which drove the rear propeller.

Dornier's extensive flying-boat experience gave him a wealth of knowledge in simple centreline thrust arrangements, where two engines were mounted back-to-back over the centreline of many of his designs. By the mid-1930s he saw the possibility of using this concept to power a high-speed fighter, but first the rear engine extension shaft arrangement had to be proved. To that end Ulrich Hütter was commissioned to design a small test-bed for the arrangement. Designated the Göppingen Gö 9, and built by Schempp-Hirth, the test-bed featured a pencil-slim fuselage contained a 59.6-kW (80-hp) Hirth HM 60R engine mounted at the centre of gravity beneath the shoulder-set wing. Stalky main undercarriage units retracted into the wing, while a nosewheel unit retracted forward into the extreme nose. Behind the wing a long and slender tail boom hid the drive shaft which extended past a cruciform tail to a four-blade wooden propeller.

Flying for the first time in 1940, the Gö 9 proved that the rear pusher principle was both efficient and safe, which gave Dornier new impetus to his fighter designs taking shape on the drawing boards. However, the Technische Amt of the RLM decreed that Dornier abandon his work with fighters and return to the main job in hand of producing bombers and flying-boats, despite some initial interest in his radical designs. Nevertheless, in 1942 the Technische Amt issued a requirement for a high-speed unarmed intruder aircraft, and Dornier submitted his Projekt 231 design, incorporating the tractor-

The second production Do 335A-0 wears werk-nr 102 on its tail. To the RLM, the German air ministry, the Pfeil was projekt 231, but its prominent nose saw it dubbed ameisenbär (anteater) by its crews.

The Do 335 V1 differed most obviously from subsequent prototypes in having an extra oil cooler intake underneath. The first aircraft (CP+UA) took to the air on 26 October 1943.

Designed by Ulrich-Hütter, the all-wooden Göppingen G.9 was the testbed for the Do 335's aft-mounted prop design. Its Hirth engine was mounted below the wing and with it the G.9 reached a speed of 220 km/h (37 mph).

pusher engine arrangement. After evaluation, Dornier was awarded a development contract in the face of opposition from Arado and Junkers, and the designation Do 335 was assigned to Projekt 231.

As design got underway, the RLM issued a new directive to re-design the Do 335 as a multi-purpose day fighter, night fighter, fighter-bomber, Zerstörer and reconnaissance platform, which caused a delay in production of the prototype. By the autumn of 1943 the Do 335 was ready for flight.

Dornier's concept had emerged as a fearsome looking aircraft, appearing as purposeful as a fighter could. In the forward fuselage a Daimler-Benz DB 603 featured an annular-ring cowl, while exhaust stubs just aft of the trailing edge belied the position of the rear engine. Underneath the rear fuselage a large airscoop aspirated the second unit, which powered a three-blade propeller mounted behind

*The **Pfeil** was the first production aircraft to be fitted with an ejection seat; however, the system for actually escaping was a complicated one. German pilots told of how, during the test programme, two aircraft crashed and their pilots were found still in the cockpit but with their arms missing. This was supposedly due to too firm a grip being taken on the handles, which first jettisoned the canopy before the seat could be fired out.*

a cruciform tail. Under the centre-section of the wing were doors for a small weapons bay, capable of carrying a single 500-kg (1,100-lb) or two 250-kg (550-lb) bombs. The undercarriage was a tricycle arrangement, with the wide-track main units retracting inwards into the wing and the nosewheel retracting backwards (following a 90° rotation) into the area beneath the cockpit.

Remarkable shape, remarkable performance

The broad wing was set well back, and although the name Pfeil was used semi-officially, the service pilots who became acquainted with this extraordinary machine soon dubbed it 'Ameisenbär', thanks to its long nose. A Dornier pilot was at the controls for the first flight from Oberpfaffenhofen, this taking place on 26 October 1943 with the Do 335 V1 first prototype (CP+UA). After initial Dornier trials, the aircraft moved to Rechlin to begin extensive official trials. Reports from Oberpfaffenhofen and Rechlin were favourable, with only slight longitudinal stability problems encountered. Most pilots were surprised at the speed, acceleration, turning circle and general handling of the type, and development continued smoothly. Further prototypes joined Dornier and Rechlin trials, introducing new improvements such as redesigned undercarriage doors and blisters in the canopy accommodating mirrors for improved rearward vision.

By the fifth prototype, armament was installed, this comprising two MG 151 15-mm cannon in the upper fuselage decking and a single MK 103 30-mm cannon firing through the forward propeller hub. Subsequent prototypes were used for further flight trials and engine tests, culminating in the Do 335 V9 built to pre-production standards. The first Do 335A-0 pre-production aircraft (VG+PG) followed shortly in mid-1944, with full armament and ready to start operational evaluation. In September of that year, the Erprobungs-kommando 335 was established to conduct tactical development using many of the 10 Do 335A-0s built. Service trials began with the Do 335 V9 with the Versuchsverband des Oberfehlshabers des Luftwaffe.

By late autumn in 1944, the Do 335A-1 full production model appeared at Oberpfaffenhofen, this introducing the definitive DB 603E-1 engine and two underwing hardpoints capable of carrying fuel or 250-kg (550-lb) bombs. Similar in airframe details to the Do 335A-1 was the Do 335A-4 unarmed reconnaissance version. Only one was completed, adapted from a Do 335A-0 with two Rb 50/18 cameras in the weapons bay and increased external fuel. DB 603G engines were to have been fitted with higher compression ratio and more powerful superchargers.

Two-seat night fighter

Next in the line of Pfeil variants was the Do 335A-6 (prototype Do 335 V10) which was the night fighter variant. Armament remained unchanged from the fighter-bomber, but FuG 217J Neptun airborne intercept radar was added, the aerials being located forward of the wing (lateral beam port and vertical beam starboard). To operate the radar a second crewman was needed, and to accommodate him a cockpit was incorporated above and behind that of the pilot. Giving the Pfeil an even stranger appearance than before, the second cockpit also meant a considerable restructuring of the fuel system, with the weapons bay area given over to fuel carriage. The negative effect on performance of the extra cockpit, aerials, weight and other modifications such as flame-damping tubes over the exhaust ports was in the region of 10%, but production aircraft would have offset this partially by being fitted with water-methanol boosted DB 603E engines, instead of the DB 603A units retained by the sole example. Production was scheduled to have been undertaken by Heinkel in Vienna, but this plan was overtaken by events and the tooling never assembled.

The final pair of Do 355A variants were the Do 335A-10 and Do 335A-12, both featuring the second cockpit for use as conversion trainers. The former was powered by the DB 603A engine (prototype Do 335 V11) and the latter by the DB 603E (prototype Do 335 V12). With full controls in the raised cockpit for the instructor, the two prototypes were both delivered without armament, but this was rectified in the pair of Do 335A-12 production aircraft.

After development of fighter-bomber, reconnaissance, trainer and night fighter variants, the role of heavy Zerstörer was next to be developed, as a direct result of the worsening war situation. During the winter of 1944/45, the Do 335 V13 emerged from the

This was the seventh Do 335A-0 fighter to be built and was one of 10 evaluated by Erprobungskommando 335 which was formed in September 1944 to develop operational tactics for the type. The aircraft were armed with a 30-mm MK 103 cannon and a pair of 15-mm MG 151 machine-guns.

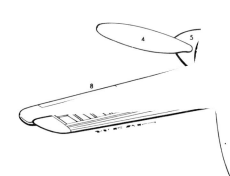

Dornier Do 335B-2 cutaway drawing key

1 Upper rudder trim tab
2 Upper rudder
3 Upper tailfin (jettisonable by means of explosive bolts)
4 VDM airscrew of 3.30 m (10.83 ft) diameter
5 Airscrew spinner
6 Airscrew pitch mechanism
7 Starboard elevator
8 Elevator tab
9 Metal stressed-skin tailplane structure
10 Ventral rudder
11 Tail bumper
12 Tail bumper oleo shock-absorber

23 Coolant radiator
24 Fire extinguisher
25 Ventral air intake
26 FuG 25a IFF
27 FuG 125a blind landing receiver
28 Rear engine access cover latches
29 Exhaust stubs
30 Supercharger intake
31 Coolant tank
32 Engine bearer

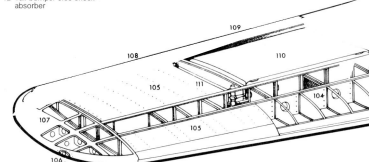

13 Ventral tailfin (jettisonable for belly landing)
14 Coolant outlet
15 Rear navigation light
16 Explosive bolt seatings
17 Rudder and elevator tab controls
18 Hollow airscrew extension shaft
19 Rear airscrew lubricant feeds
20 Aft bulkhead
21 Coolant trunking
22 Oil cooler radiator

33 Aft Daimler-Benz DB 603E-1 12-cylinder inverted-Vee liquid-cooled engine rated at 1340 kW(1,800 hp) for take-off and 1415 kW (1,900 hp) at 1800 m (5,905 ft)
34 Supercharger
35 Aft firewali
36 FuG 25a ring antenna
37 Fuel filler cap
38 Main fuel tank (1 230-litre/270 Imp gal capacity)
39 Secondary ventral fuel tank

Oberpfaffenhofen factory as the Do 335B-1. This aircraft featured the replacement of the weapons bay by a fuel tank, and the replacement of the 15-mm cannon by 20-mm MG 151 cannon. More heavily armed was the Do 335 V14 which, intended for service as the Do 335B-2, featured the same armament and an added Mk 103 30-mm cannon mounted in the wings.

In the event, these were the only B-series aircraft to be completed, although others were on the construction line at the termination of the project. These included more B-1 and B-2 prototypes, and a pair of Do 335B-6 prototypes, these being night fighters similar to the Do 335A-6 but with the heavy armament of the Do 335B-1. Other prototypes would have featured DB 603LA engines with a two-stage supercharger. One other development deserves mention, the B-4, B-5 and B-8 models which featured a 4.3 m (14 ft 10 in)

The nose-mounted Daimler-Benz DB603A-2 engine was provided with an annular nose radiator, while the ventral scoop intake was for the aft powerplant. The tractor propeller was pitch-reversible.

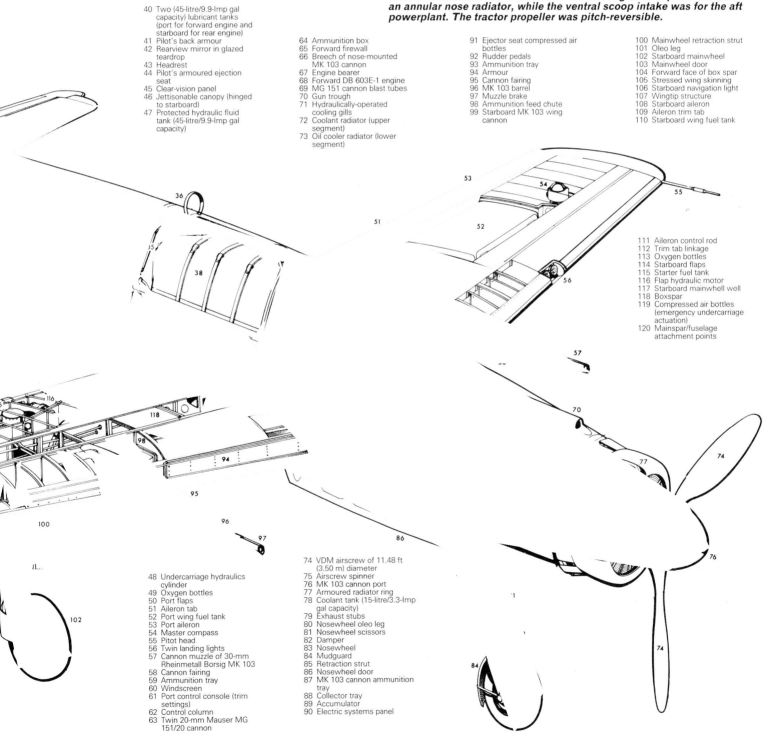

40 Two (45-litre/9.9-Imp gal capacity) lubricant tanks (port for forward engine and starboard for rear engine)
41 Pilot's back armour
42 Rearview mirror in glazed teardrop
43 Headrest
44 Pilot's armoured ejection seat
45 Clear-vision panel
46 Jettisonable canopy (hinged to starboard)
47 Protected hydraulic fluid tank (45-litre/9.9-Imp gal capacity)

64 Ammunition box
65 Forward firewall
66 Breech of nose-mounted MK 103 cannon
67 Engine bearer
68 Forward DB 603E-1 engine
69 MG 151 cannon blast tubes
70 Gun trough
71 Hydraulically-operated cooling gills
72 Coolant radiator (upper segment)
73 Oil cooler radiator (lower segment)

91 Ejector seat compressed air bottles
92 Rudder pedals
93 Ammunition tray
94 Armour
95 Cannon fairing
96 MK 103 barrel
97 Muzzle brake
98 Ammunition feed chute
99 Starboard MK 103 wing cannon

100 Mainwheel retraction strut
101 Oleo leg
102 Starboard mainwheel
103 Mainwheel door
104 Forward face of box spar
105 Stressed wing skinning
106 Starboard navigation light
107 Wingtip structure
108 Starboard aileron
109 Aileron trim tab
110 Starboard wing fuel tank

111 Aileron control rod
112 Trim tab linkage
113 Oxygen bottles
114 Starboard flaps
115 Starter fuel tank
116 Flap hydraulic motor
117 Starboard mainwhell well
118 Boxspar
119 Compressed air bottles (emergency undercarriage actuation)
120 Mainspar/fuselage attachment points

48 Undercarriage hydraulics cylinder
49 Oxygen bottles
50 Port flaps
51 Aileron tab
52 Port wing fuel tank
53 Port aileron
54 Master compass
55 Pitot head
56 Twin landing lights
57 Cannon muzzle of 30-mm Rheinmetall Borsig MK 103
58 Cannon fairing
59 Ammunition tray
60 Windscreen
61 Port control console (trim settings)
62 Control column
63 Twin 20-mm Mauser MG 151/20 cannon

74 VDM airscrew of 11.48 ft (3.50 m) diameter
75 Airscrew spinner
76 MK 103 cannon port
77 Armoured radiator ring
78 Coolant tank (15-litre/3.3-Imp gal capacity)
79 Exhaust stubs
80 Nosewheel oleo leg
81 Nosewheel scissors
82 Damper
83 Nosewheel
84 Mudguard
85 Retraction strut
86 Nosewheel door
87 MK 103 cannon ammunition tray
88 Collector tray
89 Accumulator
90 Electric systems panel

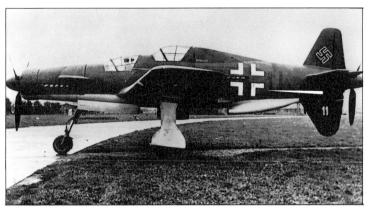

V11 was the prototype for the Do 335A-10 two-seat trainer. Both this and a second example (V12) were delivered unarmed, but the intention was to equip production models with the armament of the Do 335A-1.

increase in wing span for greater altitude performance. The development of these new outer wing panels had been undertaken by Heinkel, but they remained on the drawing board. Derivative designs included the Do 435 night fighter, with side-by-side seating, cabin pressurisation and long-span wings, the Do 535 mixed-power-plant fighter with the rear DB 603 replaced by a jet engine and the Do 635 long range reconnaissance platform which aimed to mate two Do 335 fuselages together with a new centre-section. At the termination of production, 37 Pfeils had been completed, with others awaiting final assembly and components for many more finished.

As far as is known, the Pfeil never entered into combat, although US pilots reported seeing the strange aircraft in the sky during forays over Germany. In it single-seat version it was one of the fastest piston-engined fighters ever built, with a claimed top speed of around 765 km/h (475 mph). Despite this high performance, it was the much slower two-seat night fighter version which would prob-

ably have proved the most effective if the war had continued. Equipped with excellent radar and powerful weapons, and blessed with good visibility, combat persistence and performance, the night fighter would have been excellent against the RAF bomber streams.

A complicated escape

Flying the Pfeil was an experience thanks to its high performance and unusual configuration. While the performance provided an exhilarating ride for the pilot, the configuration gave him a few consternations. His main concern was the ejection seat, the Do 335 being only the second production type to feature this. Before firing the seat, explosive bolts which held the upper vertical tail surface and rear propeller on were fired to clear a way for the egressing pilot. Despite the ejection seat he had to jettison the canopy manually. As another safety feature, the lower vertical tail surface was jettisonable in case a wheels-up landing was undertaken.

To conclude, the Pfeil proved to be a sound design with no major pitfalls. If development had been allowed to continue at a steady pace, the teething problems which remained with the type could have been ironed out at an early stage, and the Pfeil could have emerged as a warplane of major importance to the Luftwaffe. However, as the military situation facing Germany darkened during 1944/45, so development was rushed through at great speed. Also hampering development and production attempts was the state of Germany industry, which could not provide the sub-contracted components such as propellers, engines and radios fast enough.

No matter what the problems, the aviation enthusiast has been left the experience of witnessing one of the world's most exciting warplanes, and another chapter in the story of 'Might Have Been . . .'

The Do 335A-1, the initial production version, started to appear in the autumn of 1944. Emphasis soon switched to the Do 335B, the more heavily armed Zerstörer single-seat heavy fighter.

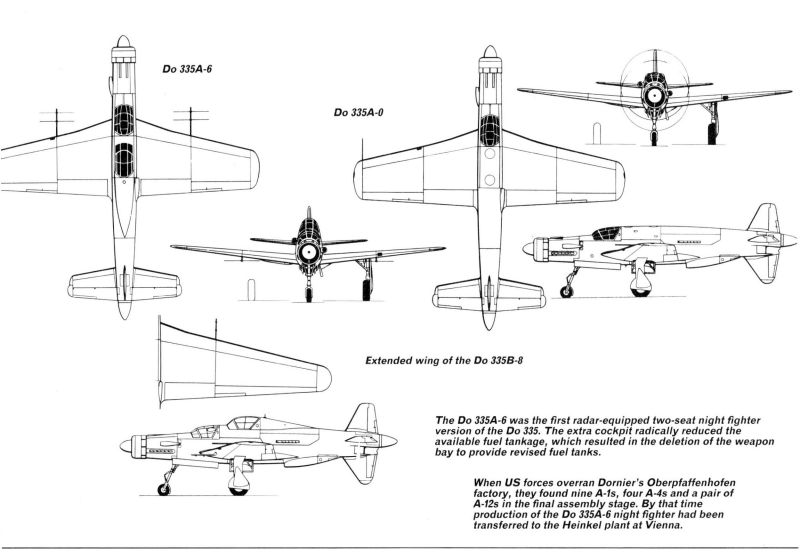

Do 335A-6

Do 335A-0

Extended wing of the Do 335B-8

The Do 335A-6 was the first radar-equipped two-seat night fighter version of the Do 335. The extra cockpit radically reduced the available fuel tankage, which resulted in the deletion of the weapon bay to provide revised fuel tanks.

*When **US** forces overran Dornier's Oberpfaffenhofen factory, they found nine A-1s, four A-4s and a pair of A-12s in the final assembly stage. **By** that time production of the Do 335A-6 night fighter had been transferred to the Heinkel plant at **V**ienna.*

Arado Ar 196

Like many of the new German warplanes developed clandestinely during the 1930s, the Ar 196 was blooded in the Spanish Civil War. Unlike most of its compatriots, however, it did not go on to enjoy a place in aviation history. Instead, Arado's torpedo-bomber fulfilled an unsung role aboard the Kriegsmarine's battleship fleet.

Although it exerted only a minor influence on World War II, the Arado Ar 196A was nevertheless an important type. Possessed of quite a useful performance, and remarkably heavily armed – typically with two cannon and three machine-guns – it served all round the coastal areas of Hitler's Europe and was also the standard aircraft carried aboard major surface warships of the German navy, the biggest battleships (*Bismarck* and *Tirpitz*) carrying four each.

The first shipboard aircraft of the resurrected German navy was the Heinkel He 60, a conventional biplane. All such aircraft had to be stressed for catapult launching, possibly while the ship was rolling or pitching in a heavy sea, and for subsequent recovery by crane after alighting on the open ocean, possibly with severe waves. The main purpose was short-range reconnaissance, but coastal patrol, rescue of downed aircrew and even local close support of ground forces (for example in anti-partisan operations) were all to become important secondary duties.

By 1936 it was clear that the He 60 was becoming outdated. Heinkel was invited to produce a successor, but the resulting He 114 proved to have extremely poor hydrodynamic and seakeeping qualities and to be deficient in other respects. After prolonged testing and modification of the He 114, it was decided in about October 1936 to issue a fresh specification and see if Arado Flugzeugwerke or the Focke-Wulf company could offer a better product. Focke-Wulf produced a conventional biplane in the Fw 62, but the Arado offering was a monoplane, with (surprisingly) a low-mounted wing.

The Kriegsmarine and Reichsluftfahrtministerium agreed that the aircraft should be powered by a BMW 132K nine-cylinder radial engine of 716 kW (960 hp) (virtually the same as the engine of the He 114). It was further stipulated that prototypes had to be produced with twin floats and with a single central float and small stabilising floats under the wingtips. The two rival companies quickly submitted drawings and costings and the Ar 196 was judged to be the more attractive. Two prototypes of the Fw 62 were ordered as an insurance, but four were ordered of the Arado. With works numbers 2589-2591, the first two (Ar 196 V1 and V2) were A-series aircraft with twin floats, while V3 and V4 were the B-series machines with a central float.

In many ways the 'eyes of the Kriegsmarine', the Arado Ar 196 had superb water and flight handling characteristics. During its early career its heavy armament made it the scourge of lumbering enemy maritime patrollers, although this was steadily reversed as the war progressed.

All were registered as civil aircraft (respectively D-IEHK, IHQI, ILRE and OVMB).

In some respects the prototypes were interim aircraft. Their engines were 657-kW (880-hp) BMW 132Dc type, driving a Schwarz two-bladed propeller. As originally built the first aircraft had twin exhaust pipes which were led round under the left side of the fuselage. Later the standard arrangement was twin shorter pipes discharging equally to left and right of the ventral centreline. The cowling fitted the engine tightly, with blisters over the valve gear, and cooling was controlled by trailing-edge hinged gills. Overall the aircraft needed very little modification, the only visible change between the first two prototypes being elimination of the balance horn at the top of the rudder and a slight increase in fin area. The V1 was also later fitted with the three-bladed VDM constant-speed propeller that was made standard. Very small modifications were made to the floats, the water rudders being modified.

Thus, V2 and V3 were similar apart from the latter's different float arrangement. V4, however, was fitted with more streamlined stabilising floats, with a simpler arrangement of struts. It also was the first Ar 196 to be fitted with armament, comprising a 20-mm MG FF cannon in each wing, fed from a 60-round drum which left a blister in the underside, plus a single 7.92-mm MG 17 machine-gun in the right side of the forward fuselage with its muzzle firing through the forward ring of the engine cowl (at about '8 o'clock' seen from the front), and a small container on the underside of each outer wing, just outboard of the cannon, for a single SC 50 (50-kg/110-lb) bomb.

The four seaplanes were carefully evaluated at Travemünde in 1937-38, but it proved difficult to decide which was the preferred float arrangement. The central float was considered preferable in operations from choppy water, but the stabilising floats of the version could easily dip into the sea during take-off, resulting in pronounced asymmetric drag and causing tricky problems. In the event, although a further A-series prototype was built (the V5, D-IPDB), it was decided to standardise on the twin-float arrangement and this was used on the 10 Ar 196A-0 pre-production aircraft which were delivered from the Warnemünde factory from November 1938.

Structurally the Ar 196 was conventional to the point of being traditional. While the wing was a two-spar all-metal stressed-skin component, the fuselage was constructed around a strong framework of welded steel tubes with light formers and stringers supporting a skin which was light alloy from the engine firewall to the rear cockpit and fabric from thence to the tail. The tail was a stressed-skin structure but with the movable surfaces covered with fabric. The floats were Alclad light alloy. Fuel was carried in two 300-litre (66-Imp gal) tanks, one in each float, with the feed pipes passing up the forward struts. The latter also incorporated protecting rungs forming a ladder with which the crew or servicing personnel could climb up to the engine or cockpit. Each wing carried slotted flaps and Flettner tabbed ailerons, and was arranged to fold to the rear, undersurface outermost, about a skewed hinge very close to the root. Folding the wings necessitated disconnecting the wing/float bracing struts.

The crew comprised a pilot and an observer/gunner. The latter normally faced aft, and as there was no fuselage tank the seats were close together. A continuous glazed canopy covered the cockpits, the pilot having a section sliding to the rear and the observer a sliding portion which originally could be

This view of the prototype Ar 196 shows the twin-float layout that became the standard. The horn balance on the rudder was discarded for the V2, which was similar apart from this and changes to the water rudders. Both aircraft flew in the summer of 1937.

completely closed. In the production versions the rear cockpit could not be totally enclosed, but wind deflectors avoided any discomfort and the definitive arrangement made it easier to aim the rear armament, which in the initial Ar 196A-1 version comprised a single 7.92-mm MG 15 machine-gun with seven 75-round saddle-type magazines. The forward-firing armament was omitted, the two SC 50 bombs were retained. The engine was changed for the definitive BMW 132K, driving a Schwarz three-bladed propeller with no spinner. A great deal of operational equipment was added in the production A-1 version, including catapult spools (the structure being locally strengthened), large smoke canisters in the floats, and also emergency rations, extra ammunition and flares in the aft part of the floats.

From the start the Ar 196A was extremely popular. Its performance was adequate, handling was superb both on the water and in the air, its reliability was excellent and the view from the cockpits very good despite the low-mounted wing.

Deliveries of the first 20 of the A-1 version started in June 1939. All this batch were assigned to Bordfliegerstaffeln (Nos 1/196 and 5/196), one of the first to go to sea being mounted on the catapult of the pocket battleship *Admiral Graf Spee*. This sailed for the south Atlantic in mid-August 1939, and on 13 December of that year encountered three (much less powerful) cruisers of the Royal Navy. Captain Langsdorff perhaps should

The Ar 196 V3 (illustrated) and V4 tested the single main float arrangement. Although this and the twin-float arrangement had many advantages, the water handling of the twin system was deemed to be more important than the choppy water landing characteristics of the single.

have launched his brand-new seaplane, which could then have directed the fire of his 28-cm (11-in) guns, while he steamed out of range of the British cruisers. Instead he closed with the British vessels, soon suffering crippling damage. As luck would have it, the very first salvo from the British ships struck the *Graf Spee*'s catapult and destroyed the Ar 196A-1 that might have turned the tables.

Subsequently, additional seaplanes replaced the He 60 in shore units as well as aboard all the Kriegsmarine's major surface warships. The very severe winter of 1939-40 delayed flight testing from Warnemünde, but the 20 A-1s were followed from November 1939 by the A-2 version. This was intended for a wider spectrum of duties than shipboard reconnaissance. Operating from shore bases it was expected to range over the North Sea and Baltic looking for shipping to harass and hostile aircraft to destroy, and it was fitted with the forward-firing armament. The MG 17 was installed in the right side of the nose, as in the V4 prototype, and two MG FF cannon were also fitted, installed in an improved way which left the wing undersurface undisturbed, the ammunition drum causing only a modest blister in the top of the wing. The pilot could elect to use the MG 17 only. Though they were not expected to be used very much, the cannon also gave the pilot a feeling of moral superiority, with the knowledge that the Arado could probably shoot down any hostile aircraft it was likely to encounter over the open ocean.

Inevitably the empty and gross weights kept rising, but the Ar 196 never became sluggish or difficult to handle. In 1940 the factory delivered 98, this total including the first few of 24 of a version designated Ar 196A-4. This replaced the A-1 aboard the warships, differing in having the forward-firing armament and also the additional FuG 16Z radio. A further change was that the Schwarz propeller was replaced by a VDM pattern with a spinner, as fitted to the modified V1 prototype. The V4 was also slightly stronger, for harsh shipboard use. On 26 May 1941 the great battleship *Bismarck* launched her Ar 196A-4s in an

Bordfliegerstaffel 1./196 and 5./196 were the two units responsible for providing aircraft for naval vessels, based initially at Wilhelmshaven and Kiel-Holtenau. This aircraft is seen on board the Prinz Eugen heavy cruiser.

The Ar 196 was designed to meet a requirement to replace floatplanes aboard large ships of the Kriegsmarine. Here one of the prototypes is tested aboard a ship. In operation the aircraft was catapulted into the air for take-off, and hoisted back on board the ship after a sortie.

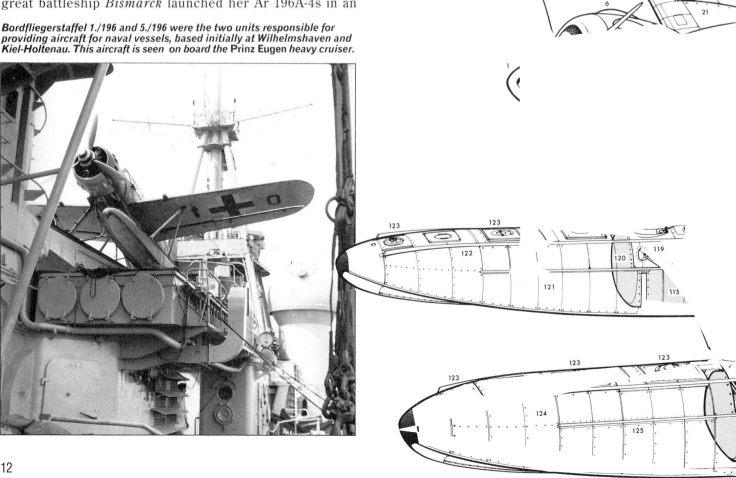

Arado Ar 196A-3 of 1./Bordfliegerstaffel 196, operating in the Lofoten Islands, Norway in February 1944.

Arado Ar 196A-3 cutaway drawing key

1 Spinner
2 Propeller hub
3 Starboard fuselage fixed 7.9-mm MG 17 gun port
4 Schwarz adjustable-pitch three-bladed propeller
5 Cowling ring
6 Cylinder head fairings
7 BMW 132K nine-cylinder air-cooled radial engine
8 Cowling panel frame
9 Quick-release catch
10 Cowling flaps
11 Engine lower bearers
12 Handholds
13 Engine accessories
14 Air louvre
15 Firewall bulkhead frame
16 Oil tank
17 Starboard MG 17 trough
18 Fuselage frame/engine support bearer attachment
19 Engine upper bearers
20 Forward fuselage decking
21 Starboard wing skinning

22 Leading-edge rib stations
23 Starboard outer rib
24 Starboard navigation light
25 Starboard wingtip
26 Starboard aileron
27 Aileron mass balance
28 Underwing access panel
29 Aileron control linkage
30 Windscreen
31 Instrument panel
32 Forward fuselage upper frame
33 Sea rudder lever
34 Handhold
35 Sea equipmenl locker (incl. drag-line and anchor/heaving-line)
36 Rudder pedal assembly
37 Seat support frame
38 Entry footstep
39 Seat adjustment handwheel
40 Armrest and seat harness
41 Control column
42 Pilot's seat
43 Sliding canopy
44 Rear-view mirror
45 Aerial mast

46 (Starboard) wing fold position
47 Pilot's headrest
48 Support frame
49 Canopy aft section
50 Aft canopy lock/release
51 First-aid kit
52 Observer/gunner's sliding seat
53 Entry footstep
54 Flare cartridge stowage
55 Chart table
56 Radio equipment
57 Fuselage frame/aft spar attachment
58 Wingroot fillet
59 Observer's sliding seat port
60 Ammunition box
61 Dorsal gun swivel mounting
62 Wind deflector plate
63 Ammunition feed
64 Ring sight
65 Twin 7.9-mm MG 81 flexible machine-guns
66 Flare bomb stowage
67 Gun support bracket
68 Fuselage aft frame

69 Master compass access
70 Fuselage skinning
71 Stringers
72 Elevator control cable linkage
73 Rudder controls
74 Tailfin/fuselage support/attachment bracket
75 Tailfin root fillet
76 Starboard tailplane section
77 Elevator mass balance
78 Starboard elevator section
79 Tailfin leading-edge
80 Rudder internal mass balance
81 Rudder tab linkage
82 Tailfin structure
83 Aerial
84 Aerial stub attachment
85 Rudder upper hinge
86 Rudder frame
87 Rudder post
88 Rudder tab
89 Elevator tab
90 Tab hinge
91 Elevator frame
92 Elevator mass balance

93 Tailplane structure
94 Elevator attachment
95 Rudder control linkage
96 Tailplane attachment
97 Elevator cable/rod link
98 Tie-down lug
99 Catapult attachment
100 Control lead
101 MG 81Z counterbalance
102 Wing attachment strengthening plate
103 Wing fold line
104 Gun charging cylinder
105 Ammunition drum 60 rounds
106 Port wing fixed 20-mm MG FF cannon
107 Cannon aft mounting bracket
108 Cartridge collector box
109 Cannon barrel support sleeve
110 Watertight muzzle cap
111 Forward spar attachment
112 Float forward strut/fuselage attachment
113 Tubular strut fairing
114 Inner Vee-strut

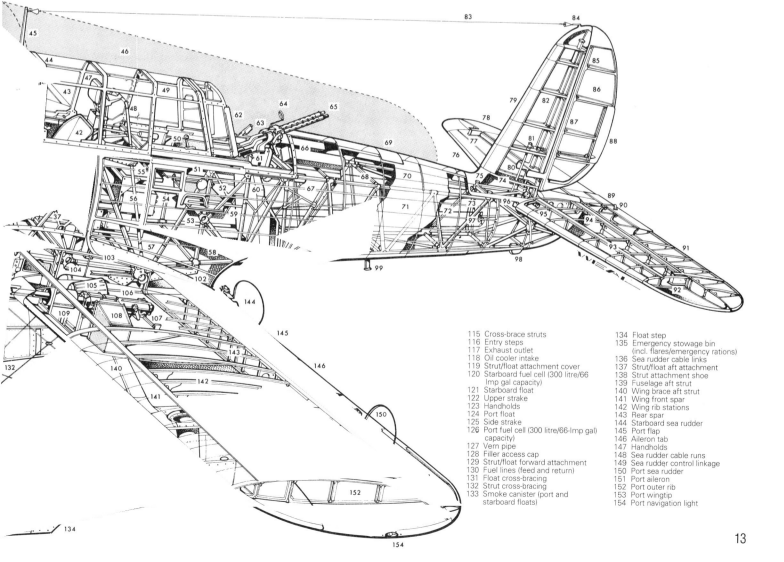

115 Cross-brace struts
116 Entry steps
117 Exhaust outlet
118 Oil cooler intake
119 Strut/float attachment cover
120 Starboard fuel cell (300 litre/66 Imp gal capacity)
121 Starboard float
122 Upper strake
123 Handholds
124 Port float
125 Side strake
126 Port fuel cell (300 litre/66-Imp gal capacity)
127 Vern pipe
128 Filler access cap
129 Strut/float forward attachment
130 Fuel lines (feed and return)
131 Float cross-bracing
132 Strut cross-bracing
133 Smoke canister (port and starboard floats)

134 Float step
135 Emergency stowage bin (incl. flares/emergency rations)
136 Sea rudder cable links
137 Strut/float aft attachment
138 Strut attachment shoe
139 Fuselage aft strut
140 Wing brace aft strut
141 Wing front spar
142 Wing rib stations
143 Rear spar
144 Starboard sea rudder
145 Port flap
146 Aileron tab
147 Handholds
148 Sea rudder cable runs
149 Sea rudder control linkage
150 Port sea rudder
151 Port aileron
152 Port outer rib
153 Port wingtip
154 Port navigation light

Arado Ar 196

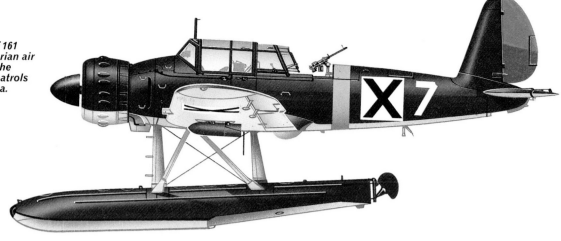

An Arado Ar 196A-3 of 161 Eskadra, Royal Bulgarian air force. This unit flew the Arado for Black Sea patrols from the base at Varna.

attempt to destroy or drive away the RAF Coastal Command Catalina flying-boat that was looking for the battleship as it raced for a home port. They did not succeed, and the 'Cat' called up Swordfish torpedo aircraft which, by crippling Bismarck's steering gear, sealed the ship's fate (it was sunk on 28 May).

On the other hand, on 5 May 1940 two A-2 seaplanes from 1/Küstenfliegergruppe 706, based at recently occupied Aalborg in Denmark, spotted a British submarine, HMS *Seal*, which had been damaged by a mine in the Kattegat. Unable to dive, the British submarine had to lie helplessly on the surface while an A-2 flown by Lt Günther Mehrens attacked with cannon and two bombs. When a second A-2 joined in the submarine surrendered. Mehrens alighted and took on board the submarine's commanding officer, taking him back to Aalborg.

Production in 1941 comprised 97 Ar 196s, almost all being of the definitive A-3 sub-type, which incorporated a few further structural changes and additions to the equipment. Production

Ar 196s were active over most European waters, from Norway to the Mediterranean. This Ar 196A-3 belonged to 4./Bordfliegergruppe 196, operational in the Adriatic in 1943. This aircraft often scouted ahead for warships, spotting targets at long range and warning of danger.

Ar 196A-1s were delivered for the shipborne patrol mission, 20 of which were followed by the Ar 196A-2 (illustrated). Intended for the coastal patrol mission, these were the first aircraft to feature the forward-firing armament for nuisance attacks against vessels.

in 1942 totalled 94 A-3s, and between July 1942 and March 1943 a further 23 were delivered from the French SNCA du Sud-Ouest factory at Bougenais (St Nazaire). The parent factory delivered 83 seaplanes in 1943, nearly all being of the final main production model, the A-5. This had a much more effective rear armament, comprising an MG 81Z twin-gun installation, with automatic mass balance and no fewer than 2,000 rounds in a continuous pair of belts. The MC 81 fired at 1,800 rounds per minute per gun. Other changes included the FuG 25a, and later the FuG 141, as well as the FuG 16Z radios. Cockpit instrumentation was improved and there were other minor changes.

In summer 1943 the Fokker works at Amsterdam was brought in to build the A-5 version, producing 69 by termination in August 1944. At Warnemünde production was terminated in March 1944 after the delivery of 22 of the A-5 version, bringing the total production of all versions to 541, including the 10 A-0s and five prototypes.

Almost all this considerable total operated from shore bases, mainly with See Aufklärungsgruppen, often in units partly equipped with the Bv 138 flying-boat. Two of the chief units were gruppen of SAGr.125, based first in the Baltic and later from Constanza for operations over the Black Sea, and SAGr.126 based on Crete and other locations for operations over the eastern Mediterranean and Balkans. Other units included SAGr.128, which operated over the western part of the Channel and the Bay of Biscay, and SAGr.131 which operated off the west coast of Norway until the autumn of 1944. Further Ar 196 seaplanes flew over the Black Sea with the 101st and 102nd coastal reconnaissance squadrons of the Royal Romanian air force, as well as the 161st coastal squadron of the Bulgarian air force. Most of these operations ceased by the late summer of 1944 as a result of the westward movement of the Eastern battlefront.

In 1940-41 Arado also built a small number of Ar 196B-0 seaplanes with the single central float configuration. Otherwise similar to the A-2, the B-series was for a time on the strength of Bordfliegerstaffel 1/196 at Wilhelmshaven. There was also a project for an Ar 196C, which would have been improved in equipment and in streamlining, but it was never built.

The crew of a 2./SAGr Ar 196A-3 prepare for launch from their Crete base in the summer of 1943. As the war neared its end, the Ar 196 gradually disappeared from service, although a few served through to the end. It was to be the last fighting floatplane built in Europe.

Arado Ar 196

The last and definitive model of the float plane was the Ar 196A-5, which featured improved radio equipment and improved defensive armament in the form of the MG81Z installation. Mounted in the rear cockpit, this paired two MG 81 7.9-mm (0.311-in) machine-guns on a single mount, with a maximum load of 2,000 rounds. Fixed forward-firing armament remained two 20-mm MG FF cannon in the wings and one MG 17 7.9-mm (0.311-in) machine-gun in the starboard cowling. This armament could be used against slow-moving aircraft, and for strafing surface targets. In the latter role the Ar 196 had underwing racks for a pair of SC 50 bombs (50 kg/227 lb). This Ar 196A-5 served with 2./Seeaufklärungsgruppe (SAGr) 125 in the eastern Mediterranean and Aegean Seas during 1943, alongside the Blohm und Voss Bv 138. The unit later became 4./SAGr 126 under the control of Luftwaffenkommando Südost.

Iain Wyllie

Messerschmitt Me 410 Bomber-Hunter

Several months before the Luftwaffe's much-vaunted Bf 110 Zerstörer received such a mauling at the hands of the RAF, Messerschmitt was already flying its successor. However, the new aircraft (Me 210) proved extremely troublesome, and it took a considerable redesign to produce an acceptable combat type. This aircraft, the Me 410, became widely respected in the latter part of the war.

In February 1944 a Staffel of the Luftwaffe's II/KG51, commanded by Maj Puttfarken, began flying intruder missions over England. Missions over the enemy country by long-range bomb-carrying night fighters had been almost unheard-of for more than a year. The aircraft used for the resumption was the Messerschmitt Me 410, and it was clear by this time that it was an outstanding aircraft: fast, heavily armed and a really formidable fighting machine. Puttfarken himself achieved five kills before he was shot down near Canterbury on 23 April.

All this was a great relief to Professor Dr-Ing Willy Messerschmitt, because to everyone's surprise the development programme for this aircraft could hardly have been a greater disaster. This shattered the previously sky-high reputation of Messerschmitt AG, and also was of great concern to the Luftwaffe.

Back in 1938 the Reichsluftfahrtministerium was wisely taking a long-term view and planning well ahead to make sure that all the Luftwaffe's future requirements would be met in good time. There was nothing wrong with Messerschmitt's Bf 110 twin-engined long-range fighter, but the Luftwaffe high command regarded this 'Zerstörer' class of aircraft as so overwhelmingly important that Messerschmitt was requested to prepare plans for a Bf 110 successor. The company's proposal was accepted in the summer of 1938, and contracts were placed for prototypes of rival designs, the Me 210 and Arado Ar 240. But the Arado submission was regarded as a mere backup. Messerschmitt's reputation was so high that the Me 210 contract included provisions for mass production of long-lead parts, such as wing spars and landing gears, and an option on the first 1,000 aircraft off the assembly line.

Messerschmitt's famed test pilot Dr-Ing Hermann Wurster made the maiden flight of the first prototype Me 210 on 5 September 1939, just after the start of World War II. He reported that handling in both the yawing and pitching planes was totally unacceptable, in fact dangerous. Seldom has a first-flight test report been so damning. This was a big setback, because the Augsburg-Haunstetten design team had tried to create a worldbeating multi-role aircraft able to fly the 'all can do' Kampfzerstörer missions as originally considered by the air staff in Berlin in 1934. These missions included air fighting, ground attack, dive bombing and reconnaissance. Now, it seemed, the new prototype was unfit even to fly.

Though it naturally made the maximum use of experience with the successful Bf 110, the Me 210 introduced many totally new features. One was that the nose was deep but very short. In fact the tip of the nose was well behind the propeller spinners. The pilot was right at the front, the forward-firing armament of two of the new Mauser MG151/20 cannon and two 7.92-mm MG17 machine-guns being under the floor, instead of in front of the instrument panel as in the Bf 110. Even more remarkable, under the cockpit floor was a substantial bomb bay, with two doors, able to accommodate two SC500 bombs of 500 kg (1,102 lb) each. Above and below the outer wings were large Venetian blind airbrakes for use during steep dive bombing attacks. A totally new feature was the very advanced rear defen-

With its neatly cowled engines and purposeful nose contours, the Messerschmitt Me 210 certainly looked the part, but it was plagued by vicious and unpredictable handling problems during its development. To rectify the matter the fuselage was considerably lengthened, as demonstrated by this aircraft.

sive armament. In the fuselage just aft of the wing was a large drum mounted transversely, rotated up or down by an electric motor. On this drum's left and right ends were mounted single 13-mm MG131 guns, pivoted so that they could swing out to the 90° abeam position. Each of these heavy machine-guns had 450 rounds. The whole FDL131 assembly was under the control of the observer, who faced aft and had an optical sight and remote aiming pistol-grips. These barbettes promised good firepower over the entire rear hemisphere with very little drag.

The Me 210 introduced several other new features. The tandem cockpits were covered by a multi-panel glazed Plexiglas canopy which wrapped round at the sides to give the backseater some vision downwards, so that he could fire at any fighter trying to find a 'blind spot' at six o'clock below and to the rear. The big main landing wheels were mounted inboard of single straight legs which during the retraction sequence turned to stow the wheels flat in the shallow rear of the nacelles, as in the Ju 88. The pilot and observer had hinged canopies, but instead of the roof opening up on transverse hinges each complete canopy section hinged to the right. A structural detail was that in the Bf 109 and 110 the engines were hung on bearers forged in solid Elektron (magnesium alloy), but the bearers in the Me 210 were hollow box-sections welded from steel sheet. The engines were Daimler-Benz DB601A-1s virtually identical to those fitted to the 1939 Bf 109 and 110, but the new fighter was expected to be faster than either.

New styling

Immediately after the first flight the prototype was rebuilt with a huge single-fin tail and new tapered tailplane. This resulted in only a small improvement, and throughout 1940 the increasing number of prototypes (suddenly reduced by the crash of the second on 5 September 1940) were exhaustively flown by company pilots and the Rechlin test centre. With production building up it was imperative to find complete solutions, but these proved elusive. By 1941 Me 210A-0s and A-1s were coming off the assembly lines at Augsburg

After some initial reservations regarding the aircraft's past, the Me 410 was found to be a potent warplane by Luftwaffe pilots, and achieved considerable success as a day-fighter against bomber formations. Against Allied fighters, however, it was cut to pieces.

and Regensburg and from the MIAG plant at Braunschweig, but eventually, after prolonged arguments, it was decided that the whole programme had to be terminated. Manufacture stopped at the three factories between January and March 1942. One of the results was the enforced resignation of Willy Messerschmitt.

Testing continued at full pressure, and on 14 March 1942 an Me 210A-0 flew with a longer and deeper rear fuselage, slatted outer wings and various other changes. It proved a great improvement. Work accordingly was rushed ahead on a new aircraft embodying these changes, as well as revised outer wings with straight taper instead of 5° sweepback, and much more powerful DB603 engines. To avoid the stigma attached to the number 210 this new aircraft was designated the Me 410.

While this work went ahead, many modifications were made to the dozens of Me 210s that were available. Existing A-1 and A-2 aircraft were fitted with the new rear fuselage and slats and issued to 16./ KG6 and later to III/ZG1, the latter unit also receiving many A-1s and A-2s which Messerschmitt received permission to complete in late 1942. These saw action in Sicily, Tunisia and Sardinia. Following tests with an A-0 fitted with DB605B engines, the Me 210C was put into production at Duna (Danube) aircraft works for both the Luftwaffe and Hungarian air force, using DB605B engines made by Manfred Weiss. Meanwhile there were schemes to replace the MG131 barbettes, which were troublesome, one featuring

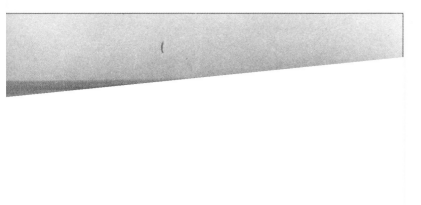

Me 410A-1 cutaway drawing key

1 Starboard navigation light
2 Starboard detachable wingtip
3 Main spar
4 Wing leading-edge slat
5 Aileron control rods
6 External balance (underwing)
7 Starboard aileron
8 Tab (ground-adjustable only)
9 Aileron trim tab
10 Trim tab control
11 Slatted airbrakes (above and below wing)
12 Wing centre/outer section join
13 Starboard underwing radiator
14 Boundary layer bleed
15 Radiator flap section
16 Radiator flap motor (in flap section)
17 Starboard oil filter
18 Cowling panelling
19 Starboard engine supercharger intake
20 Starboard nacelle
21 Exhaust stub cover
22 Oil cooler intake (adjustable flap)
23 Auxiliary intake
24 Coolant filter access
25 Spinner
26 Three-bladed constant-speed VDM propeller
27 Starboard mainwheel
28 Bomb-bay doors (open)
29 Two 7.9-mm MG 17 machine-gun ports
30 Two 20-mm MG 151 canno ports
31 Cabin air intake
32 Cabin air heater
33 Nose glazing
34 Rudder pedals
35 Instrument panel side sections
36 Instrument panel lower section
37 Control column
38 Pilot's heelboards
39 MG 151 cannon blast tube
40 Bomb bay
41 Bomb winch cable hoist
42 Port instrument console
43 Throttle quadrant
44 Pilot's seat
45 Starboard instrument console (weapons/oxygen)
46 Revi C/12D weapons sight
47 Armoured windscreen
48 Hinged cockpit canopy section
49 Pilot's armoured head/backrest
50 Canopy internal bracing
51 Ammunition magazines (1,000 rounds 7.9-mm/350 rounds 20-mm)
52 Pilot's entry handhold
53 Ammunition feed chutes
54 Port weapons breeches
55 Mainspar centre-section carry-through
56 Observer's seat
57 Electrical main distribution panel
58 Beam armament master switch and ammunition counter
59 Sighting head for FDSL beam barbettes
60 Hinged cockpit canopy section
61 Aerial mast (angled to starboard)
62 D/F loop aerial housing

63 Optically flat side windows
64 Barbette elevation input shaft
65 Barbette traverse input shaft
66 Observer's entry handhold
67 EZ2 D/F receiver remote control unit
68 FuG 10 radio receiver
69 EZ2 D/F receiver
70 FuG 10 radio transmitter
71 Rear spar centre-section carry-through
72 Wingroot fairing
73 Barbette electrics junction box
74 Access panel/handhold
75 Barbette torque amplifier
76 Barbette ring gears
77 Barbette centre rotating drum
78 Ammunition around drum (500 rpg)
79 Port beam gun fairing
80 13-mm MG 131 beam gun
81 Aerial unit
82 Rear fuselage access panel

83 FuG 25 IFF transformer
84 FuG 25 transponder
85 Aerial lead-in
86 Master compass
87 Fuselage frames
88 Course control drive

In Luftwaffe service the Me 210 proved up to the job, although its performance was less than sparkling. Its main problem by the time it entered service was its appalling reputation, which was also to dog the Me 410 soon after.

twin 20-mm MG151 cannon fixed to fire to the rear and aimed by the pilot via a tall aft-facing periscopic sight. A few Me 210B reconnaissance aircraft were built, and Blohm und Voss fitted seven A-1s as tandem dual trainers (the backseater, of course, facing forward).

In Hungarian service the Me 210C-1 and Ca-1 did well and were very popular. The Duna works delivered 267 aircraft before switching to the Bf 109G in March 1944, and the Hungarians used the speedy twin intensively on the Eastern Front.

Obviously the faults had been cured, and when the first Me 410 began flight testing in autumn 1942 it was the basis for an extremely useful aircraft. The new fuselage and new wing completely cured the previously terrible handling and tendency to flick into a spin, and the 1380-kW (1,850-hp) DB603A engines resulted in outstanding performance. With the MG131 barbettes now working well the Me 410A-1 Schnellbomber and Me 410A-2 Zerstörer began to come off the assembly lines in December 1942, and while production built up the Messerschmitt company and Luftwaffe armament and equipment centres developed a remarkable variety of schemes for different armament and mission equipment.

Comprehensive weapons fit

The basic models in production from January 1943 until September 1944 comprised the Me 410A series with DB603A engines and the Me 410B with 1417-kW (1,900-hp) DB603Gs and other minor changes. The standard armament was the same as for the Me 210A series: two MG151/20 and two MG17 firing forward and the MG131 barbettes at the rear. Aircraft with suffix /U1 had the MG17s removed and a single vertical reconnaissance camera installed in the rear fuselage. Those designated /U2 were equipped for the Zerstörer role with two MG151/20 cannon in the bomb bay, firing ahead. The /U2/R2 versions had the bomb bay fitted with two 30-mm MK103 or MK108 guns, the lower Plexiglas pane in the nose being replaced by a metal plate. The /U2/R5 conversion – like the others intended mainly for shooting down heavy bombers by day – installed four MG151s in the bomb bay, giving six 20-mm firing ahead. Equally heavy armament was provided by the /U2/R4, which added the two MG151s in the bomb bay, in a Waffenbehälter, followed by two further MG151s underneath in a Waffentropfen. The /U4 conversion fitted a single BK5 50-mm gun. The first conversions had no other forward-firing armament. Newly built A-2/U4s followed with the BK5 plus the twin MG151s and twin MG17s, and a further 100 field conversion kits were supplied comprising the BK5 plus two 30-mm

Despite its new designation, the Me 410 was very similar to its predecessor. This is the Me 410 V1, which had previously been one of the Me 210A-0 pre-production aircraft. Principal differences were the adoption of the DB 603A engine and a revised wing planform.

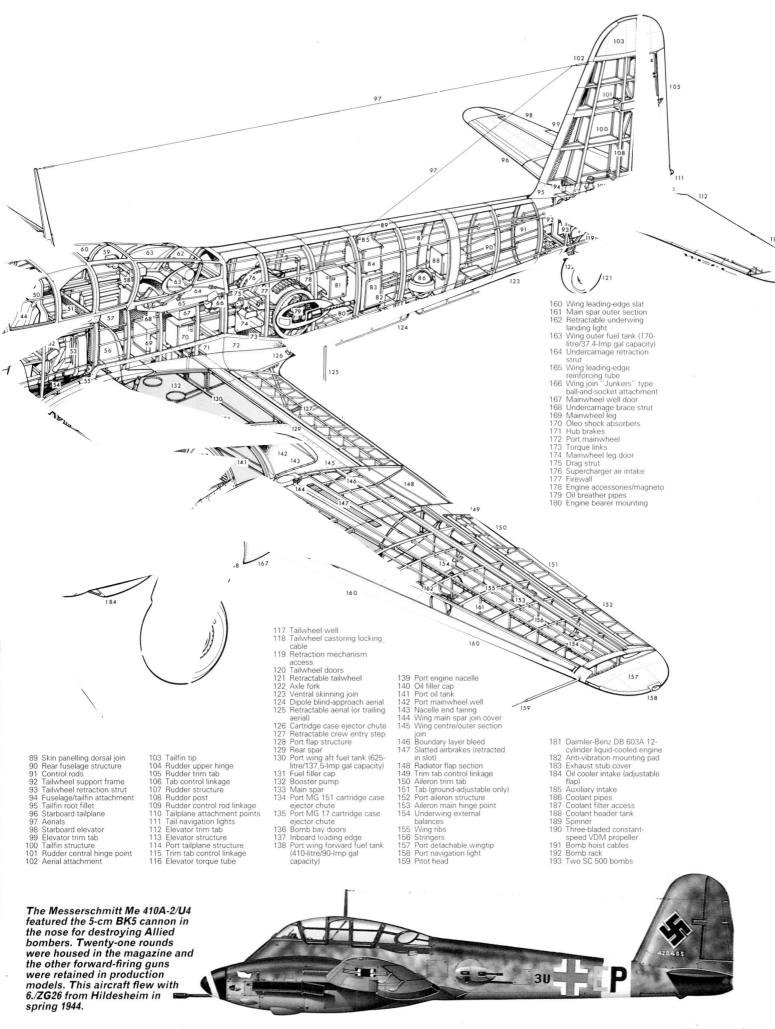

160 Wing leading-edge slat
161 Main spar outer section
162 Retractable underwing landing light
163 Wing outer fuel tank (170-litre/37.4-Imp gal capacity)
164 Undercarriage retraction strut
165 Wing leading-edge reinforcing tube
166 Wing join ''Junkers'' type ball-and-socket attachment
167 Mainwheel well door
168 Undercarriage brace strut
169 Mainwheel leg
170 Oleo shock absorbers
171 Hub brakes
172 Port mainwheel
173 Torque links
174 Mainwheel leg door
175 Drag strut
176 Supercharger air intake
177 Firewall
178 Engine accessories/magneto
179 Oil breather pipes
180 Engine bearer mounting

117 Tailwheel well
118 Tailwheel castoring locking cable
119 Retraction mechanism access
120 Tailwheel doors
121 Retractable tailwheel
122 Axle fork
123 Ventral skinning join
124 Dipole blind-approach aerial
125 Retractable aerial (or trailing aerial)
126 Cartridge case ejector chute
127 Retractable crew entry step
128 Port flap structure
129 Rear spar
130 Port wing aft fuel tank (625-litre/137.5-Imp gal capacity)
131 Fuel filler cap
132 Booster pump
133 Main spar
134 Port MG 151 cartridge case ejector chute
135 Port MG 17 cartridge case ejector chute
136 Bomb bay doors
137 Inboard leading edge
138 Port wing forward fuel tank (410-litre/90-Imp gal capacity)

139 Port engine nacelle
140 Oil filler cap
141 Port oil tank
142 Port mainwheel well
143 Nacelle end fairing
144 Wing main spar join cover
145 Wing centre/outer section join
146 Boundary layer bleed
147 Slatted airbrakes (retracted in slot)
148 Radiator flap section
149 Trim tab control linkage
150 Aileron trim tab
151 Tab (ground-adjustable only)
152 Port aileron structure
153 Aileron main hinge point
154 Underwing external balances
155 Wing ribs
156 Stringers
157 Port detachable wingtip
158 Port navigation light
159 Pitot head

181 Daimler-Benz DB 603A 12-cylinder liquid-cooled engine
182 Anti-vibration mounting pad
183 Exhaust stub cover
184 Oil cooler intake (adjustable flap)
185 Auxiliary intake
186 Coolant pipes
187 Coolant filter access
188 Coolant header tank
189 Spinner
190 Three-bladed constant-speed VDM propeller
191 Bomb hoist cables
192 Bomb rack
193 Two SC 500 bombs

89 Skin panelling dorsal join
90 Rear fuselage structure
91 Control rods
92 Tailwheel support frame
93 Tailwheel retraction strut
94 Fuselage/tailfin attachment
95 Tailfin root fillet
96 Starboard tailplane
97 Aerials
98 Starboard elevator
99 Elevator trim tab
100 Tailfin structure
101 Rudder central hinge point
102 Aerial attachment

103 Tailfin tip
104 Rudder upper hinge
105 Rudder trim tab
106 Tab control linkage
107 Rudder structure
108 Rudder post
109 Rudder control rod linkage
110 Tailplane attachment points
111 Tail navigation lights
112 Elevator trim tab
113 Elevator structure
114 Port tailplane structure
115 Trim tab control linkage
116 Elevator torque tube

The Messerschmitt Me 410A-2/U4 featured the 5-cm BK5 cannon in the nose for destroying Allied bombers. Twenty-one rounds were housed in the magazine and the other forward-firing guns were retained in production models. This aircraft flew with 6./ZG26 from Hildesheim in spring 1944.

Messerschmitt Me 410: Bomber-Hunter

Although never rivalling the de Havilland Mosquito in terms of versatility or performance, the Me 410 did however introduce a welcome increase in performance over the Messerschmitt Bf 110 that had previously equipped the Zerstörergeschwader. The aircraft certainly had some notable features, including the bomb bay which was mounted under the nose and forward cockpit. Able to take two bombs of up to 500-kg (1,102-lb) size, these were attached to a lowered rack which was then hoisted back into the bomb bay. The 13-mm MG131 beam guns were also notable, these traversing through 70° above and below the horizon and through 40° of azimuth, with contact breakers interrupting the firing if the guns pointed at the aircraft structure.

Specification
Messerschmitt Me 410A-1/U2

Type: two-seat heavy fighter (Zerstörer)

Powerplant: two Daimler Benz DB 603A inverted V-12 engines, each rated at 1305.5 kW (1,750 hp) for take-off, 1380 kW (1,350 hp) at 2100 m (6,890 ft) and 1212 kW (1,625 hp) at 5700 m (18,700 ft)

Performance: maximum speed 507 km/h (315 mph) at sea level, 624 km/h (388 mph) at 6700 m (21,980 ft) and 600 km/h (373 mph) at 8000 m (26,250 ft); maximum cruising speed 587 km/h (365 mph); range at maximum cruising speed 1200 km (746 miles); range at economical cruise 1690 km (1,050 miles)

Weights: empty equipped 7518 kg (16,574 lb); loaded 9651 kg (21,276 lb)

Dimensions: wing span 16.35 m (53 ft 7¾ in); length 12.48 m (40 ft 11½ in); height 4.28 m (14 ft 0½ in); wing area 36.20 m² (389.687 sq ft)

Armament: two 20-mm (0.79-in) MG 151 cannon with 350 r.p.g. and four 7.9-mm (0.31-in) MG 17 machine-guns with 1,000 r.p.g. in lower fuselage firing forwards; two 13-mm (0.51-in) NG 131 machine-guns with 500 r.p.g. in remotely-controlled FDSL lateral barbettes

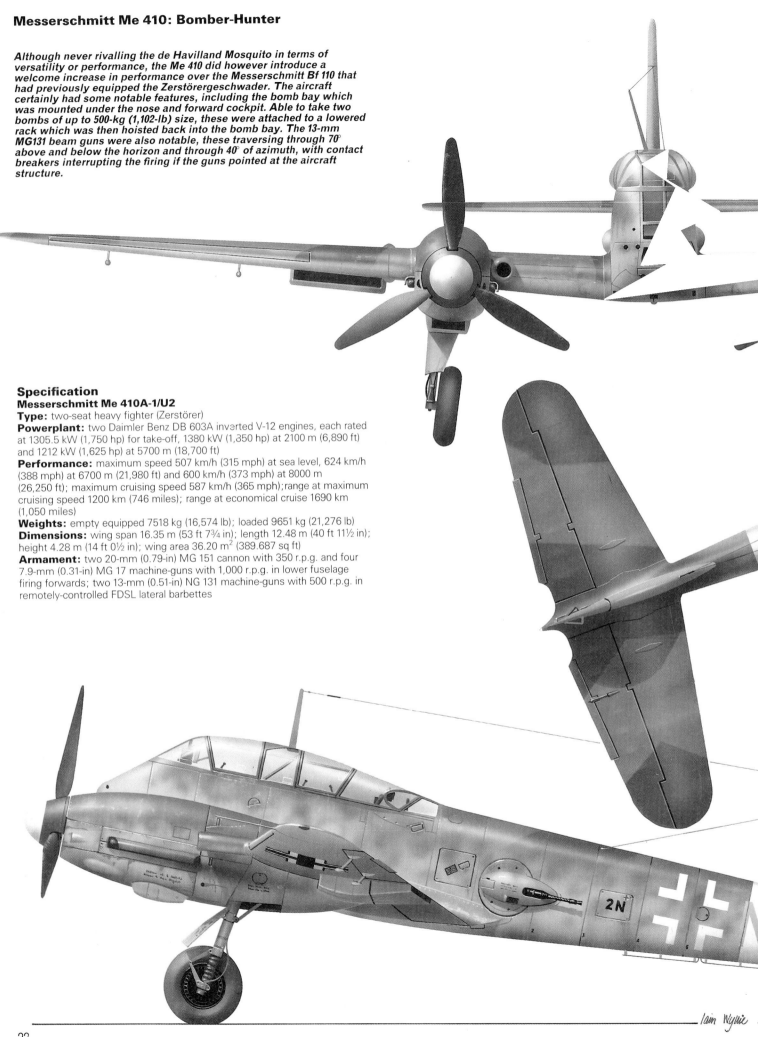

Iain Wyllie

Messerschmitt Me 410: Bomber-Hunter

Messerschmitt Me 410s served on Eastern, Mediterranean and Western fronts. This aircraft flew with I./SG 152 during the winter of 1943/44, when the unit was based at Deblin-Irena in Poland.

MK103 and the associated ZFR 4a gunsight, the resulting designation again being B-2/U4. The rare Me 410B-6 had the twin MK103s in the bomb bay and two MG131s in place of the MG17s. Another rarity was the B-5 torpedo bomber which carried any of a variety of torpedoes slung under the left side of the fuselage. Forward-firing armament was reduced to just the two MG151s, and most of these aircraft were fitted with FuG 200 Hohentwiel search radar. As well as the special Friedensengel gliding torpedo, B-5s tested the SB800RS Kurt 800-kg (1,765-lb) rolling bomb for use against surface ships, and the SB1000/410 blast weapon specially designed for external carriage by the B-5, with an elliptical low-drag cross-section and small drag chute to stabilise its fall. I/ZG1 used the B-6 variant, which had twin MG151/20s, twin MG131s and two MK103s plus Hohentwiel radar. They operated in the anti-ship role before being thrust into the anti-bomber battle, the radar then usually being removed.

Defence of the Reich

By mid-1944 almost all surviving Me 410s were engaged in the defence of the Reich against day bombers. With their speed and firepower they brought down many bombers, but overall the scoring rate was probably about even because the big twins were easy meat for escorting P-51s and P-47s. More fortunate were the Me 410A-3 and B-3 reconnaissance versions, which from December 1943 were built in numbers and, except over England, were fast enough to do much good work with modest attrition. Unlike the inadequate A-1/U1 they had a properly designed installation of two Rb 20/30, 50/30 or 75/30 cameras in the deepened underside of the nose in what in other versions was the bomb or heavy gun bay.

The Me 410 had by 1944 fully established a good reputation in the Luftwaffe, and because of the wide publicity given to II/ZG26 as the Hornissengeschwader it became unofficially known as the Hornet. Many were used for special test and trials programmes. At least one tested the experimental rapid-fire 210-mm rocket launcher. Many Luftwaffe fighters had used the 210-mm rocket using clumsy Wfr.Gr.21 mortar tubes under the wings. The auto launcher was a big drum mounted inside the Me 410 weapon bay, tilted up at the usual angle and with the 'six o'clock' tube exposed underneath the aircraft. On lining up on a bomber the pilot could blast off all six rockets from the drum in less than two seconds. Initial trials seriously damaged the Me 410, but after much effort the system was made to work and it was subjected to combat trials in several Me 410Bs, though the results appear to have been lost.

Swan song

By early 1944 the Messerschmitt design team was busy with a stretched version, the Me 410C. This was intended to have much higher performance at high altitudes, even though it was intended to carry heavier loads of weapons and, in some versions, night interception radar. Two new wings were designed, with span increased to 18.25 m (60 ft) or 20.45 m (67 ft). More powerful engines fitted with turbosuperchargers were to be used, either the DB603JZ, Jumo 213E/JZ or BMW 801TJ. All were to drive propellers with four very broad blades, and the Daimler-Benz engine was to have annular nose radiators replacing the usual ones under the rear part of the wings. At least two Me 410s tested the annular-cowled engines and the 410C's proposed revised forward fuselage and new main landing gears with twin wheels retracting straight to the rear without a 90° twist. Such were the problems afflicting the industry that before any 410C could be completed the programme was abandoned. In its place came the Me 410D, with the new twin-wheel gears, annular-cowled 603JZ engines and revised forward fuselage (which was expected to give better pilot view and lower drag). A further feature was outer wing panels which, though similar aerodynamically to those previously in production, were made of wood to conserve strategic materials.

Even this achieved nothing. Other wood programmes were in severe difficulty with adhesives and structural failures, and in summer 1944 the 410D was itself replaced by an interim Me 410H with no major change from the 410B-2 except the addition of extra untapered wing panels between the engines and the outer wings. These would have extended span to 23 m (75 ft) but the first conversion was never completed.

Test flights with the elongated fuselage revealed the Me 210 to be an adequate warplane, and the few that had been built were modified and cleared for service. Here a pre-production Me 210A-0 (background) formates on an Me 210A-1.

The lengthening of the fuselage and fitment of automatic wing slots mostly cured the instability problem, allowing some Me 210As to see action with the Luftwaffe. These aircraft are of III./ZG1, seen operating in Tunisia during March/April 1943.

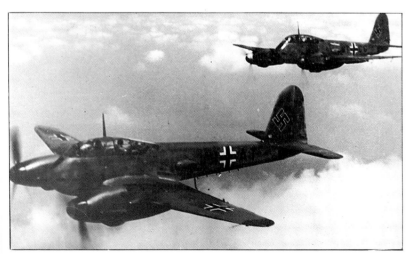

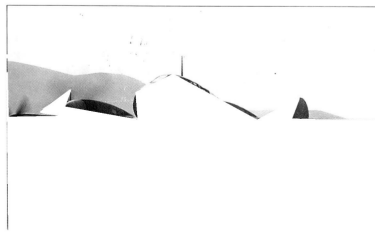

Dornier's Flying Pencil

From the outset, Dornier's Do 17 was an impressive design. It worried the Royal Air Force, as it was faster than any of their front-line fighters of the time, and with the coming of the Spanish Civil War it showed its deadly potential to maximum effect. Its speed made Hitler's Blitzkrieg possible, while later versions became the scourge of the Allied bomber effort.

It is commonly thought that the fast new bombers of the Luftwaffe in the late 1930s were developed clandestinely in the guise of civil transports. Certainly, anyone who studied the Do 17 V1, the first prototype of a totally new high-speed landplane built by the Dornier-Werke GmbH at Friedrichshafen in mid-1934, would have said such a conclusion was obvious. So slim that it was soon dubbed 'fliegender breistift' (flying pencil), the type looked every inch a fast bomber with its superb lines, small single-finned tail, blended wing/fuselage aerodynamics and landing gear units retracting into the nacelles of the BMW engines. As an airliner it was a joke, with a cramped cubbyhole for two immediately aft of the flight deck and a four-seat box aft of the wing with headroom of 1.22 m (4 ft). Anyone could see the wing was placed in the shoulder-high position in order to leave room for a big bomb bay under it.

From the first flight on 23 November 1934 the Do 17 handled well, but though two further prototypes were speedily completed and tested by the airline Deutsche Lufthansa, it was reluctantly agreed that the type was not suited to carrying passengers. For, despite all appearances, the Do 17 really had been designed as a fast six-passenger mailplane! The prototypes languished in a hangar at the Löwenthal factory, where by chance they were spotted by Flugkapitän Robert Untucht, famed Luthansa test pilot and RLM (air ministry) liaison officer. He instantly drew the obvious conclusion, which apparently had not occurred to anyone else, and tested one of the aircraft. His enthusiasm led to the Do 17 V4, a bomber prototype with twin fins. Further prototypes followed, the Hispano-engined Do 17 V5 reaching 391 km/h (243 mph). As this was well above the

speed of any fighter in the service it was hoped defensive guns would not be needed, but eventually the Do 17E-1 went into production at the company's new factories at Löwenthal, Manzell and Allmansweiler in 1936 with hand-aimed MG 15s firing above and below at the rear, and with a bomb load of up to 750 kg (1,653 lb). With a shortened glazed nose, the Do 17E-1 and corresponding Do 17F-1 reconnaissance aircraft were not quite so elongated, but when a staffel of 15 F-1s went to Spain in spring 1937 its Do 17s easily outpaced Republican fighters, and aircraft of this type quickly replaced the Heinkel He 70 in reconnaissance wings. Do 17E-1s also served in Spain, with 1 and 2/K 88, along with a more powerful version, the Do 17P with 645-kW (865-hp) BMW 132N radials. Both remained standard types, serving with Grupo 27 of the Spanish EdA (air force) until 1949.

Foreign service and operations

In July 1937 the Do 17 V8 (also known as the Do 17M V1) appeared at the prestigious International Military Aircraft Competition at Zurich. It impressed everyone with its clean lines, and when it easily won the Circuit of the Alps, pulling far ahead of every fighter at the meeting, the media had a field day. What was not reported was that its 746-kW (1,000-hp) DB 600A engines had been earmarked for

Fitted with BMW-Bramo 323P Fafnir engines rated at 745.7 kW (1,000-hp) for take-off, the Dornier Do 17Z-2 appeared in 1939 capable of carrying a 1000-kg (2,205-lb) bomb load. This example was one of the last in front-line service, fighting on the Eastern Front in 1942 with 15.(Kroat)/KG 53.

Many of the Do-17s surviving into 1941 served with **KG 2**, and this Do 17Z-2 flew with that unit's I Gruppe based at Tatoi, Greece, in May 1941. Do 17Zs could undertake shallow diving attacks at speeds up to 595 km/h (370 mph) on account of their sturdy structure. **KG 2** was soon to take its Do 17s to the **USSR**.

Early in 1942, Hermann Goering presented 15 ex-Luftwaffe Do 17Z-2s to the Finnish air force where they supplanted Bristol Blenheims with PLeLv 46 and enjoyed considerable success against the Russians. This example survived the war and was flown for several years after by PLeLv 43 on reconnaissance duties.

fighters, so the production Do 17M bomber had Bramo 323A-1 Fafnir radial engines of the same power. They also had the short rounded nose of the Do 17E and Do 17F, but Yugoslavia was so impressed at Zurich that its delegation bought 20 Do 17Ks plus a manufacturing licence, this model retaining the original long nose but being powered by Gnome-Rhône 14N radials of 731 kW (980 hp). The Do 17K had a 20-mm cannon and three machine-guns, but still reached 417 km/h (259 mph). When Germany invaded Yugoslavia on 6 April 1941 70 Do 17Ks of various sub-types were on strength, 26 being destroyed on the ground but others seeing prolonged and hectic action. A few were eventually put into servce by the Croatian puppet air force against Soviet partisans, while on 19 April 1941 two escaped to Heliopolis, Egypt, with cargoes of gold, subsequently serving with the RAF as AX706/707.

Fighting over Spain against the Polikarpov I-16 had suddenly showed the Dornier's vulnerability, and in late 1937 a completely new forward fuselage was designed to provide much more room for an enlarged crew and better arcs of fire for the guns. First flown in early 1938 on the DB-engined Do 17S and Do 17U versions, the new front end went into major production with the Do 17Z series of bombers, reconnaissance aircraft and night-fighters, all powered by the Fafnir. With a maximum load of 1000 kg (2,205 lb) the Do 17Z-2 was virtually the standard 'Dornier' during the great battles of 1940. Over 500 had been built when production was stopped in mid-year, and these aircraft saw much service with KG 2, KG 3, KG 53 (Croatian) and the Finnish air force.

The Do 17Z-6 Kauz (screech-owl) was a night-fighter fitted with the nose of a Ju 88C-2 complete with one cannon and three MG 17s. This was followed by the properly planned Do 17Z-10 Kauz II, with the world's first FLIR (forward-looking infra-red) detector, two cannon and four machine-guns. The first of several Do 17Z-10 kills

was gained by Oberleutnant Becker on 18 October 1940; it was a Vickers Wellington over the Zuyder Zee. By late 1940 the Do 17Z-10 was being replaced by the Do 215B. The 215 designation was chosen by the RLM for export versions of Do 17Z, the only sale being to Sweden in late 1939, which selected the 820-kW (1,100-hp) DB 601A engine. The 18 Do 215B-1 aircraft involved were never exported, but were taken over by the Luftwaffe as fast reconnaissance machines. At least 20 of the last batch of Do 215B-4s were completed as Do 215B-5 night-fighters with not only the IR sensor but also the first Lichtenstein radar. Again Becker scored the first kill, on 9 August 1941, with four more by 2 October to become the first night ace.

In 1937 the RLM had called for an enlarged Do 17Z with much heavier bomb load and considerably greater fuel capacity, able to accept any of a range of engines, and equally capable at level or dive bombing. First flown in August 1938, the Do 217 V1 was powered by 802-kW (1,075-hp) DB 601A engines, but despite its similar appearance to the Do 17/215 it was a totally new design. It soon showed that it was less pleasant to fly, and in fact crashed, but development continued. Prototypes flew with Junkers Jumo 211A and BMW 139 engines before the big BMW 801 was used in the Do 217 V9 prototype of January 1940. By this time handling was acceptable, the leading edges of the fins being slotted, but the unique dive brake, which opened like a giant cross at the extreme tail, caused endless difficulty. In mid-1941, after wing brakes had been tried and several aircraft lost, the RLM abandoned its stance that the heavy Do 217 had to be a dive bomber.

The heavyweight arrives

First to enter service, in late 1940, the Do 217E-1 was the first bomber model, with the massive bomb load of 4000 kg (8,818 lb), of which 2517 kg (5,550 lb) was inside the bomb bay. A handful to fly,

The original 'flying pencil': Dornier's Do 17V1 fast mailplane caused much anxiety in Britain and France when it appeared in late 1943, as its military potential was both obvious and frightening. A year later all fears were realised when the twin-fin Do 17V4 bomber prototype was rolled out.

The initial production bomber version was the Do 17-1, which began equipping the Kampfgeschwader in 1937. It was soon to receive its baptism of fire in Spanish skies, alongside the similar Do 17F-1 reconnaissance version. This E-model of 7./KG 255 is seen with national insignia painted over for the 1938 war games.

KG 2 became the only Geschwader to be completely equipped with the Do 217. Originally beginning replacement of the Do 17Z in 1941, KG 2 pulled back from the Russian front and relocated to the Netherlands for bombing and anti-shipping strikes over the North Sea. This is a Do 217E-2/ R19 of 9./KG 2 with two MG 81 machine-guns in the tailcone.

but still a most effective bomber, the Do 217E-1 had a hand-held 20-mm MG FF in the nose, used by KG 40 against ships in the Atlantic, and seven MG 15s. The Do 217E-2 introduced the EDL 131 electric dorsal turret with the excellent MG 131 gun, a hand-aimed MG 131 being in the ventral position, a fixed MG 151/15 firing ahead and three hand-aimed MG 15s completing the defence, though R19 (the 19th in the *Rüstsatz* series of field kits) added twin or quadruple MG 81 machine-guns firing aft from the tailcone. Other *Rüstsätze* added barrage cable cutters and various weapon kits, by far the biggest of which hung two Hs 293 anti-ship missiles under the wings, with Kehl/Strassburg radio command guidance link. The first operational missile carrier was the Do 217E-5, flown by II/KG 100, which went into action with increasingly devastating effect against British ships from 25 August 1943.

Night-fighter

With the Do 217E subtypes Dornier got the much heavier Do 217 family into service, and all subsequent models proved adequate but generally (and, in the case of the Do 217K-2, severely) underpowered. Despite this, and the absence of the 1491-kW (2,000-hp) engines that were needed, Dornier proposed in early 1941 to develop a night intruder fighter version. The result was the Do 217J, with plenty of fuel and weapons for missions over the UK, but Hitler personally stopped further such flights from 12 October 1941 so the Do 217J served only over Germany and, from September 1942, over Italy with the Regia Aeronautica. Equipped with early radar, usually FuG 202 Lichtenstein BC, the Do 217J-2 retained the turret and lower rear gun of the Do 217E-2 but had a new nose with four MG FFs and four MG 17s. Eight 50-kg (110-lb) SC50 bombs could be carried in the rear bomb bay, though this provision was removed from the Do 217J-2 version.

On 31 July 1942 Dornier flew the first Do 217N, with 1380-kW (1,850-hp) DB 603A engines. A much better, but still not brilliant, night-fighter, the Do 217N carried a heavier load of avionics and, for use on the eastern front, restored the rear bomb bay. The Do 217N-2 had wooden fairings in place of the turret and lower rear gun, but most had the new SN-2 radar and an increasing number were fitted with *schräge Musik* oblique upward-firing cannon, the usual fit being four 20-mm MG 151 of the type which by the start of Do 217N-2 production had also replaced the forward-firing MG FFs. Only 364 Do 217Js and Do 217Ns were delivered, and they had faded from the NJG (night fighter wings) front line by mid-1944.

Proven in action

In 1941 Dornier had again enlarged the crew compartment, this time eliminating the windscreen and glazing the whole nose as in many other German types of the period. The Do 217K-1 bomber entered service with KG-2, replacing the last of the Do 17Z-2s, in October 1942. Crews initially felt vulnerable surrounded by Plexiglas, but the Do 217K-1 was better arranged and also introduced a braking parachute made of Perlon, a nylon-like material. In December 1942 the Do 217K-2 followed it into service, this having the span greatly increased to lift two of the formidable FX, or FX 1400 or Fritz X, guided bombs. Each of these weighed 1570 kg (3,461 lb) and the Kehl/Strassburg command link steered it in azimuth and pitch. Major Bernhard Jope's III/KG 100 at Istres had a field-day on 9 September 1943 when the Italian fleet sailed from La Spezia to join the Allies. One of the world's biggest battleships, the brand-new *Roma*, took two direct hits, blew up and sank in minutes; and her sister *Italia* just reached Malta with 800 tons of water on board. Later FX sent many other ships to the bottom. Most Do 217K-2 aircraft had a paired R19 *Rüstatz* in the tail with four aft-firing MG 81 guns.

Laid down to a Swedish air force order, this Do 215B-1 was converted on the production line for Luftwaffe use following the arms embargo in 1939. It was configured for long-range reconnaissance and served with 3.Aufkl. St./Ob.d.L. attached to the Luftwaffe High Command at Stavager in April 1940.

Featuring a redesigned nose packed with guns, the Do 217J was the night-fighter/intruder version of the Do 217E. This example, the Do 217J-2, differed from the J-1 by having no rear bomb bay. Do 217Js often operated in concert with Messerschmitt Bf 110s, whose manoeuvrability and speed were greater than that of the Do 217.

Dornier Do 217K-1 cutaway drawing key

Seen wearing hastily-applied RAF roundels and Air Ministry registration, this Do 217M-1 shows the Daimler-Benz DB 603A engines which distinguished it from the BMW 801D-powered Do 217K-1. Later Do 217M version featured carriage for Fritz-X and Hs 293A missiles, but these did not attain series production.

1 Starboard rudder tab	52 Hot-air duct	83 Armoured turret ring
2 Rudder controls	53 Balloon-cable cutter in leading-edge	84 Aerial mast
3 Rudder mass balance (lead insert)	54 Starboard outer fuel tank (35 Imp gal/160 litre capacity)	85 Gun safety guard
4 Starboard tailfin		86 Starboard beam-mounted 7.9-mm MG 81 machine-gun (750 rounds)
5 Leading-edge slot	55 Starboard oil tank (51.7 Imp gal/235 litre capacity)	87 13-mm MG 131 machine-gun (500 rounds)
6 Tailplane/tailfin attachment		88 Electrically-operated dorsal turret
7 Elevator	56 Flame-damping exhaust pipes	89 Revi gunsight
8 Elevator mass balance	57 Sliding-ring cooling air exit	90 Angled side windows
9 Fixed tab	58 BMW 801D 14-cylinder two-row radial engine	91 Jettisonable decking
10 Trim tab	59 Annular oil cooler	92 Bomb-aimer's folding seat
11 Tailplane construction	60 VDM Three-blade metal propeller of 12.79 ft (3.90 m) diameter	93 Navigator's
12 Elevator controls		94 Pilot's contoured table seat
13 Rear navigation light	61 Cooling fan	95 Rear-view gunsight
14 Four aft-firing 7.9-mm MG 81 machine-guns (*Rüstsatz* [field conversion set] 19)	62 Cowling sliding nose-ring	96 Upper instrument panel
	63 Propeller boss	97 Nose glazing
15 Ammunition boxes	64 Starboard inner fuel tank (175 Imp gal/795 litre capacity)	98 Control horns
16 Tailplane trim control		99 Engine controls
17 Fuel emergency jettison		100 One 13-mm MG 131 in strengthened nose glazing (alternatively twin 7.9-mm MG 81Z)
18 Mudguard		101 Balloon-cable cutter in nose horizontal frame
19 Tailwheel		102 Cartridge ejection chute
		103 Ammunition feed
		104 Lotfe 7D bombsight
		105 Bomb aimer's flat panel
		106 Control column counterweight

Last production Do 217 was the Do 217M, essentially a Do 217K-1 with DB 603As, or alternatively a bomber version of the Do 217N. Only a few were built, the priority being the Do 217N night-fighters, but one hit by AA fire near London on 23 February 1944 was abandoned by its crew and then flew on to make an excellent belly landing near Cambridge! Even at light weights height could not be maintained on one engine, and as with all the Do 217s the feeling was that there was too much aeroplane for the available wing area and power. Last of the Do 217s, and by far the fastest, the Do 217P family was for high-altitude use and had the same complex *HZ-Anlage* system as the Henschel Hs 130: a DB 605T in the rear fuselage drove a giant two-stage blower which supercharged the two DB 603B propulsion engines, the underside of the fuselage and inboard wings being filled by giant radiators and intercoolers. The three engines provided 2148 kW (2,880 hp) at 13715 m (45,000 ft), and aircraft of this family reached heights up to 16155 m (53,000 ft) and speeds of over 644 km/h (400 mph). (Dornier's literature states 785 km/h, or 488 mph, but this is an error.)

The end, and beyond

Total Do 217 production amounted to 1,541 bombers and 364 night-fighters, not including the five Do 217Rs. These were five of the six prototypes of the Do 317, Dornier's bid to win the advanced 'Bomber B' contract for a fast pressurised long-range bomber (to flatten the UK) and defended by remote turret guns. The Do 317 V1 began its flight trials in 1943 looking like a Do 217M with triangular fins, and the Do 317B with 2140-kW (2,870-hp) DB 610A/B double engines never even flew. The last five Do 317 prototypes were completed without pressurisation and fitted as Hs 293 missile carriers for III/KG 100 under the designation Do 217R.

The Do 317 was an advanced extension of the Do 17/217 line, featuring a pressurised cabin. No real increase in performance over the Do 217P was found, and apart from the Do 317V1 (illustrated), the other five prototypes were completed without pressurisation and used by KG 100 as missile carriers.

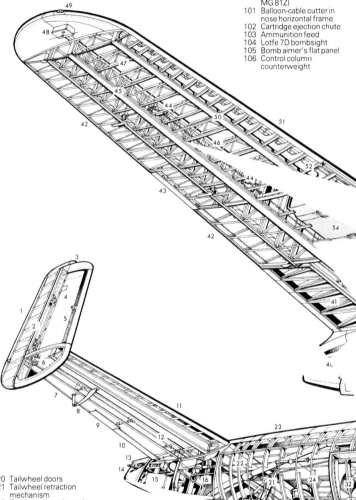

20 Tailwheel doors	65 Fuselage main fuel tank (231 Imp gal/1050 litre capacity)	
21 Tailwheel retraction mechanism		
22 Tailplane carry-through	66 Wing spar carry-through	
23 Fuselage skinning	67 Bomb bay top hinge line	
24 Master compass	68 Load-bearing beam	
25 Dipole antenna	69 Bomb shackle	
26 Anti-collision beacon	70 Bomb bay centre hinge line	
27 Elevator mass balance	71 Typical bomb load: two 2,250-lb (1000-kg) SC 1000 bombs	
28 Port tailfin		
29 Leading-edge slot	72 Forward bomb doors	107 Nose armour
30 Bomb bay division	73 13-mm MG 131 machine-gun in ventral position (1,000 rounds)	108 Ventral gunner's quilt
31 Bomb bay hinge line		109 Ammunition box (nose MG 131)
32 Bomb bay rear bulkhead entry/inspection hatch	74 Ammunition ejection chute	110 Cartridge collector box
33 Spherical oxygen cylinders	75 Ventral gunner's station	111 Entry hatch
34 Starboard mainwheel	76 Armoured bulkhead	112 Entry hatch (open)
35 Mudguard	77 Cartridge collector box	113 Entry ladder
36 Mainwheel doors	78 Batteries (two 24-Volt)	114 Port mainwheel doors
37 Mainwheel retraction mechanism	79 Radio equipment	115 Mudguard
38 Mainwheel well	80 Dorsal gunner's seat support	116 Port mainwheel
39 FuG 25 (A-A recognition)		117 Mainwheel leg cross struts
40 FuG 101 radio altimeter	81 Cabin hot-air	118 Port engine cowling
41 Outer section split flaps	82 Dorsal gunner's station	119 Landing light (swivelling)
42 Starboard aileron		120 Control linkage
43 Aileron tab		121 Pitot head
44 Control lines		122 Port navigation light
45 Rear spar		123 Port aileron
46 Braced wing ribs		124 Aileron trim tab
47 Intermediate ribs		
48 EGS 101 antenna		
49 Starboard navigation light		
50 Front spar		
51 Leading-edge hot-air de-icing		

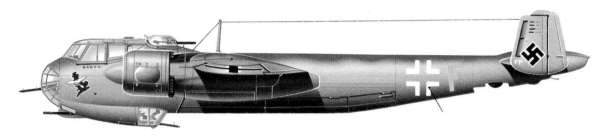

Do 217Es served with KG 40 in France on anti-shipping strikes under the command of Fliegerführer Atlantik from March 1941 onwards. The type was successful in this role and was later adapted to carry the Henschel Hs 293A and Fritz-X anti-ship missiles.

Dornier Do 17, 215 and 217 variants (simplified, omitting many prototypes)

Do 17V1: original civil mailplane prototype, two 559-kW (750-hp) BMW V1 engines, wing area 55 m² (592 sq ft), speed 435 km/h (270 mph)

Do 17V4: first bomber prototype, twin fins, BMW V1

Do 17V8: first Do 17 M-series, DB 600 engines, long glazed nose

Do 17E: initial production bomber, 559 kW (750 hp) BMW V1, short rounded nose, speed 355 km/h (221 mph)

Do 17F: initial production reconnaissance version, similar to Do 17E

Do 17VJ: bomber, similar to Do 17E but 597-kW (800-hp) BMW 132F engines

Do 17K: Yugoslav aircraft, **Do 17Ka-1** and **Do 17Ka-2** reconnaissance/bombers and **Do 17Kb-1** bomber, long glazed nose, 634-kW (850-hp) GR 14Na/2 engines

Do 17M: bomber, 671-kW (900-hp) Bramo 323A engines, broadly similar to E

Do 17P: day/night reconnaissance, 645-kW (865-hp) BMW 132N engines

Do 17R: testbeds with 820-kW (1,100-hp) DB 601A or other engines

Do 17S: new forward fuselage with roomy crew compartment, 746-kW (1,000-hp) DB 600G engines

Do 17U: five-seat pathfinder (two radio/radar operators) with new nose and DB 600A engines (according to Dornier, Bramo 323A)

Do 17Z: four-seat bomber with new nose, basically Do 17M with modified crew compartment; later **Do 17Z-2** with 746-kW (1,000-hp) Bramo 323P engine, **Do 17Z-3** reconnaissance bomber, **Do 17Z-4** crew trainer and **Do 17Z-5** maritime reconnaissance aircraft

Do 17Z Kauz: Do 17Z-6 Kauz I night-fighter with nose of Ju 88C-2, followed by **Do 17Z-10 Kauz II** designed from the start for role, both with Bramo 323P engines

Do 215 V3: export demonstration bomber with Do 17Z-0 airframe and 802-kW (1,075-hp) DB 601A engines

Do 215B: most four-seat reconnaissance/bomber with 820-kW (1,100-hp) DB 601A; **Do 215B-5** night-fighter with first Lichtenstein radar

Do 217 V1: new enlarged bomber/dive bomber with 57-m² (614-sq ft) wing and 802-kW (1,075-hp) DB 601As

Do 217 V2/3/4: prototypes with 895-hp (1,200-hp) Jumo 211As

Do 217 V7/8: prototypes with 1156-kW (1,550-hp) BMW 139

Do 217A: long-range reconnaissance/bomber, long-span 65-m² (700-sq ft) wing, 1008-kW (1,350-hp) DB 601 R/C3

Do 217C: similar to Do 217A but regular 57-m² (614-sq ft) wing, revised ventral contour, no cameras, more defensive guns

Do 217E: major family of four-seat bombers, 1178-kW (1,580-hp) BMW 801MA or ML engines; **Do 217E-2** introduced turret; **Do 217E-4** BMW 801C engines; **Do 217E-5** either HS 293 or FX 1400 missiles

Do 217G: bomber float seaplane, 1156-kW (1,550-hp) BMW 801A; not flown

Do 217J: interim three-seat night-fighter, 1178-kW (1,580-hp) BMW 801L, FuG 202 Lichtenstein BC radar

Do 217K-1: four-seat night bomber; 1268-kW (1,700-hp) BMW 801D engines, new fully glazed bulbous nose

Do 217K-2: carrier for FX 1400 missiles, long-span 67-m² (721-sq ft) wing, R19 art-firing tail guns

Do 217L: high-altitude reconnaissance aircraft, 1491-kW (2,000-hp) DB603HC-3 engines, 70-m² (753-sq ft) wing, 580 km/h (360 mph), ceiling 13000 m (42,650 ft)

Do 217M: bomber, 1380-kW (1,850-hp) DB 603A engines

Do 217N: four-seat night-fighter and intruder, 1380-kW (1,850-hp) DB 603A engines

Do 217P: ultra-high altitude pressurised bomber with third supercharging engine to boost DB 603B main engines, Do 217K-2 wing

Do 217R: Hs 293 missile carrier modified from Do 317A prototypes

Do 317A: four-seat high-altitude bomber, 1305-kW (1,750-hp) DB 603A engines

Do 317B: unbuilt bomber, 2140-kW (2,870-hp) DB 610A/B double engines

60

56

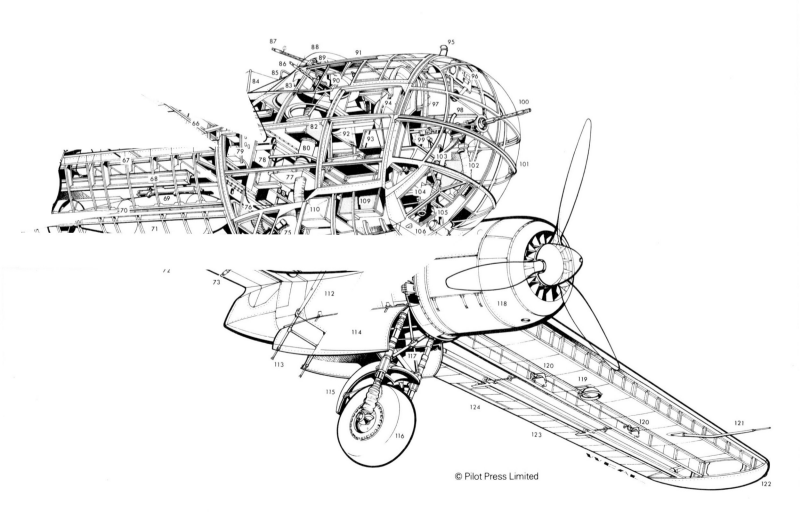

© Pilot Press Limited

*One of the ultimate sub-types of the basic
Do 217E series was the E-5, built from the start
with wing pylons for the Hs 293A stand-off
radio-guided anti-ship missile, together with
the associated Kehl/Strassburg guidance
system. This model entered service with
II/KG 100 in April 1943 and quickly made its
mark against Allied ships in the Bay of
Biscay and the Atlantic, the first attack being
against British destroyers on 25 August 1943.
This Do 217E-5, from 6/KG 100, is very unusual
in retaining its fixed MG 151 cannon under the
nose; normally this was removed when the
20-mm MG FF hand-aimed cannon was added
in the glazed part of the nose.*

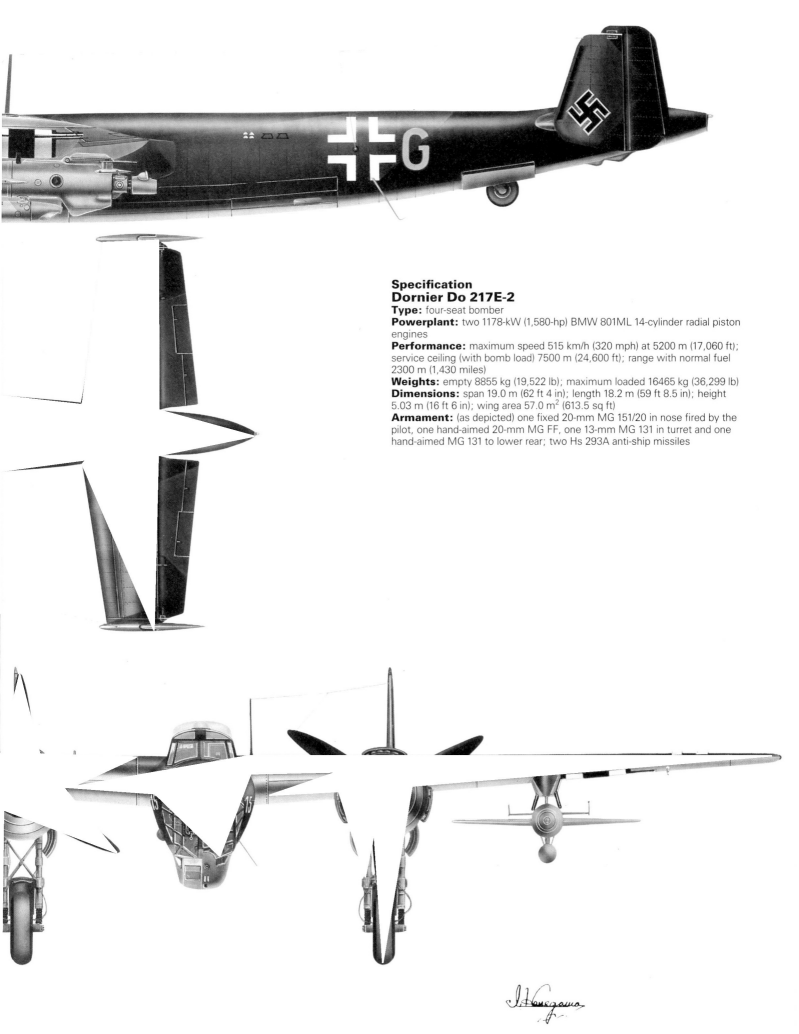

Specification
Dornier Do 217E-2

Type: four-seat bomber

Powerplant: two 1178-kW (1,580-hp) BMW 801ML 14-cylinder radial piston engines

Performance: maximum speed 515 km/h (320 mph) at 5200 m (17,060 ft); service ceiling (with bomb load) 7500 m (24,600 ft); range with normal fuel 2300 m (1,430 miles)

Weights: empty 8855 kg (19,522 lb); maximum loaded 16465 kg (36,299 lb)

Dimensions: span 19.0 m (62 ft 4 in); length 18.2 m (59 ft 8.5 in); height 5.03 m (16 ft 6 in); wing area 57.0 m^2 (613.5 sq ft)

Armament: (as depicted) one fixed 20-mm MG 151/20 in nose fired by the pilot, one hand-aimed 20-mm MG FF, one 13-mm MG 131 in turret and one hand-aimed MG 131 to lower rear; two Hs 293A anti-ship missiles

Junkers Ju 188
'Rächer'

The versatility and success of the Ju 88 were beyond question, and a follow-on aircraft was a logical step, resulting in the Ju 188, an excellent bomber, reconnaissance platform and anti-ship weapon. However, despite the capabilities of the new aircraft, it was a case of 'too few, too late' for the Luftwaffe.

By the start of World War II it was obvious to the German Reichsluftfahrtministerium that the Ju 88 was an aircraft of outstanding merit. Indeed, its very excellence was to some extent a drawback to Junkers, in that any major development was considered unnecessary. Right at the start of the programme in January 1936 the company had sketched a Ju 85B and Ju 88B with a revised crew compartment forming a fully glazed forward fuselage of smooth aerodynamic shape, with no separate windscreen, and developments of these designs were projected with new and more powerful engines such as the BMW 139 and Jumo 213.

Junkers was at last allowed to try out this new crew compartment in a single Ju 88B, and began its flight test programme in early 1940. Apart from having 1194-kW (1,600-hp) BMW 801 radial engines the rest of the 88B was virtually the same as an 88A, though a bomb rack was added under each outer wing, outboard of the dive brakes. In 1940 Junkers also built 10 pre-production Ju 88B-0 aircraft, but though these proved efficient and popular it was considered there was no point in disrupting Ju 88A production. The B-0s were adapted as reconnaissance aircraft, with bomb racks removed and extra fuel in the bomb bay. One was modified with a different version of the BMW 801 engine and a dorsal turret mounting an MG 131 gun, and

this machine, the Ju 88E-0, was used sporadically during 1941 for various tests.

A growing need for aircraft

For the future, all hopes rested on the next generation, the so-called Bomber B. The contenders for this programme were eventually whittled down to three: the Do 317, Fw 191 and Ju 288. But by the autumn of 1942 it was increasingly clear that none of these programmes looked like producing anything that the Luftwaffe could use for a long time to come. This threw increased emphasis on the possibility of major improvements to the existing aircraft, and none seemed a better candidate than the Ju 88. Junkers had never completely halted such developments, and had managed to make major changes to the airframe which improved handling at high gross weights.

The Ju 88 V27, flown in September 1941, had an airframe resembling the Ju 88E-0 but with extended outer wings, the new

The Ju 88 V44 was the second of the Ju 188 development vehicles, and introduced the enlarged tail surfaces. As such it was redesignated as the Ju 188 V1 during mid-1942, joined on the flight test programme by another aircraft to hasten development.

The first operational unit to receive the Ju 188 was I/KG 6, and it used its aircraft for pathfinder duties. The wing was heavily involved in the spring 1944 'Little Blitz' over England, during which time this Ju 188A-2 is seen being loaded for a mission.

pointed tips having a span increased from 20 m to 22 m. The Ju 88 V44, flown in the spring of 1942, continued the improvements with an enlarged tail, the span of the horizontal tail being increased and the fin and rudder being enlarged into an almost rectangular shape (this tail was later adopted for the Ju 88G night fighter, and the new wing on the 88G-7).

The programme speeds up

In October 1942 the critical decision was made to transfer some staff from the Ju 288 and put full development resources into a development of the Ju 88 designated Ju 188. The basis was to be the Ju 88 V44, which thereupon became the Ju 188 V1. By January 1943, a second prototype was in the air at the Bernburg plant, which had been selected as the Ju 188 assembly centre (Dessau remaining the main design centre). The RLM decreed that the initial production Ju 188A-0 should be a bomber, capable of both level and dive bombing, and fitted with the same slatted dive brakes and automatic pull-out gear as the Ju 88A. The ministry further stipulated that, to avoid delays due to engine shortages, the 188 should be able to be powered by either the BMW 801 or Jumo 213, each in the form of a 'bolt on' power egg requiring the minimum of aircraft modification.

In fact the first production aircraft to leave the assembly line were actually Ju 188E-0s and E-1s, because they had BMW engines (the A-series were powered by the Jumo 213). The E-0 and E-1 entered service with Ekdo d.Lw 188 and KG 6 in May 1943, the first operational Gruppe being I/KG 6 which began missions in the Pathfinder role on 20 October 1943. By the end of that year production of the Ju

188, so long ignored, was in full swing. Bernburg had delivered 283 aircraft, and other assembly lines were in action at ATG (Leipzig) and Siebel (Halle).

In fact there were differences apart from the engines between the two initial production versions. Both the Ju 188A-1 and E-1 were four-seat medium bombers with the same airframe, from which the dive brakes and pull-out gear had been eliminated (dive bombing no longer being a requirement). The dorsal turrets were the main difference, the A-series having the EDL 151 with an MG 151/20 cannon and the E-series having the originally proposed EDL 131 with the MG 131 of 13-mm calibre. In general, the A-series had slightly higher performance, especially when using the MW50 power boosting system. The A-3 version was a torpedo bomber, able to carry two LT 1B or F5b torpedoes under the inner wings, and with a long bulge along the right side of the forward fuselage to accommodate the torpedo aiming and steering gear. The equivalent BMW-engined version was the E-2, and this often had the dorsal turret not fitted. Both the A-3 and E-2 often carried FuG 200 Hohentwiel anti-ship radar.

At the start of the programme Junkers had proposed fitting the FA15 type of remotely sighted and power controlled tail barbette, housing an MG 131Z (twin 13-mm guns). This complex and weighty

The BMW 801-powered Ju 188E series was delivered to the Luftwaffe slightly ahead of the Jumo 213-powered Ju 188A. This pre-production Ju 188E-0 was modified to serve as a fast staff transport for General-Luftzeugmeister Erhard Milch.

Torpedo-bomber versions were produced of both A- and E-series, this aircraft being a Ju 188E-2. Racks under the wing roots could carry an 800-kg (1,763-lb) LT 1B or 765-kg (1,686-lb) LT F5b torpedo each, while guidance equipment was contained in a fairing on the side of the nose. FuG 200 Hohentwiel radar was fitted.

installation was flown in the Ju 188C-0, a converted A-0. It was concluded that poor aiming accuracy and reliability, coupled with the other penalties, made the scheme not worthwhile. On the other hand, the urgent need of the Luftwaffe for a high-performance reconnaissance aircraft led to many Ju 188As being completed as Ju 188D-1 or D-2 aircraft. These had no forward-firing MG 151 cannon, only three crew, increased fuel capacity and gross weight increased to 15200 kg (33,510 lb). These versions carried various arrangements of Rb 50/30, 70/30, NRb 40/25 or 50/25 cameras, and the D-2 invariably was fitted with FuG 200 radar for maritime operations.

Failure to up-gun

The equivalent BMW-engined versions were the Ju 188F-1 and F-2, the latter being the radar-equipped maritime aircraft. Engines were BMW 801D-2 or G-2, rated at 1268 kW (1,700 hp). Further developments of the BMW aircraft aimed at overcoming the blind spot in the defensive system directly behind the tail. Having reluctantly rejected the FA15 barbette, Junkers considered fitting a manned tail gun. One possibility was a gunner lying prone and aiming a single pivoted MG 151, this requiring only minor structural alterations. The idea was rejected in favour of a manned version of the FA15, with superimposed MG 131 guns manned by a small gunner who could just squeeze into it (and could never have got out in a hurry). The resulting aircraft, the Ju 188G-0, looked very like the C-0, but the limits of the arc of fire of the turret were very poor. In the end this answer was rejected by the Luftwaffe, and Junkers pressed for renewed effort on the FA15 barbette. This was intended for the production Ju 188G-2 bomber and the H-1 reconnaissance aircraft. In the event these projects were overtaken by developments of the generally superior Ju 388.

Junkers never did succeed in providing the Ju 188 with an adequate all-round defence system. From the summer of 1940, the start of the Battle of Britain, it had been obvious that the kind of fast bomber envisaged by the Luftwaffe in the mid-1930s, and built in enormous numbers, could not survive in the face of interception by modern fighters. Both hasty lash-ups and considered improvements (such as the EDL cannon turrets) were tested, but to the end of the war aircraft in this class had a perilous career in any part of the sky infested with Allied fighters.

In the autumn of 1943 the project staff at Dessau had rushed into a major effort on high-altitude Ju 188s, with a pressurised crew compartment. Proposals were made for the Ju 188J Zerstörer, the 188K bomber and the 188L reconnaissance aircraft. These obviously made sense, and in September 1943 Junkers was ordered to hasten these

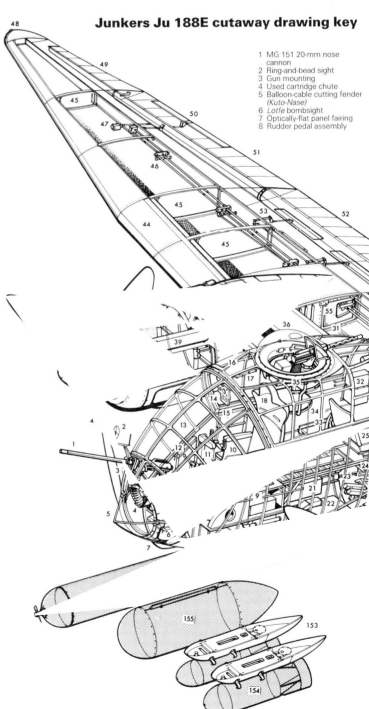

Junkers Ju 188E cutaway drawing key

1 MG 151 20-mm nose cannon
2 Ring-and-bead sight
3 Gun mounting
4 Used cartridge chute
5 Balloon-cable cutting fender (*Kuto-Nase*)
6 *Lotfe* bombsight
7 Optically-flat panel fairing
8 Rudder pedal assembly

This aircraft at Bordeaux-Mérignac is a Ju 188E-2 with its Hohentwiel radar removed. The EDL 131 turret which normally sat atop the canopy has been removed in favour of a radio aerial.

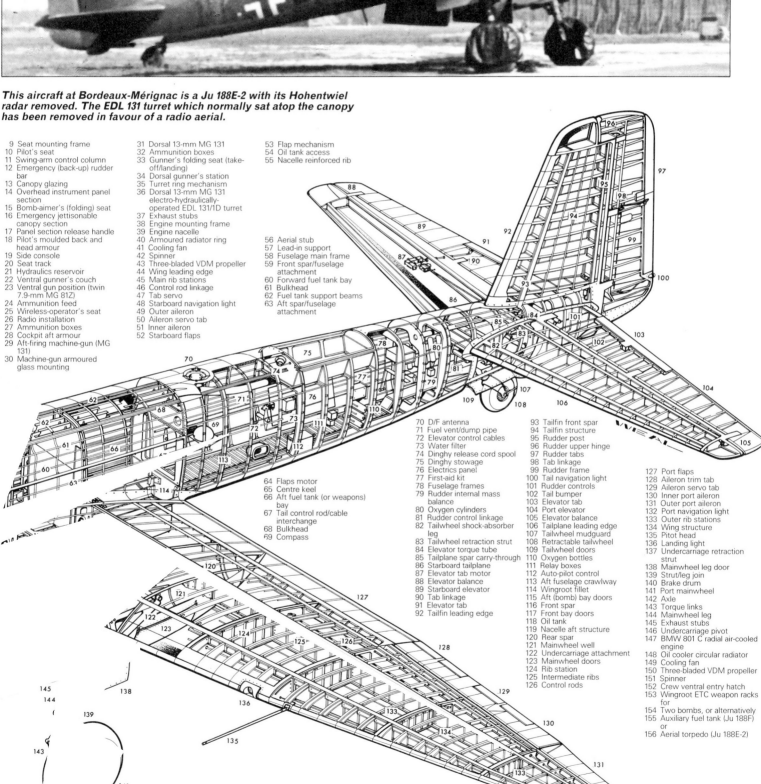

9 Seat mounting frame
10 Pilot's seat
11 Swing-arm control column
12 Emergency (back-up) rudder bar
13 Canopy glazing
14 Overhead instrument panel section
15 Bomb-aimer's (folding) seat
16 Emergency jettisonable canopy section
17 Panel section release handle
18 Pilot's moulded back and head armour
19 Side console
20 Seat track
21 Hydraulics reservoir
22 Ventral gunner's couch
23 Ventral gun position (twin 7.9-mm MG 81Z)
24 Ammunition feed
25 Wireless-operator's seat
26 Radio installation
27 Ammunition boxes
28 Cockpit aft armour
29 Aft-firing machine-gun (MG 131)
30 Machine-gun armoured glass mounting

31 Dorsal 13-mm MG 131
32 Ammunition boxes
33 Gunner's folding seat (take-off/landing)
34 Dorsal gunner's station
35 Turret ring mechanism
36 Dorsal 13-mm MG 131 electro-hydraulically-operated EDL 131/1D turret
37 Exhaust stubs
38 Engine mounting frame
39 Engine nacelle
40 Armoured radiator ring
41 Cooling fan
42 Spinner
43 Three-bladed VDM propeller
44 Wing leading edge
45 Main rib stations
46 Control rod linkage
47 Tab servo
48 Starboard navigation light
49 Outer aileron
50 Aileron servo tab
51 Inner aileron
52 Starboard flaps

53 Flap mechanism
54 Oil tank access
55 Nacelle reinforced rib

56 Aerial stub
57 Lead-in support
58 Fuselage main frame
59 Front spar/fuselage attachment
60 Forward fuel tank bay
61 Bulkhead
62 Fuel tank support beams
63 Aft spar/fuselage attachment

64 Flaps motor
65 Centre keel
66 Aft fuel tank (or weapons) bay
67 Tail control rod/cable interchange
68 Bulkhead
69 Compass

70 D/F antenna
71 Fuel vent/dump pipe
72 Elevator control cables
73 Water filter
74 Dinghy release cord spool
75 Dinghy stowage
76 Electrics panel
77 First-aid kit
78 Fuselage frames
79 Rudder internal mass balance
80 Oxygen cylinders
81 Rudder control linkage
82 Tailwheel shock-absorber leg
83 Tailwheel retraction strut
84 Elevator torque tube
85 Tailplane spar carry-through
86 Starboard tailplane
87 Elevator tab motor
88 Elevator balance
89 Starboard elevator
90 Tab linkage
91 Elevator tab
92 Tailfin leading edge

93 Tailfin front spar
94 Tailfin structure
95 Rudder post
96 Rudder upper hinge
97 Rudder tabs
98 Tab linkage
99 Rudder frame
100 Tail navigation light
101 Rudder controls
102 Tail bumper
103 Elevator tab
104 Port elevator
105 Elevator balance
106 Tailplane leading edge
107 Tailwheel mudguard
108 Retractable tailwheel
109 Tailwheel doors
110 Oxygen bottles
111 Relay boxes
112 Auto-pilot control
113 Aft fuselage crawlway
114 Wingroot fillet
115 Aft (bomb) bay doors
116 Front spar
117 Front bay doors
118 Oil tank
119 Nacelle aft structure
120 Rear spar
121 Mainwheel well
122 Undercarriage attachment
123 Mainwheel doors
124 Rib station
125 Intermediate ribs
126 Control rods

127 Port flaps
128 Aileron trim tab
129 Aileron servo tab
130 Inner port aileron
131 Outer port aileron
132 Port navigation light
133 Outer rib stations
134 Wing structure
135 Pitot head
136 Landing light
137 Undercarriage retraction strut
138 Mainwheel leg door
139 Strut/leg join
140 Brake drum
141 Port mainwheel
142 Axle
143 Torque links
144 Mainwheel leg
145 Exhaust stubs
146 Undercarriage pivot
147 BMW 801 C radial air-cooled engine
148 Oil cooler circular radiator
149 Cooling fan
150 Three-bladed VDM propeller
151 Spinner
152 Crew ventral entry hatch
153 Wingroot ETC weapon racks for
154 Two bombs, or alternatively
155 Auxiliary fuel tank (Ju 188F) or
156 Aerial torpedo (Ju 188E-2)

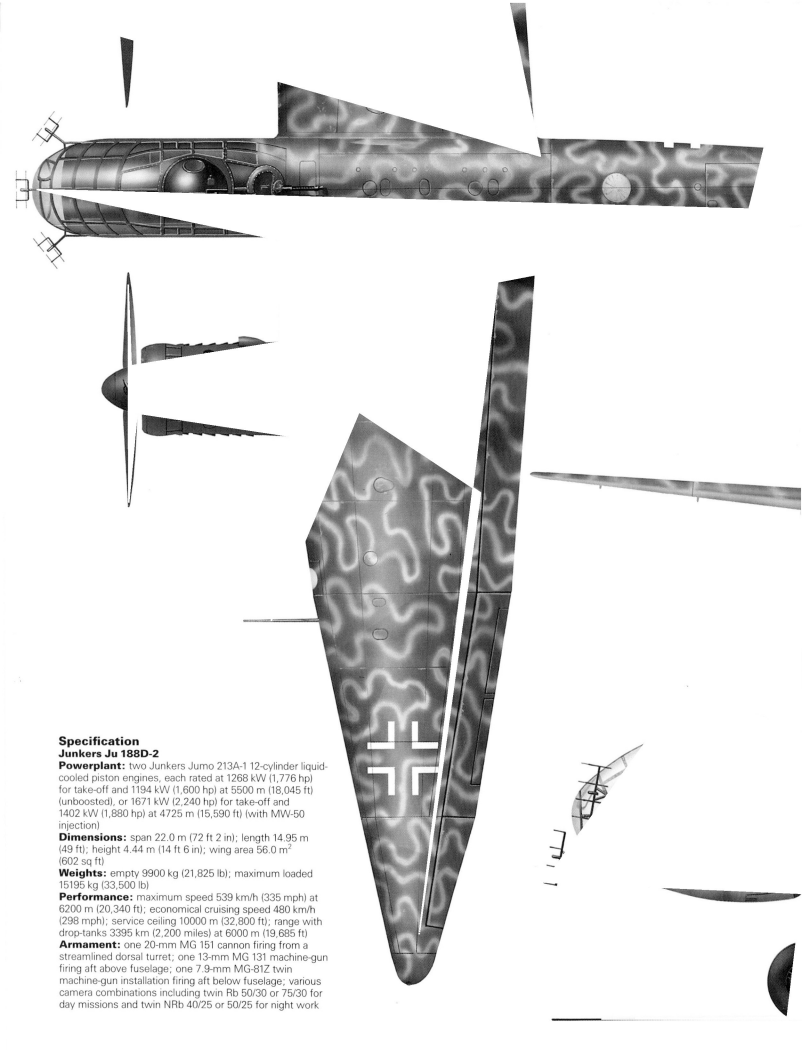

Specification
Junkers Ju 188D-2
Powerplant: two Junkers Jumo 213A-1 12-cylinder liquid-cooled piston engines, each rated at 1268 kW (1,776 hp) for take-off and 1194 kW (1,600 hp) at 5500 m (18,045 ft) (unboosted), or 1671 kW (2,240 hp) for take-off and 1402 kW (1,880 hp) at 4725 m (15,590 ft) (with MW-50 injection)

Dimensions: span 22.0 m (72 ft 2 in); length 14.95 m (49 ft); height 4.44 m (14 ft 6 in); wing area 56.0 m^2 (602 sq ft)

Weights: empty 9900 kg (21,825 lb); maximum loaded 15195 kg (33,500 lb)

Performance: maximum speed 539 km/h (335 mph) at 6200 m (20,340 ft); economical cruising speed 480 km/h (298 mph); service ceiling 10000 m (32,800 ft); range with drop-tanks 3395 km (2,200 miles) at 6000 m (19,685 ft)

Armament: one 20-mm MG 151 cannon firing from a streamlined dorsal turret; one 13-mm MG 131 machine-gun firing aft above fuselage; one 7.9-mm MG-81Z twin machine-gun installation firing aft below fuselage; various camera combinations including twin Rb 50/30 or 75/30 for day missions and twin NRb 40/25 or 50/25 for night work

When it arrived in service, the Ju 188 was an immediate and considerable improvement over the Ju 88, yet it could have been in major production much earlier had the successes of the Ju 88 not been so great. Indeed the Ju 88B, with the characteristic bulbous nose, had been flying early in 1940. However, relatively few Ju 188s were completed, and they made little difference to the course of the war, which had already turned against Germany when the first aircraft entered service. Over half of the aircraft went to reconnaissance units, for use either in an overland role or as maritime patrollers with FuG 200 Hohentwiel radar. This is one of the latter, the exhaust stubs on the engine nacelles denoting a Jumo 213-powered Ju 188D-2. It served with 1. Fernaufklärungsgruppe 124 at Kirkenes.

Iain Wyllie

This aircraft is the Ju 188 V2 after modification to serve as the prototype for the Ju 188G series. Just visible is the deepened rear fuselage which housed a manned gun turret containing twin MG 131s. Traverse of the guns was poor and the turret very cramped.

By reducing the crew to three, removing the nose cannon and replacing the bombs with drop-tanks, the Ju 188 made a capable reconnaissance platform. Jumo-powered aircraft were Ju 188Ds, while BMW-powered aircraft were Ju 188Fs. This is an F-1 for overland reconnaissace.

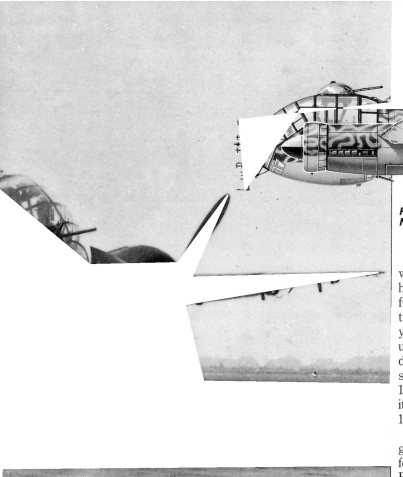

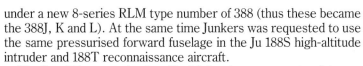

FuG 200 Hohentwiel-equipped Ju 188D-2 of 1.(F)/122 at Kirkenes, Norway in 1944.

From the outset the Ju 188 had a reputation in the Luftwaffe which, if anything, was even greater than that of the great Ju 88. It handled better, especially at high weights, and it was able to make full use of the power of the BMW 801 and Jumo 213 engines (which the Ju 88 could not do). Nevertheless, partly because of the lost two years during which Bomber B held centre stage, the Ju 188 was unable to be made in anything like adequate numbers. Whereas production of the Ju 88 exceeded 15,000, total acceptances of all versions of the Ju 188 by the Luftwaffe amounted to only 1,076 – 283 in 1943 and 793 in 1944. (Output of the Ju 388, of course, never got into its stride at all.) Of this modest total, something like 570 were Ju 188D and 188F reconnaissance aircraft.

Even the reconnaissance aircraft accomplished little. No photographs were brought back of the huge and prolonged build-up of forces in England prior to D-day, and reconnaissance flights over the British Isles were almost non-existent until the advent at the end of 1944 of the Arado Ar 234B. The same held true on the Italian front, where the Arado jet ended a long period in which Field Marshal Kesselring had been virtually devoid of any reconnaissance information.

Of the bomber versions, most were fitted with FuG 200 and operated in the anti-shipping role from Denmark and Norway. These aircraft would have been extremely valuable in the era of the desperate convoys to the northern ports of the Soviet Union in 1942, but in late 1944 there was little for them to do but wait for the order from Admiral Doenitz to surrender. They had no anti-submarine capability.

At the end of the war the excellent qualities of the Ju 188 were recognised by France's resurgent Aéronavale, which adopted the type for front-line use as its chief land-based bomber. It put at least 30 captured Ju 188Es and Fs into use, each being fully overhauled and given various different items of equipment and instruments. At least 12 new Ju 188Es were delivered by SNCASE (later Sud-Est Aviation) at Toulouse, these making use of various German components as well as many made in French factories. The Aéronavale Ju 188s (which shared the same powerplant as the Nord 1402 Noroit amphibian) had a relatively short active life with the squadrons, but nine were subsequently used for valuable test programmes. These programmes included the development of piston engines, turbojets and guided missiles.

under a new 8-series RLM type number of 388 (thus these became the 388J, K and L). At the same time Junkers was requested to use the same pressurised forward fuselage in the Ju 188S high-altitude intruder and 188T reconnaissance aircraft.

The S and T were to be devoid of defensive armament, relying on their height and speed to evade interception. Thus, both had an almost perfectly streamlined forward fuselage, the engines being Jumo 213E-1s fitted with GM-1 nitrous oxide power boosting to give 1260 kW (1,690 hp) at 9570 m (31,400 ft). The S-1 could carry 800 kg (1,763 lb) of bombs internally, and with full bomb load could reach 685 km/h (426 mph) at 11500 m (37,730 ft). The lighter T-1 with two large Rb cameras could reach 700 km/h (435 mph) at the same height, posing a major interception problem. Both versions went into limited production, and deliveries of the S-1 from the ATG factory began in about May 1944. Neither reached the Luftwaffe in quantity, however, and this was partly due to a change in priority. By late 1944 most of the S-1 aircraft, both those completed and on the assembly line, had cabin pressurisation removed, together with the GM-1 system, and equipment added to fit them for low-level ground attack. A 50-mm BK 5 gun was mounted under the fuselage, streamlined by a large blister fairing, and armour was added round the engines and crew compartment. The new designation was Ju 188S-1/U. Some did go into action, usually with a crew of two.

Small numbers (between 10 and 80) of S-1 and T-1 aircraft were transferred to the Merseburg plant, where they are reported to have been converted into Ju 388L-0 reconnaissance aircraft. Some Junkers records even suggest that other Ju 388s began life as Ju 188S or T aircraft, but the evidence was lost in the chaos at the end of the war.

This Ju 188D-2 was captured intact by the Allies and extensively tested at RAE Farnborough, where it is seen with Hohentwiel radar and dorsal gun removed. Test pilots were impressed with its good handling and performance.

The Ju 188 had a short career in Aéronavale colours after the war, used briefly as a bomber and later for test purposes. In addition to aircraft captured from the Luftwaffe, the Aéronavale purchased 12 Ju 188s from SNCASE at Toulouse, assembled from German components.

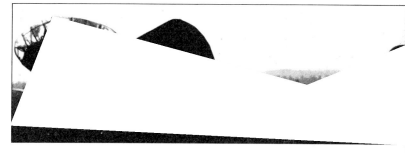

Messerschmitt Me 163

Between them, Willy Messerschmitt and Alexander Lippisch designed and built the fastest aircraft of World War II, the Me 163. It was an aircraft of last resort which was resurrected only when the streams of Allied bombers over Germany heralded the end of the war. Its performance was, quite literally, explosive, as its revolutionary engine made it dangerous and unpredictable. When it worked, it was a sight that few could have imagined as it streaked upwards into the sky. However, it came too late to save the Reich.

In three-quarters of a century of air warfare there has only been one occasion when a nation has gone into battle with an aircraft so advanced in concept that its enemies did not at first know how to tackle it. The Me 163 was very small, agile and getting on for twice as fast as most of its opponents. With relief, the Allies found that it tended to appear only in very small numbers, it clearly had a brief flight endurance, and its effectiveness was not impressive. Indeed, two were actually shot down before the type had scored a single combat success.

The story started in 1926 when Dr Alexander Lippisch built his first tailless glider. Over the next decade Lippisch built many tailless aircraft and also became involved with rocket propulsion, so it was no great surprise when in 1937 he was asked by the research section of the RLM (German air ministry) to design an aircraft to test a new rocket motor intended for manned aeroplanes, the Walter I-203, rated at 400 kg (882 lb) thrust. This operated on a mixture of two liquids which reacted violently if allowed to meet: *T-stoff*, consisting mainly of concentrated hydrogen peroxide, and *Z-stoff*, a solution of calcium permanganate in water. With such reactive propellants it was decided to design the fuselage in metal, and as the DFS (the German glider research institute) where Lippisch worked was not equipped for the task the fuselage construction was subcontracted to Heinkel.

In the event, Heinkel never built the metal fuselage, but did build the rocket-propelled He 176, whose abysmal showing in June 1939 almost caused loss of interest in any rocket aircraft. It was a very frustrated Lippisch who, early in 1939, left the DFS and teamed up with Messerschmitt. At Augsburg Willy Messerschmitt showed frosty disinterest, but Lippisch was allowed to carry on with his own team, in strict security, and in late 1939 decided that his preliminary research aircraft, the all-wood DFS 194, could in fact be flown by the rocket and not by the intended small piston engine. The machine was taken in early 1940 to Karlshagen, the test airfield at Peenemünde, where the I-203 rocket was installed. On 3 June 1940 famed glider

pilot Heini Dittmar made a successful first flight, reporting superb handling. Later this flimsy machine, designed for 300 km/h (186 mph), reached 547 km/h (340 mph) in level flight, and also demonstrated fantastic steep climbs.

Suddenly it was all systems go! The Walter company had by this time developed the II-203b motor rated at 750 kg (1,653 lb) to assist heavy aircraft to take off, and was working on a still more powerful unit. Lippisch was instructed to design a fast-climbing interceptor to use the latter motor, the short flight endurance being no problem to a target-defence aircraft which could stay on the ground until enemy bombers were almost overhead. The designation Me 163B was allocated, the Me 163A being a series of six prototypes to be powered by the II-203b modified as a permanently installed main engine.

Carefree flight

The first Me 163, with factory letters KE + SW, was completed except for its motor at Lechfeld in March 1941, and was at once put through a programme of trials as a glider, towed off by a Messerschmitt Bf 110. Dittmar again was enraptured at the handling, but the aircraft was such a good glider it consistently refused to land, and invariably almost went off the far side of the field. On one occasion Dittmar had to sideslip between two hangars and even then floated between all the airfield buildings while trying to land. The maiden flight under power took place at Karlshagen on 13 August 1941, and though he did not intend to reach high speed Dittmar was informed that the level speed as measured by ground instruments was over 800 km/h (497 mph). Soon speeds were exceeding 885 km/h (550 mph). On 2 October 1941 Dittmar was towed to over 4000 m (13,125 ft) by a Bf 110; he then cast off and started the motor. He accelerated, but suddenly lost control as the nose dropped violently.

Captured by the Allied forces during the latter stages of World War II, this Messerschmitt Me 163B-1a was preserved at RAF St Athan. Note the large dolly undercarriage unit, which was attached to the rear of the skid.

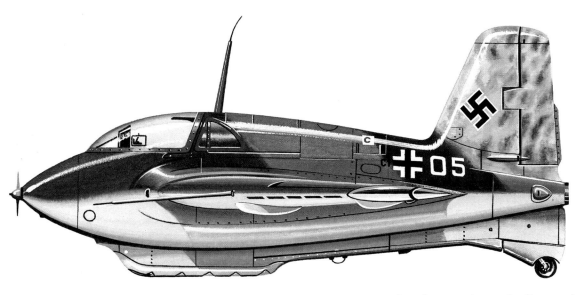

This Me-163B-1a was one of the first to become operational with the Luftwaffe in the summer of 1944. It was assigned to Erprobungskommando 16, at Bad Zwischenahn, where scorch marks on the hardstandings gave RAF photo interpreters their first clue of the existence of the Komet. The small propeller drove the generator.

It was possibly the first occasion on which a human had approached the speed of sound, compressibility trouble being experienced at about Mach 0.84. The speed of 1004 km/h (624 mph) was 250 km/h (155 mph) above the official world speed record.

Subsequent research led to a modified wing with large fixed slots over the outer leading edge, which rendered the aircraft spin-proof, though the stall remained severe. Basically the Me 163A could hardly have been simpler, but one feature was to endure into the production Me 163B and cause endless problems and catastrophic accidents. The Lippisch glider background made it seem normal to take-off from a wheeled dolly, jettisoned once airborne, and to land on a sprung skid. In fact the piloting difficulties were immense. If the aircraft was not dead into wind it would slew round and possibly overturn, the rudder being useless at low speeds. Any bump in the surface caused premature take-off or a bounce on landing, and this combined with the totally unsprung dolly to cause spinal damage to any pilot and, by shaking up the propellants, the occasional devastating explosion.

Setbacks and delays

So tricky were the liquids that for the big R II-211 motor, which was made fully controllable, the *Z-stoff* was replaced by *C-stoff* (hydrazine hydrate solution in methyl alcohol). Though testing of the motors was twice punctuated by explosions which destroyed the entire building, work went ahead on the six Me 163A prototypes, 10 Me 163A-0 pre-production aircraft and 70 pre-production versions of the Me 163B interceptor, which was given the name Komet. During 1941 procurement chief Ernst Udet had become an enthusiastic supporter of the project. His suicide in November 1941 did not help matters, because the little rocket interceptor was irrelevant to the

gigantic struggle on the Eastern Front, and attacks on Germany were as yet ineffectual and only carried out by night. So priority remained low, and Walter continued to have severe and dangerous motor problems.

Gradually more people joined the programme, though Lippisch himself took up another appointment in Vienna. A Luftwaffe officer, Rudolf Opitz, came to share the flying, and it is as well that he did because Dittmar stalled on to the poorly sprung skid and spent two years in hospital having his spine reassembled. On his first Me 163A flight Opitz almost met disaster because he was far above dolly release height before he realised he was airborne. He kept the valuable dolly attached and landed back on it; by a miracle he did not swing and overturn (which usually meant a violent explosion). Opitz made the first Me 163B flight from Lechfeld on 26 June 1942, without propellants and towed by a Bf 110. But it was to be almost a year later before, on 23 June 1943, powered flights began. Again Opitz had trouble, the dolly wrenching free during the tricky acceleration and the final part of the run being on the unsprung skid. A few seconds later the cockpit filled with choking, blinding peroxide fumes from a pipe fractured by the bumping. Opitz was on the point of baling out when the peroxide was at last all consumed by the motor.

In early 1943 a special Me 163B test squadron was formed at Karlshagen under Hauptmann Wolfgang Späte, but while this was still in its early stages Peenemünde was raided by the RAF and the unit, Erprobungskommando 16, was moved to Bad Zwischenahn. This was the centre for most Komet flying for the next year, and the aircraft became known to the Allies from high-flying reconnaissance photographs taken here in December 1943. But by this time the programme had been further delayed by a raid of the very kind the Komet had been invented to prevent. The Messerschmitt factory at Regensburg was heavily hit by Boeing B-17s on 17 August 1943,

Probably seen at Lechfeld in the spring of 1941, the Me 163A V1 formed the link between the low-speed DFS 194 and the Me 163B Komet. Seen here on its take-off trolley, with flaps down, the V1 bore factory letter code KE+SW. Trials with the rocket engine began in July, this machine being the first to exceed 800 km/h (500 mph).

The Wolf Hirth Segelflugzeugbau (glider works) built a run of 10 Me 163A-0 pilot trainers, fitted with the dangerously temperamental R II-203b motor and a large sprung take-off dolly. This particular A-0 was fitted with wooden underwing racks each carrying 12 of the R4M air-to-air spin-stabilised rockets (a local addition).

many of the pre-production batch being destroyed. The main production, however, was to be widely dispersed throughout Germany under the control of Klemm Technik, with final assembly at a secret Schwarzwald (Black Forest) centre and then guarded rail shipment to the flight-test base at Lechfeld.

This giant production plan suffered many further problems, and the flow did not begin to arrive at Lechfeld until February 1944. The production interceptor was designated Me 163B-1a, and though in many ways seemingly crude it was actually a very refined aircraft as a result of the prolonged experience with earlier variants. Nothing had been done, however, to cure the terrible danger of explosion, which was made all the more likely by the tricky and problem-ridden take-off dolly and landing skid.

The wing was smaller and simpler than those of the precursor aircraft, and though it appeared swept it was mainly its taper that gave a quarter-chord sweep angle of 23.3°. The wooden structure was simple, with two widely spaced spars and skin of fabric-covered ply usually 8 mm (0.31 in) thick. Outboard on the trailing edge were the only control surfaces, other than the rudder: large manual fabric-covered elevons used for both pitch and roll. The trim tabs were plain metal bent on the ground with pliers to give the required behaviour. Inboard were large plain hinged flaps which were lowered hydraulically by screwjacks before landing, in unison with main landing flaps ahead of them on the underside of the wing. The landing flaps caused strong nose-up trim, and the trailing-edge flaps cancelled this out with equal nose-down trim. The small fuselage was light alloy, covered mainly with detachable panels to gain access to the densely packed interior. The largest item was the *T-stoff* tank of 1040-litre (229-Imp gal) capacity which filled the space between the cockpit and the motor. Smaller *T-stoff* tanks filled each side of the cockpit. The *C-stoff* was housed in two 173-litre (38-Imp gal) tanks between the wing spars and two 73-litre (16-Imp gal) tanks in the leading edges.

Dangerous complications

The motor, which in production was called the HWK Type 509A-1, had a single chamber fed via two long straight pipes from the turbopump group located roughly in line with the trailing edge of the wing. Before each flight the entire system had to be drained and flushed through with scrupulous care using vast amounts of water. The motor was started with *T-stoff* fed from a separate starter tank in the top of the rear fuselage, while an electric motor cranked up the turbopumps. The tanks were pressurised, and once the feed reached the turbopumps the liquids were supplied under high pressure at the rate of 8 kg (17.64 lb) per second, combusting spontaneously on contact in the chamber. Sea-level thrust was about 1500 kg (3,307 lb), rising with reducing atmospheric pressure to 1700 kg (3,748 lb) at high altitude. The Type 509A could be throttled back to 100 kg (220 lb) idling rating, but it was inefficient at this level and could often stop entirely. The entire rear fuselage and motor could readily be detached. Though crude compared with later units, the Type 509A was a remarkable achievement and, though over 2.13 m (7 ft) long, weighed little over 100 kg (220 lb).

The cockpit was comfortable, though there was no system available for pressurisation other than a plain ram inlet at the front. The canopy was a flimsy Plexiglas moulding, hinged on the right side and with little ability to resist hail or birds at the speeds the Komet could attain. There was a hinged ventilation window on the left side of the hood, and another air inlet on the underside of the nose. Nose and back armour was provided, but the seat was not of the new ejection type and it was impossible to get out at high airspeeds. The nose was full of radio and other items, including the generator driven by the small windmill propeller, with access by hinging back the instrument panel. Armament comprised two cannon (one in the root of each wing between the spars). Most early armed Komets had the high-velocity 20-mm MG 151/20, but the standard production armament

was the 30-mm MK 108, fed with 60 rounds housed above the main *T-stoff* tank. Compressed-air bottles cocked the guns, and gas pressure served most of the onboard auxiliary power services, including energising the flap hydraulics. The troublesome landing skid was hydraulically retracted on take-off along with the neat steerable tailwheel. Retracting the skid automatically released the wheeled dolly, but this had a habit of bouncing up and smashing into the aircraft or even hooking on the front of the skid. If it failed to separate, a successful landing back on the dolly was not advised; it was only accomplished once. Even Hanna Reitsch tried it once, following total hang-up, and she was severely injured.

Special procedures

By learning in the most painful way, the Luftwaffe refined its Me 163B operating procedures and sloshed water everywhere during refuelling or ground running. Pilots and ground personnel wore special suits of non-organic asbestos and *Mipolamfibre*, though in a number of landings that ended inverted, the aircraft, though not exploding, managed to inflict agonising corrosive injuries when the cockpit tanks spilt substantial amounts on to the pilot before he could be got out. No combat aircraft has ever demanded so much of its operators, and in particular the landing demanded a dead-stick approach at 210 km/h (130 mph) exactly into wind and on to an exact

1 Generator drive propeller
2 Generator
3 Compressed air bottle
4 Battery and electronics packs
5 Cockpit ventilation intake
6 Solid armour (15-mm) nose cone
7 Accumulator pressuriser
8 Direct cockpit air intake
9 FuG 25a radio pack
10 Rudder control assembly
11 Hydraulic and compressed air points
12 Elevon control rocker-bar
13 Control relay
14 Flying controls assembly box

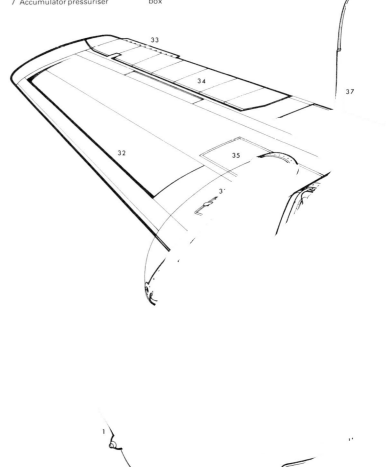

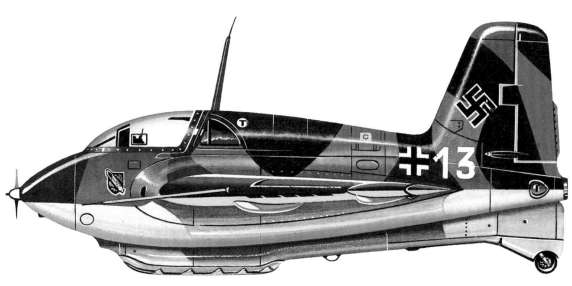

This Komet was in regular service with JG 400 at Brandis, and carried the famed badge 'Wie ein floh – aber Oh-ho!' (only a flea, but Oh-ho!). Cannon magazines were arranged in tandem in the top of the fuselage between the filling points for the highly reactive T-stoff and C-stoff.

Messerschmitt Me 163 variants

DFS 194: preliminary rocket test aircraft to explore stability and control, one only
Me 163A: six more powerful rocket test aircraft closer in design to definitive interceptor
Me 163A-0: 10 training aircraft similar to Me 163A
Me 163B Komet: production interceptor, initial **Me 163Ba-1** batch built at Regensburg with MG151/20 guns and main production **Me 163B-1a** built at dispersed plants and assembled in Black Forest, with 30-mm MK 108 guns; total completed about 320, 279 being taken on Luftwaffe charge
Me 163S: dual trainer with instructor cockpit

above centre fuselage; several built but none flown under rocket power
Me 163C: improved version with HWK 509C-1 motor with main and cruise thrust chambers; two prototypes plus three production aircraft
Me 163D/Ju 248: new design with proper tricycle landing gear and many other improvements; one Me 163D plus one Ju 248 flown only as glider
Mitsubishi Shusui: Japanese copy, produced without detailed drawings, as armed **Ki-200** and navy **J8M1**; one J8M1 flown and crashed 7 July 1945

15 Plastic rudder pedals
16 Radio tuning controls
17 Torque shaft
18 Port T-Stoff cockpit tank (13 Imp gal/60 l capacity)
19 Control column
20 Hinged instrument panel
21 Armourglass windscreen brace
22 Revi 16B gunsight
23 Armourglass internal windscreen (90-mm)
24 Armament and radio switches (starboard console)
25 Pilot's seat
26 Back armour (8-mm)
27 Head and shoulder armour (13-mm)
28 Radio frequency selector pack
29 Headrest
30 Mechanically-jettisonable hinged canopy

31 Ventilation panel
32 Fixed leading-edge wing slot
33 Trim tab
34 Fabric-covered starboard elevon
35 Position of underwing landing flap
36 Inboard trim flap
37 FuG 16yz radio receiving aerial
38 T-Stoff filler cap
39 Main unprotected T-Stoff fuselage tank (229 Imp gal/1,040 l capacity)
40 Aft cockpit glazing
41 Port cannon ammunition box (60 rounds)
42 Starboard cannon ammunition box (60 rounds)

57 Rudder trim tab
58 Rudder control rocker-bar
59 Linkage fairing
60 Fin rear spar/fuselage attachment point
61 Rocket motor combustion chamber
62 Tailpipe
63 Rudder root fairing
64 Rocket thrust orifice
65 Vent pipe outlet
66 Hydraulic cylinder
67 Lifting point
68 Tailwheel fairing
69 Steerable tailwheel
70 Tailwheel axle fork
71 Tailwheel oleo
72 Tailwheel steering linkage

91 Elevon control bell crank
92 Position of port underwing landing flap
93 Push-rod in front spar
94 Front spar
95 FuG 25a aerial
96 Pitot head
97 Wing tank connecting pipe fairing
98 C-Stoff leading-edge tank (16 Imp gal/73 l capacity)
99 Gun-cocking compressed air bottle
100 Main C-Stoff wing tank (38 Imp gal/173 l capacity)
101 Port 30-mm MK 108 short-barrel cannon
102 Expanding shell and link chute
103 Gun forward mounting frame

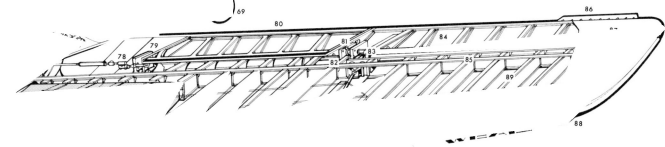

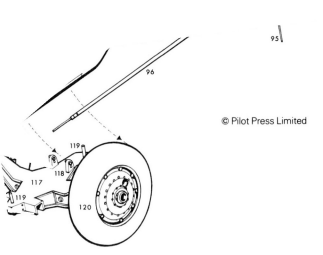

© Pilot Press Limited

43 Ammunition feed chute
44 T-Stoff starter tank
45 Rudder control upper bell crank
46 C-Stoff filler cap
47 HWK 509A-1 motor turbine housing
48 Main rocket motor mounting frame
49 Rudder control rod
50 Disconnect point
51 Aerial matching unit
52 Fin front spar/fuselage attachment point
53 Tailfin construction
54 Rudder horn balance
55 Rudder upper hinge
56 Rudder frame

73 Coupling piece/vertical lever
74 Wing root fillet
75 Combustion chamber support brace
76 Gun-cocking mechanism
77 Trim flap control angle gear (bulkhead mounted)
78 Worm gear
79 Trim flap mounting
80 Port inboard trim flap
81 Elevon mounting
82 Rocker-bar
83 Elevon actuation push-rod
84 Port elevon
85 Wing rear spar
86 Trim tab
87 Elevon outboard hinge
88 Wingtip bumper
89 Wing construction
90 Fixed leading-edge wing slot

104 Pressure-tight gun-control passage
105 Blast tube
106 Gun alignment mechanism
107 Cannon port
108 FuG 23a FF pack
109 Tow-bar attachment point
110 Compressed-air ram for landing skid
111 Hydraulics and compressed-air pipes
112 Landing skid pivots
113 Landing skid keel mounting
114 Landing skid mounting brackets
115 Trolley jettison mechanism
116 Landing skid
117 Take-off trolley frame
118 Take-off trolley retaining lugs
119 Take-off trolley alignment pins
120 Low-pressure tyre

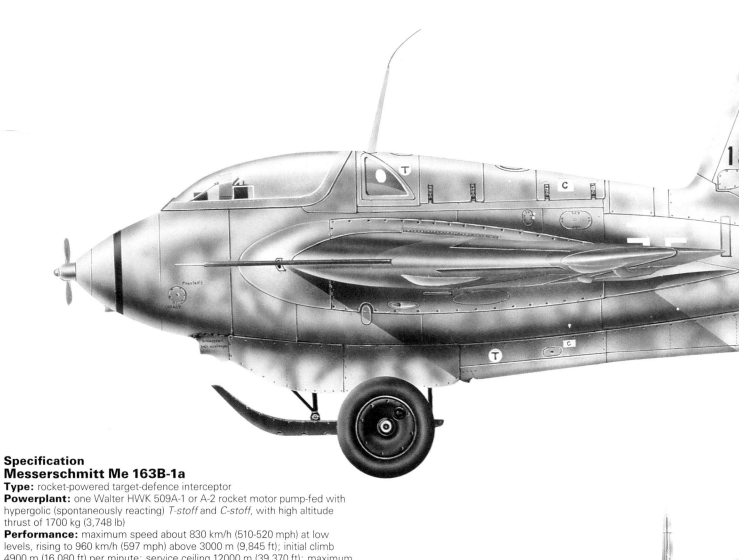

Specification
Messerschmitt Me 163B-1a

Type: rocket-powered target-defence interceptor

Powerplant: one Walter HWK 509A-1 or A-2 rocket motor pump-fed with hypergolic (spontaneously reacting) *T-stoff* and *C-stoff*, with high altitude thrust of 1700 kg (3,748 lb)

Performance: maximum speed about 830 km/h (510-520 mph) at low levels, rising to 960 km/h (597 mph) above 3000 m (9,845 ft); initial climb 4900 m (16,080 ft) per minute; service ceiling 12000 m (39,370 ft); maximum rocket endurance (allowing for periods at reduced thrust) 7 minutes 30 seconds; practical range about 130 km (80 miles) not allowing for combat

Weights: empty 1900 kg (4,190 lb); maximum take-off 4310 kg (9,502 lb)

Dimensions: span 9.40 m (30 ft 7⅓ in); length 5.85 m (19 ft 2⅓ in); height (on take-off dolly) 2.76 m (9 ft 0 ⅔ in); wing area 18.50 m² (199.1 sq ft)

Armament: two 30-mm Rheinmetall MK 108 cannon each with 60 rounds

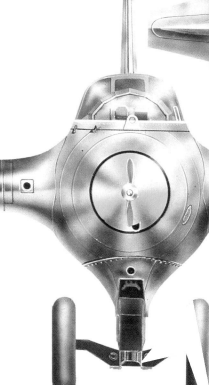

With elaborate plans for the Messerschmitt Me 163B to operate from two rings of bases covering west, northwest and northern Germany, the type could have proved one of the most important operational aircraft of World War II. In reality, however, this ambitious but unpredictable aircraft met with very limited success in the latter part of 1944 and early 1945. Evident in this illustration is the short oval-section fuselage and excellent view afforded to the pilot through the Plexiglas moulded canopy.

Messerschmitt Me 163

This colour scheme was used by the JG 400 Ergänzungsstaffel (training squadron) and also by operational elements of JG 400, to one of which the Me 163B-1a was assigned. This machine, operating from Brandis in early 1945, was unusual in having the white/yellow markings for C-stoff (hydrazine) and T-stoff (peroxide) added to the ventral drains.

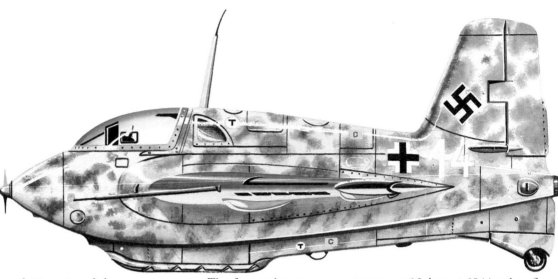

spot, with no opportunity for a second attempt, and always remembering to extend the skid and then return the lever to neutral to remove the hydraulic pressure and restore oleo springing.

Fast-moving targets

Thus, early selected pilots were above average, and after initial experience flying a clipped-wing version of the Habicht glider they progressed to towed glides in the Me 163A, then glides in water-ballasted Me 163As, then powered flights in the Me 163A, and finally to the rather dreaded Me 163B. Production Komets were accepted by the Luftwaffe from May 1944. It had been Späte's plan to build up Komet forces at a dense ring of bases each about 100 km (62 miles) apart, so that each Komet could also glide home, but covering all approach routes for bombers from British bases. This never proved possible. Though a few combat missions were flown, often by development Komets, from Karlshagen, Zwischenahn, Wittmundhafen and Udetfeld, the first proper base selected was Brandis, near Leipzig, chosen to try to protect the largest concentration of oil refineries in Germany.

The unit was I/JG 400, under Oberleutnant Robert Olejnik and formed from Erprobungskommando 16 at Zwischenahn in May 1944 and finally equipped with aircraft in late July, at Brandis. Before this there had been many attempts by Komet pilots to engage the enemy, but these had always been frustrated, on one occasion by the cut-out of the motor by negative *g* just as the pilot was about to blast two unsuspecting Republic P-47s. The first major engagement was on 28 July 1944 when six Komets got airborne to try to interfere with 596 B-17s heading for the Leuna-Merseburg oil complex. No hits were scored, mainly because of high closing speeds, and the landings were hair-raising with many near-collisions.

The first major engagement came on 16 August 1944, when five Komets took on 1,096 USAAF heavies which had not yet been instructed to avoid Brandis. The first to reach a B-17 was hit by the bomber's tail gunner. Another Komet scored hits on a B-17 of the 305th BG, but was then destroyed by Lieutenant Colonel John Murphy's North American P-51. But on 24 August Feldwebel Siegfried Schubert destroyed two B-17s, and other Komets bagged two others. Such success was not to be repeated, and among the casualties was Schubert, who blew up on take-off because of the troublesome dolly. Never did the growing armada of Komets strike a telling blow, largely because of the difficulty of aiming accurately in the very brief firing time available. To overcome this the SG 500 (*Sondergeräte*, or special equipment) or *Jagdfaust* was devised, with 10 vertical barrels along the wing roots firing 50-mm projectiles upwards, triggered automatically by photocells sensing the reduced light input as the rocket interceptor flashed past beneath its target. SG 500 did well in test, but was used just once, on 10 April 1945, before the final German collapse.

Komets not to be

There were many ideas for improved Komets, including a far better version, the Me 163D/Ju 248, which had a proper landing gear and a motor with main and cruise thrust chambers. But even the Soviet Union soon gave up development of this (as the MiG Zh or I-270) and the fairest overall assessment of the Me 163 is that 80 per cent of Komet losses occurred during take-off or landing, 15 per cent were due to loss of control in a compressibility dive or fire in the air, and the remaining 5 per cent were losses in combat. And in 1945, with some 300 in front-line service, only I/JG 400 was able to engage the enemy; it claimed nine bombers but lost 14 in doing so.

Messerschmitt AG built no fewer than 70 pre-production Me 163Bs at Regensburg, all assigned to particular operational or mechanical problems. Probably the most dangerous phase of each flight was the landing, which had to be perfect every time. Here the 35th Me 163B (V35), coded GH+IN, glides safely to a stop.

Two of the Me 163B prototypes, V6 and V18, were later modified with prototypes of the HWK 509C-1 motor equipped with main and cruising thrust chambers, to give much better flight endurance. Here the V6 blows steam through its propellant lines in the summer of 1944. Note the repositioned retractable tailwheel.

Heinkel He 177 Greif

The Luftwaffe failed to appreciate the value of strategic bombing, and began work on suitable designs too late to save the war. One of the few aircraft that did get off the ground was Heinkel's remarkable Greif. Not the most reliable of aircraft, it still managed some noteworthy missions, including pioneering air-to-surface missile work.

In the final three years of World War II Hitler's Germany was steadily reduced to rubble by the greatest fleets of heavy bombers the world will ever see. In reply the mighty Luftwaffe fielded just one type of heavy bomber, which achieved very little except to frighten its crews to death (often literally). Not to put too fine a point on it, it suffered from problems.

To be frank, while the RAF and US Army Air Force was deeply imbued with the urge to deploy strategic airpower, the Luftwaffe was primarily a tactical force dedicated to support the Wehrmacht in its land battles. Moreover, when in 1936 Goering was asked to back the launch of a heavy bomber, he explained the Führer was only interested in how many bombers there were, not how big they were. At that time, the Berlin air ministry was supporting the development of a 'Ural-bomber' programme with two rival types, the Do 19 and Ju 89. Had these continued, they would have been obsolescent by World War II. This programme was cancelled in 1937, and replaced by a requirement called 'Bomber A' which it was hoped would lead to a better aircraft. This requirement demanded a maximum speed of 540 km/h (335 mph) and the ability to carry a 2000 kg (4,410 lb) bombload over a radius of 1600 km (995 miles) at a cruising speed of 500 km/h (310 mph) – challenging figures. To make matters much more difficult it also required the capability of making medium-angle diving attacks.

Ernst Heinkel AG was given the job, without competition, and Projekt 1041 was actually started in late 1936. Under Technical Director Hertel, the gifted Günter twin brothers planned a bomber incorporating many radical new features, intended to give it the highest possible performance. Later designated He 177, the new bomber was marvellously clean aerodynamically. The fuselage was like a tube, with a glazed nose and a gun position in the glazed tailcone. The mid-mounted wing had high aspect ratio, for maximum efficiency, and under it was room for a large bomb bay. Clearly, power had to come from four engines of about 895.2 kW (1,200 hp) or two of 1790.4 kW (2,400 hp), but there were no 1790.4 kW (2,400 hp) engines. Boldly, in partnership with Daimler-Benz, Heinkel had designed a dive bomber, the He 119, powered by a DB 606 double engine comprising two DB 601 inverted-V12 engines side-by-side joined through a common gearbox to a single propeller. Two of these were to power the new heavy bomber, clearly offering lower drag and better manoeuvrability than four separate engines. To reduce drag further it was planned to augment the engine cooling by using surface condensation of steam in sandwich panels forming part of the wing skin. There were to be four main landing gears, one retracting inwards and another outwards under each engine to lie in the wing ahead of the main spar. Defensive guns were to be in remotely controlled turrets above the forward fuselage in the front and rear of a ventral gondola, as well as in the manned tail position. Altogether the 177 promised to have lower drag than any previous aircraft (even an unarmed civil one) of its size.

Things began to go wrong from the outset. By early 1939, when the V1 first prototype was taking shape, it was reluctantly concluded that steam cooling was impractical. Much larger radiators had to be used (they were made circular, round the front of each double

The He 177 had a checkered career in Luftwaffe service, its advantages negated by a plague of troubles mostly concerning the propulsion system. Worst of these problems was a tendency for the engines to catch fire without warning, leading to the uncomplimentary nickname 'Luftwaffenfeuerzeug'.

The He 177 V1 first flew on 19 November 1939, but was only aloft for 12 minutes before engine temperatures soared, heralding a long saga of such problems. Another problem to surface was the inadequacy of the tail surfaces, which were increased on the second prototype, and again on production machines.

Aside from the engine problems, the He 177 exhibited a nasty swing on take-off, resulting in several accidents. The A-1 version introduced larger tail surfaces and stronger damping on the tailwheel. This is the A-03 pre-production aircraft, showing the unique mainwheel arrangement.

engine). In turn this meant greater drag, which demanded extra fuel which meant increased weight, in a vicious circle. The ministry officials then decreed that this big bomber had to be able to make steep 60° dive attacks, which resulted in a considerable increase in structure weight, further reducing performance and also requiring addition of large dive brakes under the wings. To slow the landing of the overweight aircraft full-span Fowler flaps were adopted, the outer portions coming out from under the ailerons. Again there were problems because the wing had not been stressed for the large lift and drag loads of the flaps.

The V1 made its maiden flight on 19 November 1939. Despite being unarmed it failed to come anywhere near the Bomber A requirement, maximum speed being 460 km/h (285 mph) and range being inadequate. On the other hand it handled reasonably well, and the few snags recorded gave no indication of the years of toil and disaster that were to follow.

Seven further prototypes followed, each heavier than its predecessor. Vertical tail area was increased, triple bomb bays were incorporated, various types of defensive armament fitted (low-drag remotely controlled guns were replaced by conventional turrets or hand-aimed guns) and ceaseless efforts made to try to eliminate the most serious problem, which was the frequency of engine fires. V2 suffered flutter and disintegrated, V4 crashed into the sea and V5's engines caught fire at low level, the aircraft flying into the ground and exploding.

In 1939 a total of 30 He 177A-0 pre-production aircraft were ordered, plus five from Arado. These had many changes including a redesigned nose for a crew of five, armament comprising a 7.92-mm MG81 in the multi-pane hemispherical nose, a 20-mm MG FF in the front of the gondola, a twin MG81Z at the rear of the gondola, a

This He 177A-5 was captured by British forces and allocated the serial TS439. Painted with large black and white stripes, it returned to England for evaluation. A high-altitude He 177A-7 was also obtained.

In order to cure the He 177's engine problems, Heinkel redesigned the bomber with four separate engines under the spurious designation He 177B. The redesign was in fact so great that its true number was He 277. This is the prototype, a converted He 177A-3.

Early A-5 series aircraft retained the three bomb bays of the A-3, with the forward unit blanked off. However, the A-5/R6 dispensed with two of the weapons bays for the maritime attack role. These aircraft of II./KG 40 are seen at Mérignac after the adoption of the Atlantic reconnaissance role in spring 1944.

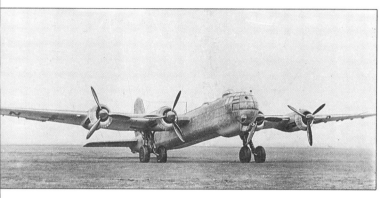

13-mm MG 131 in the roof turret and a hand-aimed MG 131 in the tail. In the course of A-0 production the dive brakes were removed, partly because the 177 was structurally unable to meet the requirement and partly because the dive bomber had shown itself to be vulnerable. There were many other changes, but the most urgently needed ones concerned the powerplants.

When one studies the detailed reports on some of the many hundreds of serious He 177 engine fires one marvels that the usually impressive Germanic design efficiency could have been so often forgotten. Many features of the DB 606 installation might almost have been deliberately arranged to give trouble. The oil scavenge pumps were oversized, and at heights over 6000 m (19,685 ft) the oil tended to aerate and foam, leading to breakdown in lubrication and to seizures, con-rods breaking through the crankcase and fires. Almost always the oil dripped on to the white-hot exhaust manifold serving the two inner banks of cylinders, and radiant heat from this frequently ignited oil and fuel that collected in the bottom of the cowling. Many other fires resulted from fuel leaks from the high-pressure injection pumps and rigid piping, and the whole engine was installed so

tight up to the main spar that there was no room for a firewall and the piping, electric cables and other services were jammed in so tightly that, especially when soaked in leaking fuel and oil, the fire risk was awesome. There were even problems caused by the handing (opposite rotation) of the big 4.52 m (14 ft 8 in) four-bladed propellers. Seen from behind, the left propeller rotated anti-clockwise and the right propeller clockwise, and the engines with inserted idler wheels to reverse output rotation often suffered from torsional vibration causing crankshaft failure. At least seven A-0 aircraft were badly damaged in take-off accidents caused by uncontrollable swing to left or right, despite enlargement of the fin and rudder, and it became standard practice on take-off to keep the tailwheel on the ground as long as possible.

Production system

Over 25 of the 35 A-0s were destroyed from various causes, and the rest were used for crew training at Ludwigslust. Whereas at the start Heinkel had predicted the He 177 would be in service in 1940, by the end of that year production had not even begun. Indeed, for various reasons Heinkel's Oranienburg factory never built the initial production model at all, partly because, despite increasing pressure for the 177 to get into action, the A-1 version was still seen to be imperfect to the point of being dangerous. All 130 examples of the He 177A-1 were made by Arado, between March 1942 and June 1943, with the tails and parts of the fuselage being supplied from a factory at Mielec in Poland. The A-1 retained 2014-kW (2,700-hp) DB606 engines, and incorporated only a few of the dozens of planned improvements, but it could carry very heavy bombloads weighing up to 6000 kg (13,230 lb). It could not, however, carry the FX1400 or Hs 293 guided bombs, though Field Marshal Milch thought it could. Hitler urged the aircraft be brought into service, to range far beyond the Eastern Front at night and to escort U-boats and blockade runners in the Atlantic.

At last, in October 1942, Heinkel began delivering the improved He 177A-3, but far from a tempo of 70 per month the huge Oranienburg plant found it hard to get beyond five per month. The A-3 did its best to eradicate the faults. The engine remained the 606, though it had been hoped to fit the 2312.4-kW (3,100-hp) DB 610 (made up of a pair of DB 603s). However, the engines were mounted 20 cm (7 in) further forward, the exhaust system was redesigned and many other dangerous features were altered. To balance the engines the rear

6 Staffel of Kampfgeschwader 100 was based at Toulouse-Blagnac during May 1944, using its He 177A-5s on bombing missions. Most were maritime-orientated, flying either to the Mediterranean or the Bay of Biscay.

fuselage was extended by 1.6 m (5 ft 2 in) and a second dorsal turret added. Like the A-1, the A-3 was produced with different Rüstsätzen giving different armament, almost all sub-types having an MG 151/20 in the front of the gondola and a second of these hard-hitting cannon in the tail, aimed by a gunner who did not lie but sat comfortably under a Plexiglas bulge under the rudder. Other weapons carried included the Hs 293 radio-controlled attack missile and, in the R-7 and all A-5 versions, a range of anti-ship torpedoes.

Heinkel made 170 A-3s, following which, from February to December 1943, Heinkel and Arado delivered 261 He 177A-5s, which in the final year of war was the chief operational version. The main advantage of the A-5 was that it introduced the more powerful DB 610 engine, and as the weights were only fractionally heavier than those of the first versions the performance was improved, especially in ceiling which went up from a poor 7000 m (22,965 ft) to just over 8000 m (26,245 ft). Standard features of the A-5 included a strengthened airframe, shorter main-gear legs, normal ailerons without Fowler flaps extending to the wingtips, and racks under the forward fuselage and outer wings for three Hs 293s, or two Hs 294s or two FX 1400 bombs. Like the A-3/R7 the A-5 could also release the LT50 glider torpedo, which was fitted with a small glider airframe enabling it to be released from a height of 250 m (820 ft) several kilometres from a target.

Bombing London

Until manufacture of all aircraft other than fighters was virtually abandoned in October 1944, Heinkel and Arado together delivered no fewer than 565 He 177A-5s, and their operational record was much better than that of earlier versions. By far the most important Luftwaffe units to use the He 177 were KG40 and KG100, the former being concerned chiefly with the Battle of the Atlantic with the Hs 293 and both taking part in Operation Steinbock, the revenge attacks on London in the early weeks of 1944. In Steinbock experienced crews found they could climb to almost 9000 m (29,527 ft) before nearing England. Then, at full power and in a shallow dive, they stood a chance of avoiding interception by keeping speed at about 700 km/h (435 mph). On the other hand the effectiveness of these missions was extremely low. On 13 February 1944 Goering was at Rheine to watch 2. and 3./KG100 set off for England; 14 taxied out, 13 took off, eight soon returned with overheated or burning engines, four reached London and three came back.

Operational training was undertaken by the Flugzeugführerschule (B) 16 at Burg near Magdeburg, initially with ex-KG 40 He 177A-1s but later with improved models such as this He 177A-3/R2. The A-3 had a lengthened fuselage and redesigned engine mountings.

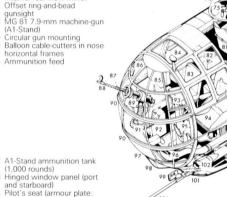

Heinkel He 177A-5 cutaway drawing

1 Starboard navigation light
2 Detachable wingtip
3 FuG 101 radio altimeter (FM)
4 Aileron control runs
5 Starboard aileron
6 Aileron trim tab
7 Spring-loaded geared tab
8 Aileron counter-balance
9 FuG 102 radio altimeter (pulsed)
10 Tab mechanism
11 Fowler flap outboard track
12 Fowler flap position (extended)
13 Aileron tab control linkage
14 Flap actuating cylinder (hydraulic)
15 Control cables
16 Main spar (outboard section)
17 Wing ribs
18 Auxiliary front spar
19 Heated leading edge
20 Oil radiator intake
21 Starboard Hs 293 radio-controlled glide-bomb
22 Starboard outer mainwheel door (open position)
23 Starboard outer mainwheel well
24 Balloon cable-cutter in leading edge
25 Starboard ETC weapons rack
26 Twin oil radiators (starboard engines)
27 Radiator outlet flap
28 Hot-air ducting
29 Mainwheel door actuating cylinder
30 No. 8 (starboard outer) fuel tank of 1,120 litre/246.5 Imp gal capacity (flexible bag)
31 Fuel filler cap
32 Fowler flap outer section
33 auxiliary rear spar
34 Wing dihedral break point
35 Fowler flap track
36 Starboard fuel starting tank (9 litre/2 gal capacity)
37 Starboard oil tanks
38 Main hydraulic tank (starboard only) (32 litre/7 gal capacity)
39 Fuel filler cap
40 No. 3 (starboard inner) fuel tank of 621 litre/136.5 Imp gal capacity (metal/self sealing)
41 Fowler flap inner section
42 Main spar (inboard section)
43 Starboard inner mainwheel well
44 Engine supercharger
45 Nacelle fairing
46 Wing spar attachment point and fairing
47 Engine accessories
48 Daimler-Benz DB 610A-1 24-cylinder liquid-cooled engine
49 Anti-vibration side-mounting pad
50 Supercharger and wing de-icing intakes
51 Nacelle former
52 Coolant vents
53 Engine forward mounting
54 Cooling gills
55 Double-gear crank casing
56 Single propeller shaft
57 Propeller de-icing saddle tank
58 Nacelle cooling profile

59 Propeller variable-pitch mechanism
60 Propeller boss
61 Blade cuffs
62 VDM four-bladed propeller (right-handed)
63 Chin intake
64 Flame damper exhaust
65 Starboard outer mainwheel leg
66 Starboard inner mainwheel leg
67 Starboard outer mainwheel
68 D/F loop in dorsal blister
69 Emergency hydraulic tank (25 litre/5.5 Imp gal)
70 No. 7 fuselage frame
71 C-Stand ammunition tank (1,000 rounds)
72 Dorsal barbette remote drive motor
73 Revi gunsight with slotted 10-mm armour protection
74 Remote control sighting cupola
75 Barbette traverse control handle
76 Barbette elevation control handle
77 Main radio panel (FuG 10P; general-purpose set) (FuG17Z: VHF communication and homing) (FuG BL 2F: Blind-approach)
78 First-aid pack
79 Navigator's take-off/landing station
80 Window
81 Gunner's seat
82 Emergency jettison panels (port and starboard)
83 Bomb aimer's seat (raised)
84 External rear-view mirror
85 Engine control panel (starboard)
86 Internal rear-view mirror
87 Offset ring-and-bead gunsight
88 MG 81 7.9-mm machine-gun (A1-Stand)
89 Circular gun mounting
90 Balloon cable-cutters in nose horizontal frames
91 Ammunition feed

92 A1-Stand ammunition tank (1,000 rounds)
93 Hinged window panel (port and starboard)
94 Pilot's seat (armour plate: 9-mm back, 6-mm seat)
95 Rudder pedals
96 Cockpit hot-air
97 Lower glazed section often overpainted/armoured
98 Lotfe 7D bombsight fairing
99 'Boxed' gunsight
100 MG 151 20-mm cannon (A2-Stand)
101 Bullet-proof glass in nose of 'bola'
102 De-icing intake
103 Ventral crew entry hatch
104 Telescopic ladder
105 Actuating arm
106 MG 151 20-mm cannon ammunition feed
107 De-icing air heater/blower
108 A2-Stand ammunition tank (300 rounds)
109 Toilet installation
110 C-Stand ammunition feed
111 Thermos flasks
112 Circular vision port
113 MG 151 13-mm machine gun (C-Stand) at rear of 'bola'
114 'Fritz X' (Kramer X-1) radio-controlled bomb
115 Cruciform main fins
116 SAP warhead
117 Tail fin structure
118 Air-brake attachment
119 Ventral bomb rack (only fitted if forward bomb bay blanked off)
120 Forward-bomb bay (often blanked off)
121 Fuel tank retaining strap lugs
122 Internal bomb shackle
123 Bomb bay central partition

124 No. 4 (fuselage) fuel tank (1520 litre/334 Imp gal) (Replaced by 3450 litre/759 Imp gal tank if bomb bay blanked off) (metal/self-sealing)
125 Fuel filler cap
126 Barbette remote drive cooling duct and linkage
127 Remote control dorsal barbette (B1-Stand)
128 Twin 13-mm MG 131 guns
129 No. 13 fuselage frame
130 Barbette structure
131 B1-Stand double ammunition tank (1,000 rounds per gun)
132 Central bomb bay (often blanked off)
133 Bomb bay door (outer section)
134 Port inner mainwheel well
135 No. 5 (fuselage) fuel tank (1520 litre/334 Imp gal) (Replacd by 3450 litre/759 Imp gal tank if bomb bay blanked off) (metal/self sealing)
136 Fuel filler cap
137 No. 19 fuselage frame
138 Main spar carry-through
139 Main spar/fuselage attachment points
140 Aft bomb bay
141 Auxiliary rear spar/fuselage attachment points
142 No. 1 (Fuselage) main fuel tank (1140 litre/330 Imp gal) (metal/self sealing)

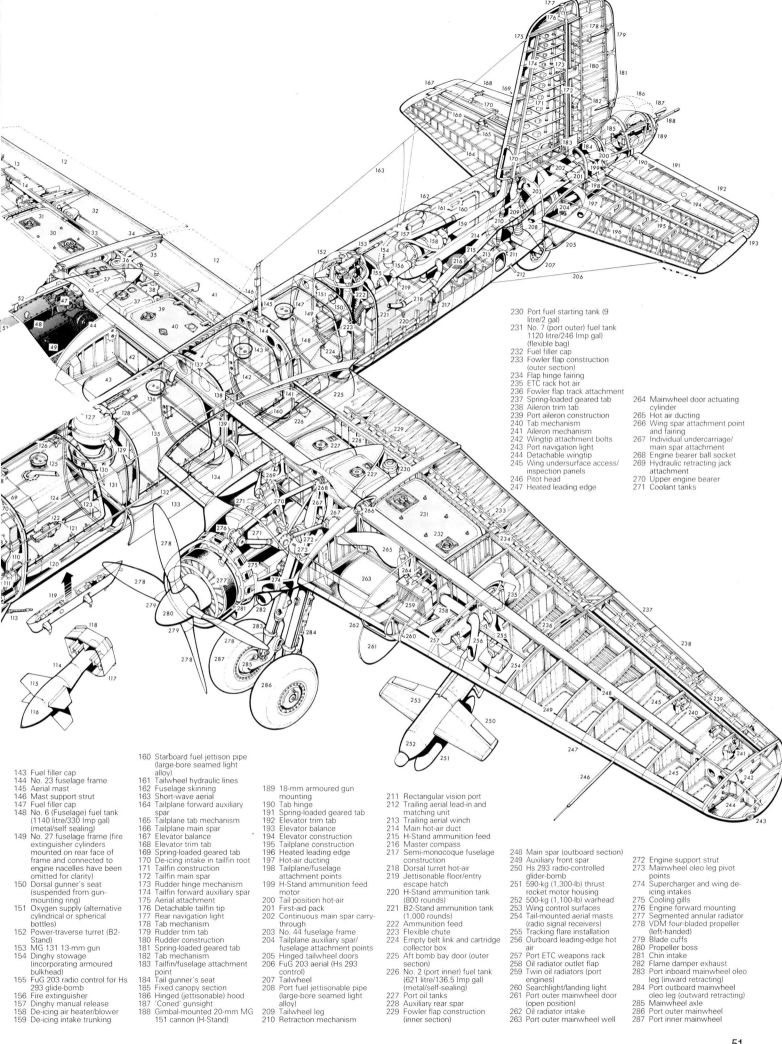

230 Port fuel starting tank (9 litre/2 gal)
231 No. 7 (port outer) fuel tank 1120 litre/246 Imp gal) (flexible bag)
232 Fuel filler cap
233 Fowler flap construction (outer section)
234 Flap hinge fairing
235 ETC rack hot air
236 Fowler flap track attachment
237 Spring-loaded geared tab
238 Aileron trim tab
239 Port aileron construction
240 Tab mechanism
241 Aileron mechanism
242 Wingtip attachment bolts
243 Port navigation light
244 Detachable wingtip
245 Wing undersurface access/ inspection panels
246 Pitot head
247 Heated leading edge
264 Mainwheel door actuating cylinder
265 Hot air ducting
266 Wing spar attachment point and fairing
267 Individual undercarriage/ main spar attachment
268 Engine bearer ball socket
269 Hydraulic retracting jack attachment
270 Upper engine bearer
271 Coolant tanks

143 Fuel filler cap
144 No. 23 fuselage frame
145 Aerial mast
146 Mast support strut
147 Fuel filler cap
148 No. 6 (Fuselage) fuel tank (1140 litre/330 Imp gal) (metal/self sealing)
149 No. 27 fuselage frame (fire extinguisher cylinders mounted on rear face of frame and connected to engine nacelles have been omitted for clarity)
150 Dorsal gunner's seat (suspended from gun-mounting ring)
151 Oxygen supply (alternative cylindrical or spherical bottles)
152 Power-traverse turret (B2-Stand)
153 MG 131 13-mm gun
154 Dinghy stowage (incorporating armoured bulkhead)
155 FuG 203 radio control for Hs 293 glide-bomb
156 Fire extinguisher
157 Dinghy manual release
158 De-icing air heater/blower
159 De-icing intake trunking

160 Starboard fuel jettison pipe (large-bore seamed light alloy)
161 Tailwheel hydraulic lines
162 Fuselage skinning
163 Short-wave aerial
164 Tailplane forward auxiliary spar
165 Tailplane tab mechanism
166 Tailplane main spar
167 Elevator balance
168 Elevator trim tab
169 Spring-loaded geared tab
170 De-icing intake in tailfin root
171 Tailfin construction
172 Tailfin main spar
173 Rudder hinge mechanism
174 Tailfin forward auxiliary spar
175 Aerial attachment
176 Detachable tailfin tip
177 Rear navigation light
178 Rudder trim tab
179 Rudder trim tab
180 Rudder construction
181 Spring-loaded geared tab
182 Tab mechanism
183 Tailfin/fuselage attachment point
184 Tail gunner's seat
185 Fixed canopy section
186 Hinged (jettisonable) hood
187 'Coned' gunsight
188 Gimbal-mounted 20-mm MG 151 cannon (H-Stand)

189 18-mm armoured gun mounting
190 Tab hinge
191 Spring-loaded geared tab
192 Elevator trim tab
193 Elevator balance
194 Elevator construction
195 Tailplane construction
196 Heated leading edge
197 Hot-air ducting
198 Tailplane/fuselage attachment points
199 H-Stand ammunition feed motor
200 Tail position hot-air
201 First-aid pack
202 Continuous main spar carry-through
203 No. 44 fuselage frame
204 Tailplane auxiliary spar/ fuselage attachment points
205 Hinged tailwheel doors
206 FuG 203 aerial (Hs 293 control)
207 Tailwheel
208 Port fuel jettisonable pipe (large-bore seamed light alloy)
209 Tailwheel leg
210 Retraction mechanism

211 Rectangular vision port
212 Trailing aerial lead-in and matching unit
213 Trailing aerial winch
214 Main hot-air duct
215 H-Stand ammunition feed
216 Master compass
217 Semi-monocoque fuselage construction
218 Dorsal turret hot-air
219 Jettisonable floor/entry escape hatch
220 H-Stand ammunition tank (800 rounds)
221 B2-Stand ammunition tank (1,000 rounds)
222 Ammunition feed
223 Flexible chute
224 Empty belt link and cartridge collector box
225 Aft bomb bay door (outer section)
226 No. 2 (port inner) fuel tank (621 litre/136.5 Imp gal) (metal/self-sealing)
227 Port oil tanks
228 Auxiliary rear spar
229 Fowler flap construction (inner section)

248 Main spar (outboard section)
249 Auxiliary front spar
250 Hs 293 radio-controlled glider-bomb
251 590-kg (1,300-lb) thrust rocket motor housing
252 500-kg (1,100-lb) warhead
253 Wing control surfaces
254 Tail-mounted aerial masts (radio signal receivers)
255 Tracking flare installation
256 Outboard leading-edge hot air
257 Port ETC weapons rack
258 Oil radiator outlet flap
259 Twin oil radiators (port engines)
260 Searchlight/landing light
261 Port outer mainwheel door (open position)
262 Oil radiator intake
263 Port outer mainwheel well

272 Engine support strut
273 Mainwheel oleo leg pivot points
274 Supercharger and wing de-icing intakes
275 Cooling gills
276 Engine forward mounting
277 Segmented annular radiator
278 VDM four-bladed propeller (left-handed)
279 Blade cuffs
280 Propeller boss
281 Chin intake
282 Flame damper exhaust
283 Port inboard mainwheel oleo leg (inward retracting)
284 Port outboard mainwheel oleo leg (outward retracting)
285 Mainwheel axle
286 Port outer mainwheel
287 Port inner mainwheel

51

Heinkel He 177 Greif

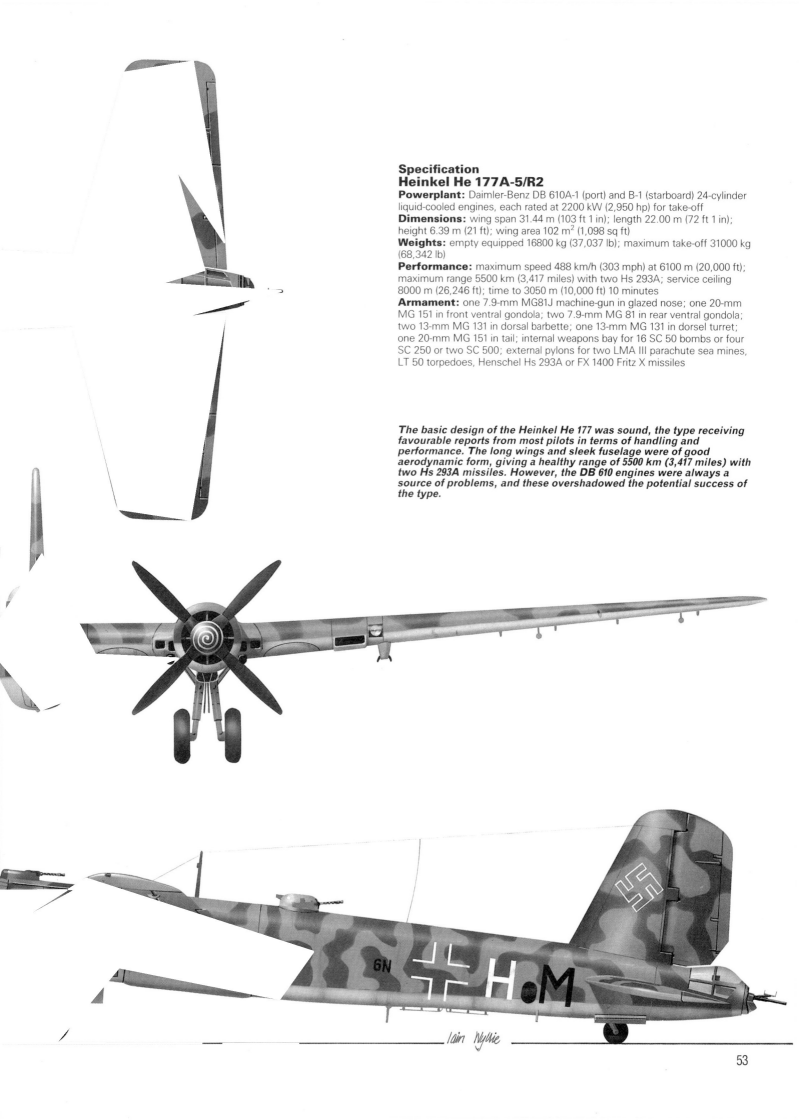

Specification
Heinkel He 177A-5/R2

Powerplant: Daimler-Benz DB 610A-1 (port) and B-1 (starboard) 24-cylinder liquid-cooled engines, each rated at 2200 kW (2,950 hp) for take-off

Dimensions: wing span 31.44 m (103 ft 1 in); length 22.00 m (72 ft 1 in); height 6.39 m (21 ft); wing area 102 m² (1,098 sq ft)

Weights: empty equipped 16800 kg (37,037 lb); maximum take-off 31000 kg (68,342 lb)

Performance: maximum speed 488 km/h (303 mph) at 6100 m (20,000 ft); maximum range 5500 km (3,417 miles) with two Hs 293A; service ceiling 8000 m (26,246 ft); time to 3050 m (10,000 ft) 10 minutes

Armament: one 7.9-mm MG81J machine-gun in glazed nose; one 20-mm MG 151 in front ventral gondola; two 7.9-mm MG 81 in rear ventral gondola; two 13-mm MG 131 in dorsal barbette; one 13-mm MG 131 in dorsal turret; one 20-mm MG 151 in tail; internal weapons bay for 16 SC 50 bombs or four SC 250 or two SC 500; external pylons for two LMA III parachute sea mines, LT 50 torpedoes, Henschel Hs 293A or FX 1400 Fritz X missiles

The basic design of the Heinkel He 177 was sound, the type receiving favourable reports from most pilots in terms of handling and performance. The long wings and sleek fuselage were of good aerodynamic form, giving a healthy range of 5500 km (3,417 miles) with two Hs 293A missiles. However, the DB 610 engines were always a source of problems, and these overshadowed the potential success of the type.

Heinkel He 177 Greif

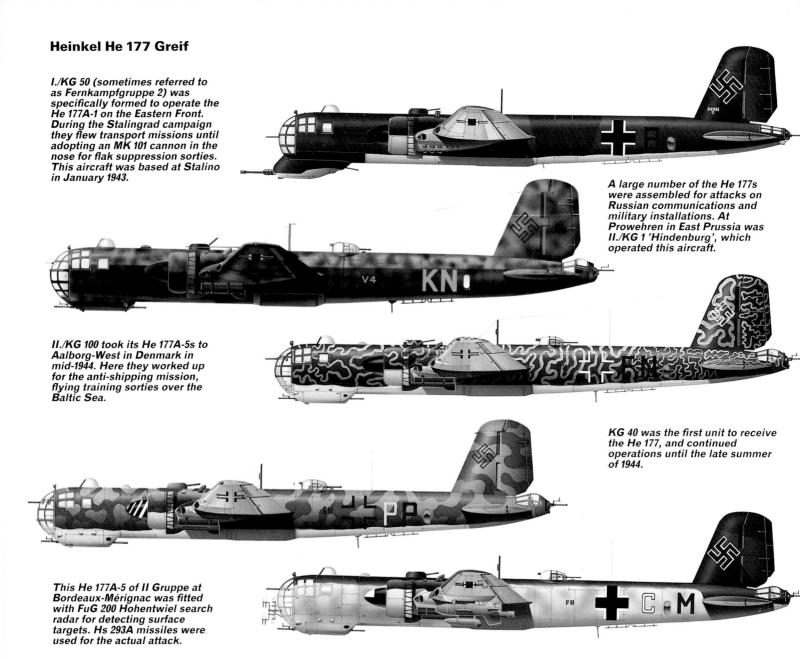

I./KG 50 (sometimes referred to as Fernkampfgruppe 2) was specifically formed to operate the He 177A-1 on the Eastern Front. During the Stalingrad campaign they flew transport missions until adopting an MK 101 cannon in the nose for flak suppression sorties. This aircraft was based at Stalino in January 1943.

A large number of the He 177s were assembled for attacks on Russian communications and military installations. At Prowehren in East Prussia was II./KG 1 'Hindenburg', which operated this aircraft.

II./KG 100 took its He 177A-5s to Aalborg-West in Denmark in mid-1944. Here they worked up for the anti-shipping mission, flying training sorties over the Baltic Sea.

KG 40 was the first unit to receive the He 177, and continued operations until the late summer of 1944.

This He 177A-5 of II Gruppe at Bordeaux-Mérignac was fitted with FuG 200 Hohentwiel search radar for detecting surface targets. Hs 293A missiles were used for the actual attack.

There were many sub-variants made in small numbers. Front-line armourers near Stalingrad – which was resupplied at great cost by a handful of He 177s used as transports – fitted 50-mm BK5 anti-tank guns under the nose. Later the He 177A-3/R5 was fited with the 75-mm gun, but this strained the structure and was altogether too powerful and only five were built. Several were flown with an electrically powered tail turret with two MG 151/20 guns, and the planned He 177A-6 was to have either this turret or one with four MG81s. The A-6, of which six were built, had a pressurised cabin, as did the A-5/R8, the latter being a single aircraft with remotely controlled barbettes in the chin and tail locations. One of the last of the numerous development proototypes, the V38 (basically an A-5), was stripped down at the Letov factory at Prague and (it was said) prepared to carry 'the German atomic bomb'. This may have been a mere rumour, but unlike several of the later variants which deleted the front and middle bomb bays, the V38 was to have had a single gigantic bomb bay. Another unusual version was intended for destroying formations of heavy bombers. The 177 Zerstörer, three of which were produced in 1944 by conversion of bombers (believed to be A-3s), were fitted with a battery of 33 large rocket launch tubes aimed upwards, slightly ahead and slightly to the right. The idea was

The weapon most associated with Heinkel He 177 in the anti-shipping role is the Henschel Hs 293A missile. These could be carried under the wings or, as here, on a special pylon fitted to the blanked-off forward bomb bay. Releases were usually made between 10 and 14 km (6.2 and 8.7 miles) from the target.

that the He 177 should formate below, behind and to the left of the bombers, but Allied fighters made the idea impractical.

Last version to get into limited production, and then only in an interim form, the A-7 had a wing extended in span from 31.46 m (103 ft 2 in) to 36.6 m (120 ft). It was intended to have 2685.6-kW (3,600-hp) DB613 engines, but these were not ready. It carried extra fuel, and intensely interested the Japanese who considered building it under licence. They planned to fit four separate engines, but Heinkel's own He 277 with four separate engines never had official approval and only a string of prototypes were built mainly with DB603A engines.

Heinkel He 115

Within a few months of its first flight in 1938, the He 115 had captured eight world speed records. Its remarkable performance, for a seaplane of the day, made it an obvious candidate for Hitler's newly-founded Luftwaffe Seeflieger and a year later the aircraft went to war as a torpedo bomber. Rapidly overtaken by progress, perhaps the He 115's greatest claim to fame is that it managed to serve with Germany, Britain and neutral Sweden.

World War II was the last conflict in which twin-float seaplanes played a significant part. Of dozens of types used, the biggest and most powerful seaplane used in quantity was the Heinkel He 115. What makes its story even more fascinating is that it saw service not only with Germany but also with Norway, Sweden, Finland and the British RAF.

This is despite the fact that the He 115 was, like many contemporaries, obsolescent from the start. Though designed as a warplane to fly not only patrol but also torpedo and bombing missions, the 115 was always too slow and ill-defended to have any chance against fighters. This was far from obvious when the requirement for a new See-Mehrzweckeflugzeug was issued in July 1935. In early 1938 prototypes of the He 115 proved superior to the rival Ha 140, and Heinkel was awarded the first of several production contracts. These were ultimately to total 138 aircraft, of which 76 were built by Flugzeugbau 'Weser'.

The He 115 V1 made its first flight in August 1937. A conventional all-metal stressed-skin machine, it had a slim fuselage, mid-mounted wing with a rectangular centre-section and sharply tapered outer panels, braced tailplane, twin BMW 132K engines (derived from the Pratt & Whitney Hornet) each rated at 715 kW (960 hp), and single-step floats each attached by tandem struts and multiple bracing wires. The wings had simple slotted flaps, the tailplane was fixed and there were large trim tabs on all control surfaces. The fuselage was arranged to accommodate a crew of three. The pilot's cockpit was above the wing leading edge, covered by a sliding canopy. In the glazed nose was a seat for the observer who also had a bombsight and, in an upper cupola, an MG 15 machine-gun. Above the trailing edge was the cockpit for the radio operator, who also had an MG 15 for upper rear defence. The fuselage beneath the wing was designed as an internal weapons bay, able to accommodate an 800-kg (1,763-lb) torpedo or three SC250 1250-kg (550-lb) bombs.

Displaying the distinctive wing shape of the earlier Heinkel 70, a Heinkel He 115B taxis in Norwegian waters. Despite a certain amount of obsolescence, the type proved to be particularly tough, especially in rough seas, and was also able to sustain a great deal of combat damage. Water and flight handling were excellent, as was its speed.

Heinkel He 115

The first prototype flew in August 1938, and to publicise the type was later prepared with a streamlined nosecone and additional fuel for record-breaking. In this configuration it established several float seaplane records for speed with load over various distances on 20 March 1938.

Altogether the He 115 showed itself to be extremely strong, to handle well and to have no significant shortcomings. In March 1938, by which time the 115 had been picked for the Luftwaffe Seeflieger, the prototype was modified with streamlined fairings over the nose and dorsal cockpits and given greater fuel capacity, and used to gain world records for speed with load, covering closed circuits of up to 2000 km (1,242 miles) with payloads up to 2000 kg (4,410 lb) at an average speed of 328 km/h (203 mph). By this time two further prototypes had flown, the V3 being almost representative of the production aircraft. The outer wings had more taper on the leading edge and less on the trailing edge, the nose was lengthened and made more streamlined with a gun cupola on the nose, and the pilot's cockpit was joined to that of the radio operator by a continuous 'greenhouse'. The radio operator was provided with a simple control column and pedals with which it was hoped he could bring the aircraft back should the pilot be incapacitated.

In 1938 two export orders were received: six He 115s for Norway and 12 for Sweden. These were built almost to the same standard as the He 115A-1 which went into production for the Luftwaffe in January 1939. The A-1 closely resembled the V3 prototype, with the addition of underwing racks for two further SC250 bombs. Delivery to the first Küstenfliegerstaffel, 1/KüFlGr 106, began with the outbreak of war, but Heinkel's Marienehe plant terminated production at the 62nd aircraft at the start of 1940. This total comprised 10 pre-production A-0s, 18 export aircraft (called A-2s and differing in radio, guns and other equipment) and 34 A-1 and A-3 seaplanes for the Luftwaffe. The A-3s had improved radio and weapon-release equipment.

All subsequent production was handled by 'Weser' at Einswarden, starting with 10 B-0s with increased fuel capacity. By 1940 the B-1 was in production, with various Rüstsätze (conversion kits) for bombing, minelaying (for example), carrying two 500-kg (1,100-lb) bombs, LMAIII mines or a single monster LMB III of 920-kg (2,028-lb) or photo-reconnaissance. The last 18 B-series were completed as B-2s with reinforced floats fitted with steel skate-like runners for operation from ice or compacted snow. This was often to prove a considerable operational advantage, though pilots had to devise a mild rocking technique, by opening and closing the throttles, to unstick the floats if they were frozen in.

The V1's record-breaking flight led to the first export order from Norway, which purchased six for the Marinens Flyvevaben. Three of these He 115A-2s were successful in escaping to Britain after the invasion, together with one captured German aircraft. They were converted for clandestine operations for the RAF.

Production by 'Weser' was completed with various sub-types of He 115C. This basically resembled the B-series but introduced heavier armament. It had been apparent for some time that two MG 15s was not adequate defensive firepower for a large aircraft with a cruising speed of about 270 km/h (167 mph). In early 1940 the V5 prototype was tested with a 20-mm MG FF cannon aimed by hand from the nose, and one might have thought this, plus a similar cannon aimed by the radio operator, could have provided the answer. What actually happened was that the He 115C-1 went into production with an MG 151/15 fixed under the nose to fire ahead, and two MG 17 machine-guns were added in the engine nacelles firing directly to the rear. The forward-firing gun was a high-velocity weapon with excellent ballistics, but to be effective the big floatplane had to be flown like a fighter. It was virtually useless for defence. As for the aft-firing guns, these could not be aimed at all, and (assuming an attacking fighter knew of their presence) were relatively easy to evade. The C-2 had the ice/snow skids, the C-3 was a specialised minelayer, and the C-4 was an Arctic-equipped torpedo carrier with no forward-firing armament.

Up-gunning in wartime

During their active careers, in 1942, surviving He 115s of all kinds were almost all fitted with the MG 81Z twin machine-gun package in place of the MG 15 in the radio operator's cockpit. This was a neater and very much faster-firing installation which did go some way to improving defensive firepower. Some aircraft, and possibly most, were retrofitted with a powerful MG 151/20 under the nose, in a prominent box which also housed the ammunition. The gun was carried on the left side and caused a noticeable nose-down pull to the left when fired. The original nose MG 15 was retained.

In late 1939, Heinkel stopped production of the He 115, all the tooling being moved to Einswarden for the 'Weser' Flugzeugbau factory. The new production model was the He 115B, incorporating greater structural strength and more fuel. This is a He 115B-1 on pre-delivery trials in early 1940.

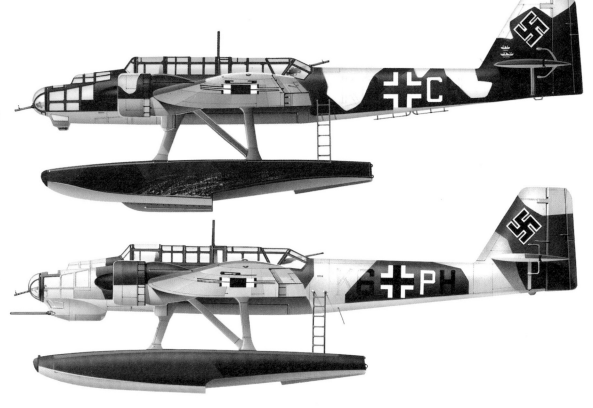

An He 115B-2 of 1./KüFlGr 406, operating in Norway. During winter a white distemper was applied to the normal splinter scheme to camouflage the aircraft in snow conditions. Note the ship kill marks on the fin.

'K6+PH' was an He 115C-1 serving with 1./KüFlGr 406 during 1942, when the unit was involved in attacking convoys taking equipment from Britain to the Soviet Union via the North Cape route.

This He 115C-1 of 3./KüFlGr 106 (code M2) shows the original 15-mm MG 151 cannon installation in the nose. Night minelaying operations were undertaken by the He 115 in British waters, and for this reason they were hastily applied with black paint to mask the light grey undersides, national insignia and white code letter.

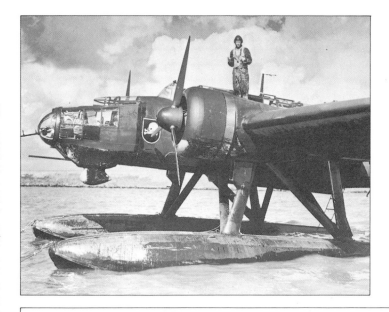

There was one attempt to increase flight performance, which had progressively deteriorated as a result of the increased weight of fuel, weapons and equipment of successive versions. In 1939 Heinkel had proposed an improved He 115 fitted with much more powerful engines, and this materialised in 1940 when an ex-Luftwaffe aircraft was returned to Marienehe and considerably modified. The structure was locally strengthened to accept bigger engines and increased gross weights, and two 1194-kW (1,600-hp) BMW 801A 14-cylinder radial engines were installed in installations generally similar to those of the early Do 217E. The fuselage was rearranged for a crew of four, with a 20-mm MG 151 under the left side of the nose, an MG 81 in the nose cupola and MG 81Z twin machine-guns in both the rear dorsal and ventral positions. Maximum speed was increased from about 295 to 380 km/h (183 to 236 mph), despite the increase in weight to 12640 kg (27,865 lb), but only the one aircraft was ever converted. Known as the He 115D-0, it later served with the Küstenfliegerstaffel.

Sturdy build

From the start the He 115 had a good reputation for strength, reliability and all-round capability. They were intensively used by both the Luftwaffe and Norwegian naval air service during the invasion of Norway in April/May 1940. At the end of this conflict one Norwegian aircraft was flown to Finland, where it was repaired and put into active service with the Ilmavoimat, where in 1943 it was joined by two He 115Cs supplied from Germany. Three Norwegian He 115A-2s and a captured B-1 were flown to Scotland, where they received RAF serial numbers BV184-187. All continued flying until there were destroyed or the spares ran out. All were modified, the

The He 115C-1 replaced the B on the production line during 1940, this adding a fixed 15-mm cannon under the nose and rearward-firing MG 17 machine-guns in the rear of the engine nacelle. During 1942-43, the 15-mm cannon was replaced by a 20-mm MG 151 in a bathtub fairing, as seen here.

Heinkel He 115

Apart from Norway, the only other export order for the He 115 came from Sweden, which purchased 12 He 115A-2s. These were used for coastal maritime reconnaissance, serving with F2 Roslagens Flygflottilj.

most obvious changes being replacement of the long 'glasshouse' by metal panels and fitting of British armament. Aircraft 185 and 187 were modified for clandestine operations, one startling change being the addition of four Browning machine-guns firing ahead from the leading edge of the wings, plus four more firing to the rear. In October 1941 BV185 was flown round via Gibraltar to Malta, where it enjoyed a charmed life in Luftwaffe markings, making numerous missions to North Africa by night and by day inserting and picking up Allied agents. On one occasion it landed in Tripoli harbour in broad daylight, took on board two agents and returned to Malta. Eventually it was destroyed at Malta by bombing. Meanwhile 187, the former Luftwaffe B-1, flew several long missions between Woodhaven, on the Firth of Tay, and points in Norway. Eventually it was decided that these missions posed too great a risk, mainly from destruction by RAF fighters.

Twilight misions

Luftwaffe He 115s had carried out minelaying operations from the the start of the war, and from 1942 surviving examples were all grouped in northern Norway for operations against Allied convoys. The most important and most successful missions were against the ill-fated convoy PQ17 in July 1942. Eight He 115C-1s of the KüFlGr 406 made torpedo attacks on 2 July, the Staffelkapitän being shot down but rescued, with his crew, by another 115 which alighted on the stormy sea. On 4 July aircraft of KüFlGr 906 disabled one ship, and subsequently aircraft of both units played a part in hunting down and sinking 23 of the 36 vessels that had comprised the convoy. A few 115s lingered on into mid-1944, but they saw little action.

Shortly before the planned invasion of Norway and Denmark, 'Weser' Flugzeugbau received instructions to prepare the aircraft for operations from snow and ice. Additional strengthening to the planing bottom and a steel skid was added, the resultant aircraft being designated He 115B-2, 18 of which were built.

Heinkel He 115B cutaway drawing key

1 7.9-mm MG 15 machine-gun
2 Gunsights
3 Ikaria nose mounting
4 Cartridge collector chute
5 Nose ring
6 Entry/escape hatch
7 Nose glazing
8 Bomb/torpedo-sight
9 Selector panel
10 Handhold
11 Bombardier's kneeling-pad
12 Ventral glazing
13 Bombardier's/navigator's hinged seat
14 Duplicate throttle controls
15 Duplicate control column
16 Instrument panel
17 Nose compartment windscreen
18 Fixed glazing
19 Electrics panel
20 Batteries
21 Cockpit/nose access
22 Smoke floats
23 Weapons bay forward doors
24 Fuselage frame
25 Cockpit floor
26 Rudder pedals
27 Throttles
28 Control column
29 Instrument panel
30 Windscreen
31 Starboard nacelle oil tank location
32 Engine bearer supports
33 Cooling gills
34 Starboard BMW 132K nine-cylinder radial engine
35 Nacelle nose ring
36 Propeller hub
37 Spinner
38 VDM three-bladed metal propeller of 10.83-ft (3.30-m) diameter
39 Nacelle hinged access/maintenance panels
40 Leading-edge hinged access/servicing panel
41 Starboard outer main fuel tank

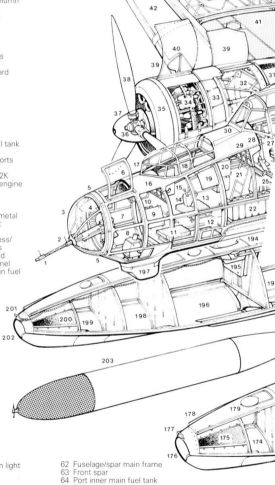

42 Leading-edge tank (provision)
43 Wing structure
44 Front spar
45 Starboard navigation light
46 Starboard outer rib
47 Aileron outer hinge
48 Starboard aileron
49 Aileron tabs
50 Rear spar
51 Aileron tab hinge fairing
52 Control linkage
53 Flap outer section
54 Aileron profile
55 Starboard flap
56 Canopy hinged section
57 Fixed section
58 Cockpit rear-sliding canopy
59 Pilot's seat
60 Leading-edge inboard hinged access/servicing panel
61 Front spar carry-through

62 Fuselage/spar main frame
63 Front spar
64 Port inner main fuel tank
65 Filler cap
66 Fuselage centre bay
67 Wireless installation

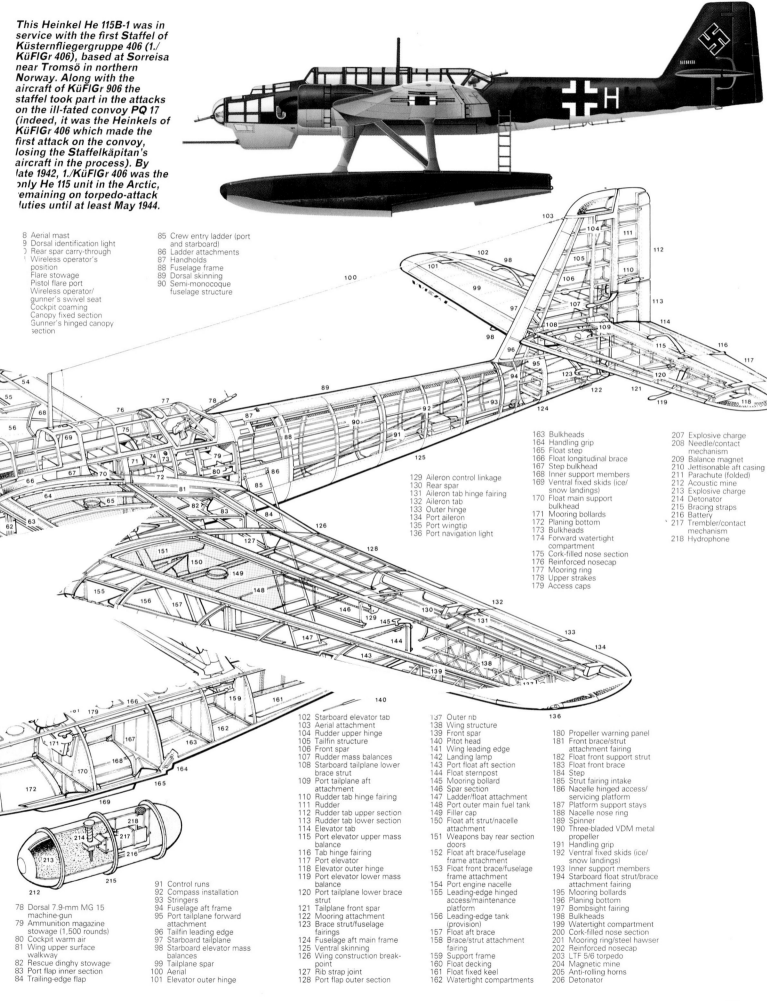

This Heinkel He 115B-1 was in service with the first Staffel of Küsternfliegergruppe 406 (1./KüFlGr 406), based at Sorreisa near Tromsö in northern Norway. Along with the aircraft of KüFlGr 906 the staffel took part in the attacks on the ill-fated convoy PQ 17 (indeed, it was the Heinkels of KüFlGr 406 which made the first attack on the convoy, losing the Staffelkäpitan's aircraft in the process). By late 1942, 1./KüFlGr 406 was the only He 115 unit in the Arctic, remaining on torpedo-attack duties until at least May 1944.

8 Aerial mast
9 Dorsal identification light
0 Rear spar carry-through
1 Wireless operator's position
Flare stowage
Pistol flare port
Wireless operator/gunner's swivel seat
Cockpit coaming
Canopy fixed section
Gunner's hinged canopy section

85 Crew entry ladder (port and starboard)
86 Ladder attachments
87 Handholds
88 Fuselage frame
89 Dorsal skinning
90 Semi-monocoque fuselage structure

129 Aileron control linkage
130 Rear spar
131 Aileron tab hinge fairing
132 Aileron tab
133 Outer hinge
134 Port aileron
135 Port wingtip
136 Port navigation light

163 Bulkheads
164 Handling grip
165 Float step
166 Float longitudinal brace
167 Step bulkhead
168 Inner support members
169 Ventral fixed skids (ice/snow landings)
170 Float main support bulkhead
171 Mooring bollards
172 Planing bottom
173 Bulkheads
174 Forward watertight compartment
175 Cork-filled nose section
176 Reinforced nosecap
177 Mooring ring
178 Upper strakes
179 Access caps

207 Explosive charge
208 Needle/contact mechanism
209 Balance magnet
210 Jettisonable aft casing
211 Parachute (folded)
212 Acoustic mine
213 Explosive charge
214 Detonator
215 Bracing straps
216 Battery
217 Trembler/contact mechanism
218 Hydrophone

78 Dorsal 7.9-mm MG 15 machine-gun
79 Ammunition magazine stowage (1,500 rounds)
80 Cockpit warm air
81 Wing upper surface walkway
82 Rescue dinghy stowage
83 Port flap inner section
84 Trailing-edge flap

91 Control runs
92 Compass installation
93 Stringers
94 Fuselage aft frame
95 Port tailplane forward attachment
96 Tailfin leading edge
97 Starboard tailplane
98 Starboard elevator mass balances
99 Tailplane spar
100 Aerial
101 Elevator outer hinge

102 Starboard elevator tab
103 Aerial attachment
104 Rudder upper hinge
105 Tailfin structure
106 Front spar
107 Rudder mass balances
108 Starboard tailplane lower brace strut
109 Port tailplane aft attachment
110 Rudder tab hinge fairing
111 Rudder
112 Rudder tab upper section
113 Rudder tab lower section
114 Elevator tab
115 Port elevator upper mass balance
116 Tab hinge fairing
117 Port elevator
118 Elevator outer hinge
119 Port elevator lower mass balance
120 Port tailplane lower brace strut
121 Tailplane front spar
122 Mooring attachment
123 Brace strut/fuselage fairings
124 Fuselage aft main frame
125 Ventral skinning
126 Wing construction break-point
127 Rib strap joint
128 Port flap outer section

137 Outer rib
138 Wing structure
139 Front spar
140 Pitot head
141 Wing leading edge
142 Landing lamp
143 Port float aft section
144 Float sternpost
145 Mooring bollard
146 Spar section
147 Ladder/float attachment
148 Port outer main fuel tank
149 Filler cap
150 Float aft strut/nacelle attachment
151 Weapons bay rear section doors
152 Float aft brace/fuselage frame attachment
153 Float front brace/fuselage frame attachment
154 Port engine nacelle
155 Leading-edge hinged access/maintenance platform
156 Leading-edge tank (provision)
157 Float aft brace
158 Brace/strut attachment fairing
159 Support frame
160 Float decking
161 Float fixed keel
162 Watertight compartments

180 Propeller warning panel
181 Front brace/strut attachment fairing
182 Float front support strut
183 Float front brace
184 Step
185 Strut fairing intake
186 Nacelle hinged access/servicing platform
187 Platform support stays
188 Nacelle nose ring
189 Spinner
190 Three-bladed VDM metal propeller
191 Handling grip
192 Ventral fixed skids (ice/snow landings)
193 Inner support members
194 Starboard float strut/brace attachment fairing
195 Mooring bollards
196 Planing bottom
197 Bombsight fairing
198 Bulkheads
199 Watertight compartment
200 Cork-filled nose section
201 Mooring ring/steel hawser
202 Reinforced nosecap
203 LTF 5/6 torpedo
204 Magnetic mine
205 Anti-rolling horns
206 Detonator

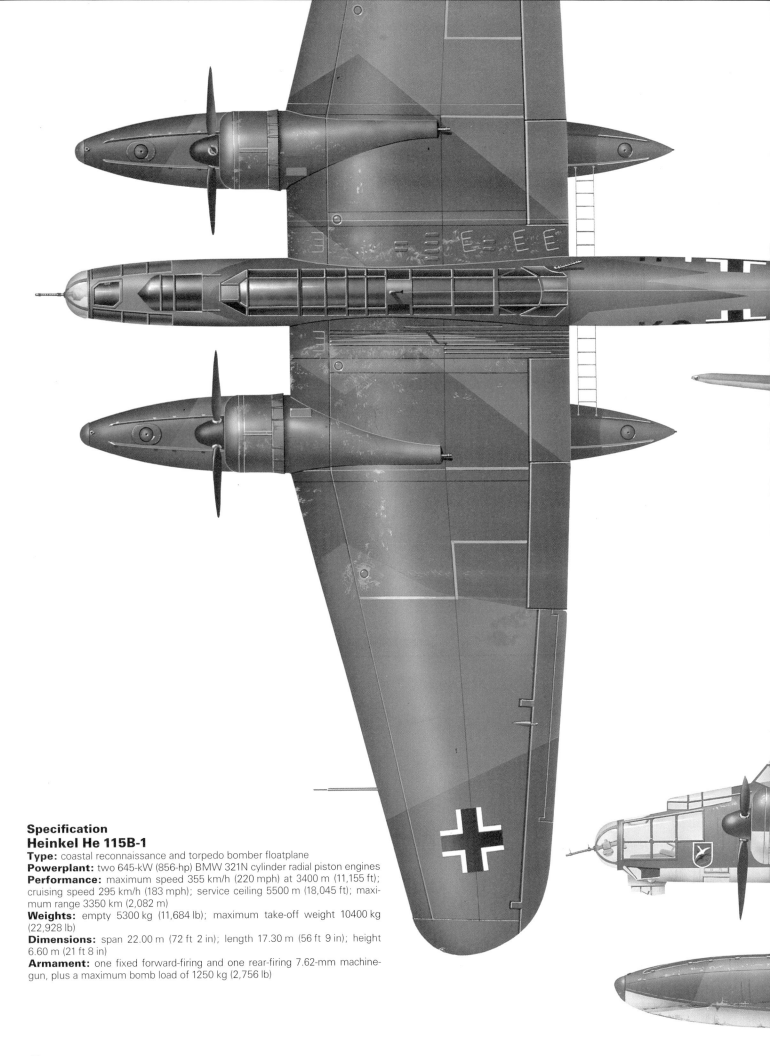

Specification
Heinkel He 115B-1
Type: coastal reconnaissance and torpedo bomber floatplane
Powerplant: two 645-kW (856-hp) BMW 321N cylinder radial piston engines
Performance: maximum speed 355 km/h (220 mph) at 3400 m (11,155 ft); cruising speed 295 km/h (183 mph); service ceiling 5500 m (18,045 ft); maximum range 3350 km (2,082 m)
Weights: empty 5300 kg (11,684 lb); maximum take-off weight 10400 kg (22,928 lb)
Dimensions: span 22.00 m (72 ft 2 in); length 17.30 m (56 ft 9 in); height 6.60 m (21 ft 8 in)
Armament: one fixed forward-firing and one rear-firing 7.62-mm machine-gun, plus a maximum bomb load of 1250 kg (2,756 lb)

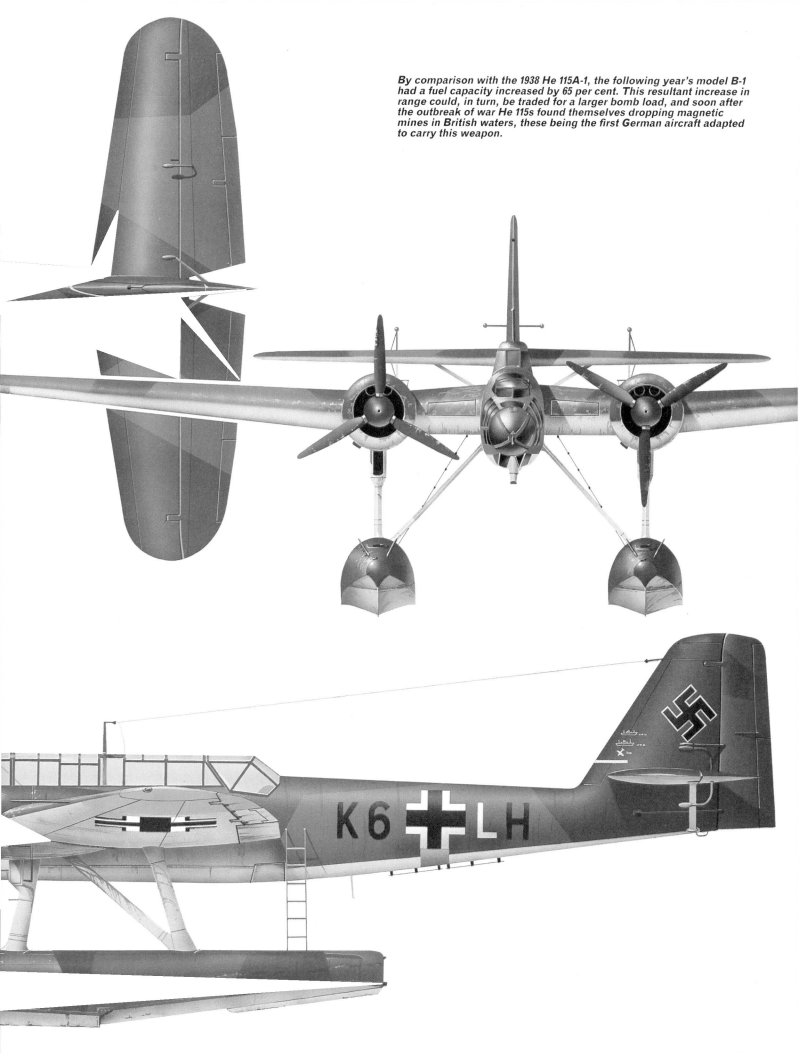

By comparison with the 1938 He 115A-1, the following year's model B-1 had a fuel capacity increased by 65 per cent. This resultant increase in range could, in turn, be traded for a larger bomb load, and soon after the outbreak of war He 115s found themselves dropping magnetic mines in British waters, these being the first German aircraft adapted to carry this weapon.

Arado Ar 234 Blitz: Strahlbomber

By the end of World War II, Germany's aviation technology easily outstripped that of the Allies. The Arado Ar 234 provided ample evidence of this lead. The world's first jet bomber, it was a sleek, fast and deftly-engineered design which was well ahead of its time.

In November 1940 many British officials thought the de Havilland company mad as it began flight testing a new reconnaissance and bomber aircraft which was thought to have such a high performance that it needed no defensive armament. How amazed they would have been had they been able to travel eastwards to the German company Arado Flugzeugwerke, where engineers Walter Blume and Hans Rebeski were beginning the design of an unarmed reconnaissance aircraft planned to fly even faster and higher that the famous Mosquito. It was to be able to do this because its engines were to be turbojets, revolutionary new engines then in the early stages of testing at the BMW and Junkers companies.

They submitted to the Air Ministry technical staff their E 370 proposal in early 1941. With it came various more radical schemes, but it was the relatively conventional 370 that was to be accepted and awarded the '8 series' type number 234.

Predictably it was an extremely clean and straightforward aircraft of all-metal stressed-skin construction, with a smooth flush-riveted exterior skin. The tapered wing was mounted on top of the slender fuselage, and the two engines were underslung below the wing in near nacelles about the same distance from the centreline that one might have expected with a piston engine. In the extreme nose was the single-seat cockpit, the entire nose being glazed with Plexiglas. The pilot got aboard by pulling down a retractable step on the left side, clambering up kick-in steps up the left side and entering via the roof hatch. This hatch could be jettisoned, but there was no ejection seat and emergency escape was a doubtful proposition. The cockpit itself, however, was roomy, comfortable and well laid out, and pressurised by engine bleed.

The challenging demand for a combat range of 2200 km meant that almost the entire fuselage aft of the cockpit had to be occupied by fuel, the tanks being filled through the top of the fuselage. All flight controls were manually operated and conventional, the ailerons

Fitted with conventional wheeled undercarriage, the Ar 234B showed considerable promise, and in service lived up to it. This aircraft is one of the early Ar 234Bs, lacking the dive-bombing periscope above the cockpit.

being of the sharp leading edge Frise type and the elevators and rudder having prominent mass balances plus a combined balance weight in the fuselage. The tailplane incidence could be varied for trimming purposes by a large lever in the cockpit, driving a screwjack. Inboard and outboard of the engines were hydraulically actuated plain flaps with a maximum of 45° for landing. It was planned that the big reconnaissance cameras would be carried in the rear fuselage.

The one feature that was truly unconventional was the landing gear. With the benefit of hindsight one can see that there should have been no serious problem, but the Arado design team could see no way to fit a normal undercarriage. With the slim fuselage full of fuel there was was no room for retracted main gears as well, nor could landing gears be accommodated in the jet nacelles or wing, the high wing meaning that ordinary wing-mounted gears would have to be very long. The company therefore proposed various unconventional arrangements, and the Air Ministry staff selected one of the most unusual. On take-off the Ar 234 was to ride on a large three-wheeled trolley. It would land on a central skid, with small stabilising skids under the engine nacelles.

Engine trouble

The engine selected was the 109-004A being developed by Junkers. Construction of the Ar 234 V1 first prototype began in the spring of 1941, Junkers having promised delivery of engines in about 10 months. Work at Arado's Warnemünde factory went ahead rapidly, but the engine suffered very serious delays and did not even begin flight testing until March 1942. What is very curious is that, whereas two 004As powered the first Me 262 in July 1942, Arado did not receive a single engine until February 1943, and could not fly the 234 V1 until 15 June 1943. By this time the engineless airframe had been waiting for 18 months. Arado considered beginning flight testing using piston engines, but there was inadequate propeller ground clearance. If a conventional landing gear had been adopted this problem would not have arisen; and if Junkers had delivered engines much earlier this outstanding aircraft would have been available up to a year earlier and in greater numbers.

As it was, the flying qualities of the 234 proved to be delightful. Based at Rheine, under chief test pilot Selle, the programme un-

For take-off the Ar 234A sat on a large trolley, which featured a steerable nosewheel and mainwheel brakes for taxiing. During the first flights of the V1, the trolley was jettisoned at altitudes, but subsequently was released on the runway.

earthed hardly any shortcomings, and from the start every pilot who flew the 234 had nothing but praise for its handling (though it took up to 10 test flights with each aircraft before the ailerons could be judged properly rigged). In contrast, the take-off/landing gear gave endless trouble. On the first flight the big trolley was correctly jettisoned at 200 ft but the parachute failed to deploy and the trolley was destroyed on hitting the ground. The same thing happened on the second flight. After this it was decided to let the aircraft rise clear, leaving the trolley on the ground, but even so both the trolley and the skid gear gave trouble. Often the skids failed to retract, pitching and porpoising on landing was severe, and on several occasions one side skid would collapse and let the wingtip drag over the ground. Moreover the aircraft could not taxi on its high-drag skids, and it was realized that on mass operations the airfield would quickly become filled with immobile Ar 234s which would obstruct following aircraft and present helpless targets to straffing aircraft. In the late summer of 1943 it was wisely decided to change to conventional landing gear. The planned Ar 234A production version was cancelled, but seven

Landing the Ar 234A was accomplished on a grass strip, the aircraft resting on a central main skid and two outrigger skids which were housed in the engine nacelles. These skids were also deployed for take-off, being used as the supports to which the trolley was attached.

Arado Ar 234 Blitz: Strahlbomber

Towards the end of the war many Arado Ar 234s were captured intact by the advancing Allied armies and several more were used by their crews to escape to neutral nations. One even got as far as Ireland, arriving on the last day of the war. The majority of these aircraft survived to become objects of study for British, American and Russian scientists.

Arado Ar 234B-2/lr Blitz cutaway key

1 Port elevator hinge
2 Tailplane skinning
3 Port elevator
4 Tab actuating rod
5 Elevator trim tab
6 Geared rudder tab (upper)
7 Rudder hinges
8 Tail navigation light
9 Plywood fin leading edge
10 T-aerial
11 Re-transmission aerial
12 Aerial matching unit
13 Tailfin structure
14 Rudder construction
15 Rudder post
16 Rudder tab (lower)

17 Lower rudder hinge
18 Rudder actuating rods
19 Parachute cable
20 Cable anchor point/tailskid
21 Starboard elevator tab
22 Elevator construction
23 Tailplane construction
24 Elevator control linkage
25 Tailplane attachment potnts
26 Elevator rod
27 Port side control runs
28 Internal mass balance
29 Parachute release mechanism
30 Main FuG 16zy panel (BZA computer)

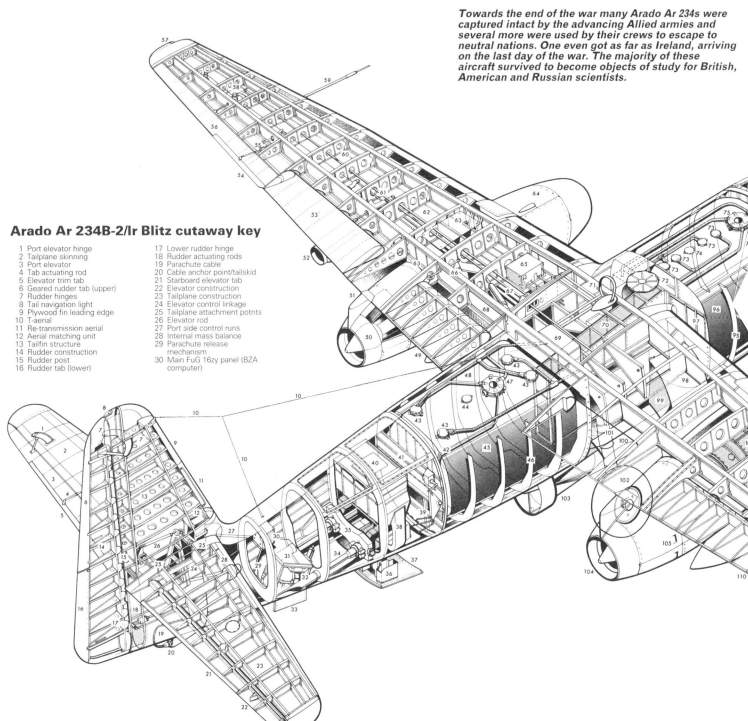

64

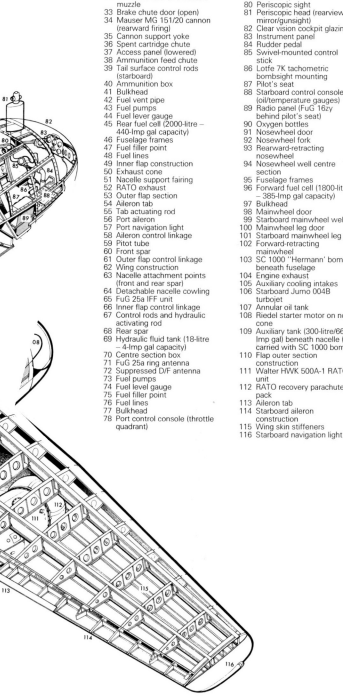

31 Brake parachute container
32 Starboard MG 151 cannon muzzle
33 Brake chute door (open)
34 Mauser MG 151/20 cannon (rearward firing)
35 Cannon support yoke
36 Spent cartridge chute
37 Access panel (lowered)
38 Ammunition feed chute
39 Tail surface control rods (starboard)
40 Ammunition box
41 Bulkhead
42 Fuel vent pipe
43 Fuel pumps
44 Fuel lever gauge
45 Rear fuel cell (2000-litre – 440-Imp gal capacity)
46 Fuselage frames
47 Fuel filler point
48 Fuel lines
49 Inner flap construction
50 Exhaust cone
51 Nacelle support fairing
52 RATO exhaust
53 Outer flap section
54 Aileron tab
55 Tab actuating rod
56 Port aileron
57 Port navigation light
58 Aileron control linkage
59 Pitot tube
60 Front spar
61 Outer flap control linkage
62 Wing construction
63 Nacelle attachment points (front and rear spar)
64 Detachable nacelle cowling
65 FuG 25a IFF unit
66 Inner flap control linkage
67 Control rods and hydraulic activating rod
68 Rear spar
69 Hydraulic fluid tank (18-litre – 4-Imp gal capacity)
70 Centre section box
71 FuG 25a ring antenna
72 Suppressed D/F antenna
73 Fuel pumps
74 Fuel level gauge
75 Fuel filler point
76 Fuel lines
77 Bulkhead
78 Port control console (throttle quadrant)

79 Pilot entry hatch (hinged to starboard)
80 Periscopic sight
81 Periscopic head (rearview mirror/gunsight)
82 Clear vision cockpit glazing
83 Instrument panel
84 Rudder pedal
85 Swivel-mounted control stick
86 Lotfe 7K tachometric bombsight mounting
87 Pilot's seat
88 Starboard control console (oil/temperature gauges)
89 Radio panel (FuG 16zy behind pilot's seat)
90 Oxygen bottles
91 Nosewheel door
92 Nosewheel fork
93 Rearward-retracting nosewheel
94 Nosewheel well centre section
95 Fuselage frames
96 Forward fuel cell (1800-litre – 385-Imp gal capacity)
97 Bulkhead
98 Mainwheel door
99 Starboard mainwheel well
100 Mainwheel leg door
101 Starboard mainwheel leg
102 Forward-retracting mainwheel
103 SC 1000 ''Hermann' bomb beneath fuselage
104 Engine exhaust
105 Auxiliary cooling intakes
106 Starboard Jumo 004B turbojet
107 Annular oil tank
108 Riedel starter motor on nose cone
109 Auxiliary tank (300-litre/66-Imp gal) beneath nacelle (not carried with SC 1000 bomb)
110 Flap outer section construction
111 Walter HWK 500A-1 RATO unit
112 RATO recovery parachute pack
113 Aileron tab
114 Starboard aileron construction
115 Wing skin stiffeners
116 Starboard navigation light

With only 840 kg (1,850 lb) of thrust available from each Jumo 004B jets, the Ar 234A was short on take-off power, particularly when loaded to the maximum weight of 8000 kg (17,600 lb). Rauchgeräte take-off rocket units were added to improve the thrust, these being jettisoned after climb-out and descending to earth by parachute.

further A-series aircraft had already been built and V2, 3, 4, 5 and 7 all flew in rapid succession (6 and 8 were set aside for fitting with four engines). In the closing months of 1943 the prototypes tested pressurisation, take-off booster rocket packs hung under the wings, the lighter and more powerful 004B engine and, in some aircraft, an ejection seat.

Dubious debut

While this work was going on at Rheine a major factory at Alt Lönnewitz was tooled up to produce the Ar 234B – popularly named the Blitz – with conventional landing gear. The first B-series prototype, the V9, was flown on 10 March 1944, the pilot being the very experienced Joachim Carl who had succeeded Selle on his predecessor's death in the crash of V7 due to engine fire. V10 introduced the RF 2C periscopic sight and racks for bombs or drop tanks under the engines and a bomb under the fuselage. V11 flew on 5 May 1944, followed by the first pre-production B-0 on 8 June. Carl had been told to make the first flight of the B-0 before 400 important guests. He insisted on making a quick test flight beforehand and was horrified to find this hastily completed machine nothing like the handbuilt prototypes. Almost everything went wrong and Carl had no idea how he managed to regain the airfield with both engines flamed out and no

The wheeled undercarriage gave the Ar 234B better flexibility of operations. This is the second B-series prototye (Ar 234 V10) which first flew on 2 April 1944. Lacking cabin pressurisation, it could be fitted with Rauchgeräte rocket-assisted take-off units under the wings.

Arado Ar 234 Blitz: Strahlbomber

In late 1944 Ar 234B-2 reconnaissance bombers were delivered to the **Stabs-Staffel** of **Kampfgeschwader 76**. Deliveries continued, allowing **KG 76** to undertake bombing missions in the Ardennes region during the winter, followed by many attacks against Allied bridgeheads during early 1945. They were particularly active during the battle for Remagen. This is one of those aircraft, seen carrying an **SC 1000 'Hermann'** bomb on the centreline. It was captured intact by the Allies at Achmer in May.

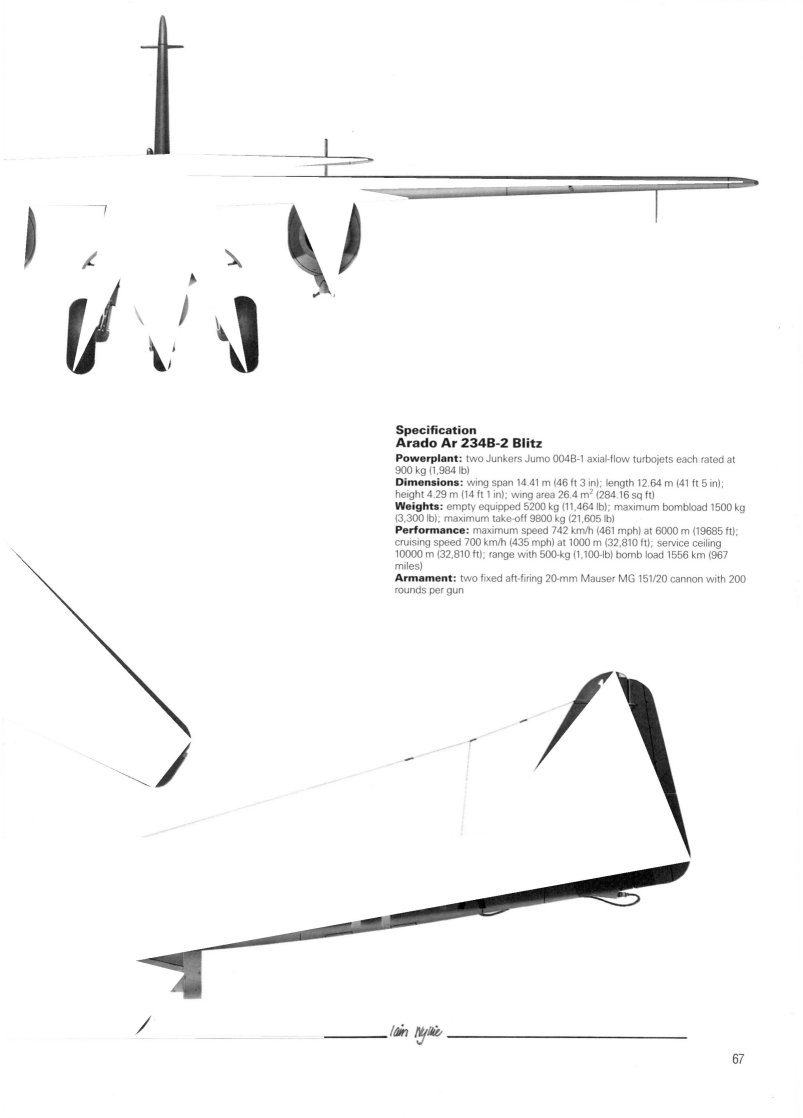

Specification
Arado Ar 234B-2 Blitz
Powerplant: two Junkers Jumo 004B-1 axial-flow turbojets each rated at 900 kg (1,984 lb)
Dimensions: wing span 14.41 m (46 ft 3 in); length 12.64 m (41 ft 5 in); height 4.29 m (14 ft 1 in); wing area 26.4 m^2 (284.16 sq ft)
Weights: empty equipped 5200 kg (11,464 lb); maximum bombload 1500 kg (3,300 lb); maximum take-off 9800 kg (21,605 lb)
Performance: maximum speed 742 km/h (461 mph) at 6000 m (19685 ft); cruising speed 700 km/h (435 mph) at 1000 m (32,810 ft); service ceiling 10000 m (32,810 ft); range with 500-kg (1,100-lb) bomb load 1556 km (967 miles)
Armament: two fixed aft-firing 20-mm Mauser MG 151/20 cannon with 200 rounds per gun

Iain Wyllie

The adoption of the tricycle undercarriage left the engine nacelles free for weapons carriage, and bomb shackles were incorporated to take up to 500 kg (1,100 lb) of bombs. A third bomb shackle was located under the centreline, capable of taking up to 1400 kg (3,000 lb).

idea whether the landing gears were up or down. Frantic work ensured that the 'official first flight' in the afternoon went off without a hitch.

Design features

Arado built 20 B-0s, 13 going at once to Rechlin test centre. The production line went straight on with a limited run of B-1 reconnaissance aircraft, followed by the standard production model, the B-2. Arado managed to fit normal landing gear by removing the centre fuselage tank, making the front and rear tanks bigger so that the total capacity of 3800 litres (835 Imp gal) was only slightly affected. Each leg with a big low-pressure tyre retracted forwards and inwards, the wheel being stowed upright. The nosewheel, fitted with spring-cam centring, retracted, all units being moved hydraulically. A braking parachute was housed in a box under the rear fuselage, its cable being attached to the rear of the tail bumper. In practice this was seldom used.

The B-2 was able to fly reconnaissance or bombing missions, and most aircraft were fitted with aft-firing defensive armament, another curious choice because the installation was heavy and the Ar 234 was virtually immune to interception by Allied fighters except in the vicinity of its airfield. The armament comprised two 20-mm MG 151 cannon, mounted horizontally and parallel in the rear fuselage and each fed with 200 rounds from a magazine overhead. The guns could be sighted by the aft-facing optics of the RF 2C periscope above the cockpit. The centreline attachment, in a fuselage recess, could take a PC 1400 1400-kg (3,000-lb) bomb, and that under each engine could take an SC 500J 500-kg (1,100-lb) bomb or a 300-litre (66 Imp-gal)

drop tank. Normal maximum bomb load was 1500 kg (3,300 lb). In the reconnaissance role various cameras could be fitted, such as two Rb 50/30 or 73/30, or one of each.

Hi-tech cockpit

The cockpit was well arranged, the only problem being that of escape in emergengy. Standard equipment included a Patin PDS three-axis autopilot, with course setting control twistgrip on the right handgrip of the pilot's control yoke. Rudder pedals were out in front with clear Plexiglas giving a view in all forward directions. Between the pilot's legs was the complex Lofte 7K tachymetric bombsight. At the start of the bombing run the pilot would swing the control yoke clear and fly the aircraft on the bombsight control knobs, looking through the optical sight. Alternatively he could fly the aircraft in the normal way and use the periscope sight and associated BZA bombing computer for a dive attack.

Handling was beautiful at all speeds, though of course a heavy bomb load made the aircraft sluggish and reduced speed by some 96 km/h (60 mph). Limiting Mach number was about 0.78, and the clean aircraft was fully aerobatic, though pilots were warned that, should they by some mischance be intercepted, they should use speed rather than manoeuvres to escape. Surprisingly, in view of the tall fin and narrow track, crosswinds were no problem, nor was an overshoot, but brakes tended to burn out after two or three landings and engine failures were common, time between engine overhauls being 10 hours.

Plugging the intelligence gap

In July 1944 two early prototypes, V5 and V7, had joined 1 Staffel of Versuchsverband Oberefehlshaber der Luftwaffe at Juvincourt, France, and following indoctrination flying formed the core of Sonderkommando Götz based at Rheine in September with four B-1s. Strength built up and from early October operational reconnaissance missions were being flown over the Allied area of north-west Europe and the British Isles. In November SdKdo Hecht and Sperling began operations, followed by Sdkdo Sommer at Udine to cover the Italian front. In each case the arrival of the Arados transformed the situation, good photo coverage having previously been perilous and almost impossible to achieve.

From October 1944 KG 76 began to convert to the B-2 bomber, beginning with II Gruppe. This began flying bombing missions during the push through the Ardennes. Later, in March 1945, III/KG 76 at last succeeded in collapsing the Remagen bridge over the Rhine, but

Several Arado Ar 234Bs were captured intact by the Allies at the war's end. Naturally they became the subject of much interest, and were extensively tested in both Britain and the United States.

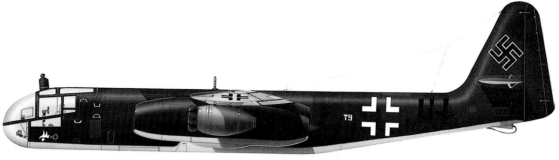

Arado Ar 234s were delivered first to Sonderkommando units for reconnaissance purposes. One of these early Ar 234B-1s is seen here in the service of Sonderkommando Sperling, flying from Rheine in late 1944. The Walter HWK 500A-1 R-gerät units are fitted.

A handful of Ar 234Bs were fitted with two 20-mm MG 151 cannon in a ventral tray and FuG 218 Neptun radar for night fighting. These served with the Erprobungskommando Bonow at Oranienburg in March 1945, this aircraft being that of Kurt Bonow himself.

by this time the loss of the bridge had little effect. Almost all surviving B-1s and B-2s ended the war in northern Germany and Jutland, from where nine were flown to England for evaluation. Total production of B-1s and B-2s was 210, but many failed to see combat duty.

The end of the war

The point was made earlier that prototypes V6 and V8 were completed with four engines. Once the beautiful handling and structural strength of the Ar 234 was established it was soon suggested that it could use greater engine thrust, and the only practical way of achieving this was to fit four BMW 003 turbojets. In the event V8 flew off its take-off trolley on 1 February 1944 powered by four 003A-0 engines in twin nacelles. V6, with four separate nacelles, followed on 8 April. It was decided at about this time to hasten the Ar 234C into production, with paired nacelles. Throughout, difficulties were experienced with the immature 003A engine. In particular, while operation on petrol was satisfactory, use of the less critically scarce J2 jet fuel was tricky, and inflight relights impossible.

The Ar 234B-1 was the initial production version and intended solely for reconnaissance. The main operating unit was Fernaufklärungsgruppe 100, which operated from southern Germany. This is one of their aircraft, captured at Saalbach by US forces.

Arado flew prototypes numbered up to V30, some directly associated with the production 234C but most to test purely experimental features. The first true 234C prototype was V19, flown in September 1944. Apart from having two pairs of 003A-1 engines the C-series aircraft had a revised nose, with a bulged roof, different side windows and double glazing throughout with improved pressurisation. Other changes included a bigger nosewheel, revised ailerons requiring less adjustment and 250 rounds for each aft-firing gun. The three main variants were to be the C-1 for reconnaissance, the gunless C-2 bomber able to take off in 889 m (2,900 ft) with a 2000-kg (4,400-lb) bomb load (only 610 m; 2,000 ft with rockets added), and the C-3 with two extra MG 151s firing forward and able to fly bomber, night fighter or attack missions.

None of these got properly into production, nor did any of the wealth of experimental versions. The latter included the V16 with a crescent-shaped wing (of the kind later used by Handley Page for the Victor), the V26 with a deep 'supercritical' wing made of wood, and the V30 with a very thin-profile metal wing with so-called laminar flow section. Some test flying was done with the Diechselschlepp method of towing an auxiliary fuel tank, an Fi 103 flying bomb or an SC1400 bomb with added wings. In another scheme a flying bomb was to be launched pick-a-back from a 234C.

Blohm und Voss BV 141

**Without doubt one of the most unusual-looking
machines ever to have taken to the air, the BV 141
shunned a traditional layout to meet the peculiar
needs of the battlefield observation role. However,
its development was littered with problems, and by
the time it matured the task was already being
undertaken by the adequate and popular Fw 189.**

Few aircraft have ever looked so freakish as the BV 141. Indeed, it seemed almost to flout the laws of nature. In fact, it was carefully planned to meet the needs of the German Air Ministry in early 1937 for a tactical reconnaissance aircraft, able to furnish a crew of three with the best possible all-round view. Secondary roles were to be light ground attack and the laying of smokescreens. Rival aircraft were the Arado 198 and Focke-Wulf Fw 189, both of which were normal designs to the extent that they were symmetrical about the major longitudinal axis. Dr Ing Richard Vogt of Blohm und Voss saw no reason why his design should not be asymmetrical!

In planning was what initially known as the Ha 141 he decided to put the crew inside a stumpy nacelle projecting in front of and behind the wing well to the right of the mid-span point. To the left of the centreline was a long 'fuselage' joining the engine at the front to the tail at the rear. Though it looked bizarre, even on paper, Vogt knew that there was no reason why such an aircraft should not be completely successful. Indeed he even calculated that the extra weight of the crew nacelle on the right of the propeller axis could be made to cancel out the torque of driving the propeller. The overall arrangement of the various weights and drags could lead to an aircraft with balance as good as in a conventional machine.

From the onset the Air Ministry distrusted Vogt's conception, but as the company was prepared to put up the money a prototype was built and flown on 25 February 1938. The engine was an 865-hp BMW 132N nine-cylinder radial, driving a VDM constant-speed propeller. Span was 15 m (49 ft 3 in) and the main landing gears had single kinked legs and retracted outwards, the wheels lying flat in the leading edges of the wing. Amazingly, not only was 'oscillation' of the landing gear almost the only trouble experienced with the odd aircraft, but landing gear problems were to dog this basic design through a long succession of contrasting prototypes.

The fact that the BV 141 flew at all seems to have surprised some officials, and an order was placed for two further prototypes. These were built in 1938, and differed in having a totally redesigned crew nacelle very like that of the Fw 189. Almost completely glazed with small flat panes of Plexiglas, this nacelle was considerably more capacious than the original, and it was utterly different inside. Instead of being seated in an isolated central cockpit on top, the pilot

The strange layout of the BV 141 was adopted to provide the maximum all-round visibility coverage in a single-engined aircraft. Certainly the forward view was unrivalled in any other observation aircraft. This is the BV 141 V12, one of the BV 141B-0 pre-production aircraft.

From certain angles the Hamburger Ha 141-0 resembled a conventional aircraft. Despite its radical layout, few problems were encountered during flight tests, apart from minor difficulties with the controls and undercarriage. Hamburger Flugzeugbau became Blohm und Voss during 1938.

From the front, the layout of the Ha 141-0 first prototype is clearly seen, including the conventional tail unit and the stepped cockpit/nose dome fuselage layout. This aircraft was later redesignated BV 141 V2, the V1 being the second aircraft built with the redesigned fuselage pod.

sat on the left side in the glass nose, with the observer/bomb aimer on the right. The observer could slide his seat along two tracks. At the front he could use the bomb sight for level bombing with four 50-kg (110-lb) bombs hung under the wings near the extremity of the rectangular centre-section. He also normally used the forward seat position in his primary (observer) role. When pushed right to the rear, and locked there, his seat could be swivelled to face aft to enable him to work the radio and to man a 7.92-mm MG15 machine-gun in a circular cupola with a ball mount. The busy observer also had charge of the vertical reconnaissance camera in the forward position. The third crew member was the gunner, who lay prone in the rear of the nacelle manning a second MG15 machine-gun firing aft from the transparent rear cone. He also had an outstanding view of the lower hemisphere, especially astern.

In addition to the two rearward-firing machine-guns the BV 141A series also had two very similar 7.92-mm MG17 fixed machine-guns, using belt-feed instead of manually loaded magazines. The MG17s

Following two further prototypes (V1 and V3), development moved to the BV 141A series, starting with this BV 141 V4. Compared to the prototypes, size was increased and the aircraft incorporated the V1's crew nacelle. A low-level bombsight was fitted.

were in the lower part of the forward nacelle firing directly ahead, aimed by a Revi sight in front of the pilot.

Several A-series prototypes were built, each introducing minor changes or refinements. The shape of the tail was changed twice, the horizontal surfaces (tailplane and elevator) being at one time asymmetric. Eventually the tail settled down to a rather forward-leaning vertical surface with a symmetric tailplane carrying a single elevator which, oddly, had slightly greater span than the fixed tailplane. The tailwheel was arranged to retract to lie aft of the end of the slim 'fuselage'. All controls were manual, balanced and fitted with tabs, and the wing had split flaps. Altogether the odd aircraft flew extremely well, being liked by the company test pilots, and in 1939 the V4 (fourth development aircraft) was due to be evaluated at the official Erprobungsstelle at Rechlin. Most annoyingly, it suffered hydraulic failure and had to be repaired following the resulting one-wheel landing. The V1 (actually the second aircraft built) had previously suffered a similar failure and made a belly landing.

As in the company test programme, the trials at Rechlin, and at the armament centre at Tarnewitz, all went very well. On the whole pilots became converted to the strange aircraft, and soon admired its docile handling and all-round capability. Both the V3 and V5 were

The adoption of the BMW 801 radial of greater power required considerable redesign in the BV 141B series. Among the most notable features was the tailplane offset to port. This is the prototype of the B series, which first flew on 9 January 1941.

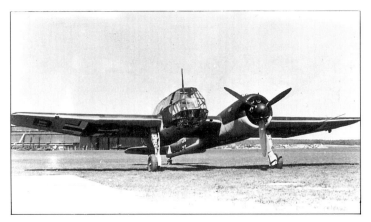

The last of the A series was the BV 141 V8, seen here during trials. Despite favourable results and a total meeting of the specification, the OKL was put off by the strange layout of the type and cancelled the BV 141A order. Development of this variant ended in January 1940.

A BV 141B at rest during trials. This variant was nowhere near as pleasant to fly as the A series, with heavy vibration levels showing up under static tests. The offset tailplane had first been tested on the V2, and was introduced to increase the field of fire available to the rear gunner.

used in bombing trials, and at the end of the evaluation it was concluded that the BV 141 fully met official requirements. The Air Ministry accordingly made plans for large-scale production, but the Oberkommando der Luftwaffe would have none of it. From a basis of ignorance and bigotry it persuaded the RLM (Air Ministry) to cancel the programme on 4 April 1940. It had to put forward a reason, and the only one the high command could think of was that the aircraft could be considered underpowered (though this was actually no problem, and it was completely safe to fly).

BV 141A is blocked

In retrospect, the attitude of the OKL was very unfortunate. Had the BV 141A been permitted to go into production there is no reason to doubt that it would have given good service, especially on the Eastern Front and in North Africa, and that it would have done all that the Fw 189 (the aircraft eventually chosen) could do. It would have been considerably faster, and had a greater range and endurance. By terminating the A series, and unwarrantably calling for greater power, the OKL merely had the effect of preventing any aircraft of this family from reaching the Luftwaffe in useful numbers.

Vogt and his design staff had, in fact, foreseen that more might be called for. Had they merely fitted a similar engine of a little more power, such as the 1,200-hp BMW Bramo Fafnir 323 R2, all might yet have been well. Unfortunately, though they stuck to the original crew nacelle, they could not resist creating a totally new aircraft around it. This is largely because they switched to the 1,560-hp BMW 801A 14-cylinder two-row engine, which meant such an increase in power, torque and weight that the airframe structure had to be restressed anyway. The wing was made much stronger, increased in span to 17.46 m (57 ft 3 in) and redesigned with outer panels tapered equally on the leading and trailing edges (previously they had had almost a sweptback appearance). The long-chord engine cowl led into a long fuselage terminating in a totally redesigned tail which (to improve field of fire for the rear guns) ended up with an asymmetric tailplane on the left side only, carried on a pylon well above the end of the fuselage. The main landing gears were redesigned with much stronger straight legs, with no kink, and with the wheels retracting into wells in the inboard ends of the dihedralled and tapered outer panels.

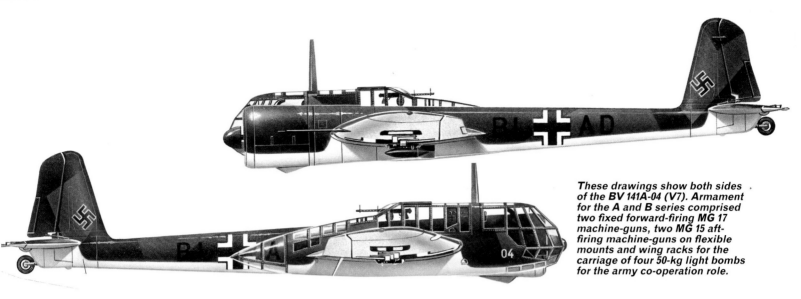

These drawings show both sides of the BV 141A-04 (V7). Armament for the A and B series comprised two fixed forward-firing MG 17 machine-guns, two MG 15 aft-firing machine-guns on flexible mounts and wing racks for the carriage of four 50-kg light bombs for the army co-operation role.

The completely redesigned aircraft was designated BV 141B. The mock-up was approved in February 1940, and the first of five development aircraft flew on 9 January 1941. The RLM entertained high hopes for it, because it was expected to reach about 480 km/h (300 mph) and to have general handling reminiscent of a fighter. But aircraft design – at least in the pre-computer age – was more an art than a science, and while the low-powered A model had been docile the powerful B was 'a dog'. It suffered from bad handling, especially in the rolling plane, severe vibration from various causes, and a succession of mechanical faults, most of them in the hydraulic system and landing gears. The test schedule was perpetually being disrupted, and it soon looked as if the new 141B would eliminate the goodwill that had been won by its predecessor.

Made it at last

Though bigger and more powerful than its predecessors, the 141B had little more capability, the gun and bomb armament and the crew vision and camera fits being unchanged. Altogether a pre-series run of five BV 141B-0 aircraft was constructed, the last (V13) not being delivered until 15 May 1943. By this time it mattered little that there were still a host of major and minor faults to be rectified, such as continuing vibration, a delay due to lack of a suitable propeller, and choking cordite fumes when the two fixed MG17 guns were fired. The Luftwaffe had already picked the Fw 189, and this was serving satisfactorily in the tactical reconnaissance role. (Even the Fw 189 was mildly unconventional, in having a central nacelle and twin tail booms.)

In fact the V10 prototype, the second BV 141B, did reach the Luftwaffe. It was delivered in the autumn of 1941 to Aufklärungsschule 1 at Grossenhain, for trials under front-line conditions. It must have made a favourable impression, despite the snags, because a little later the General-Luftzeugmeister ordered that Blohm und Voss should deliver enough BV 141Bs to form an operational staffel on the Eastern Front. This never happened, partly because the Fw 189 was doing the job and partly because the Blohm und Voss factory at Hamburg-Finkenwerder (which today works on Airbuses) was urgently needed for other work. One cannot help feeling a little regret that what was perhaps the oddest-looking aeroplane ever built never got into proper production.

The BV 141 V9 in flight. This aircraft was tested at the E-Stelle at Rechlin from May 1941 onwards, joined by other prototypes. Type evaluation and service trials both revealed many minor flaws, and this, coupled with the success of the Focke-Wulf Fw 189, led to the demise of the BV 141 project.

Blohm und Voss BV 141.

Specification
Blohm und Voss BV 141B-0

Type: army co-operation and tactical reconnaissance platform

Powerplant: one BMW 801A-0 14-cylinder two-row radial engine, rated at 1164 kW (1,560 hp) for take-off

Performance: maximum speed 368 km/h (229 mph) at sea level, 438 km/h (272 mph) at 5000 m (16,400 ft); maximum range 190 km (1,180 miles); normal operational range 1200 km (745 miles); service ceiling 10000 m (32,810 ft)

Weights: empty equipped 4700 kg (10,362 lb); normal loaded 5700 kg (12,566 lb); maximum take-off 6100 kg (13,448 lb)

Dimensions: wing span 17.46 m (57 ft 3¼ in); length 13.95 m (45 ft 9¼ in); height 3.60 m (11 ft 9¾ in); wing area 52.9 m² (569.41 sq ft)

Armament: two fixed 7.9-mm (0.31-in) MG 17 machine-guns; one 7.9-mm (0.31-in) MG 15 machine-gun firing aft from flexible mounting; underwing racks for four SC 50 50-kg (110-lb) bombs

This is the fourth BV 141B-0 pre-production aircraft (BV 141 V12), as seen when it was delivered to Tarnewitz for armament trials. During gun-firing tests, it was discovered that the gun ports were too short, meaning the cockpit rapidly filled up with cordite smoke. The B series was considerably different to the A series, with a bigger engine, larger dimensions, equi-taper outboard wing sections and the tailplane offset to port. This last improvement had been introduced to provide the gunner with an almost uninterrupted field of fire from the rear of the cockpit. The gun smoke and other problems haunted the BV 141B programme throughout, and by the time the BV 141 was ready to enter service its role was being adequately filled by the Fw 189.

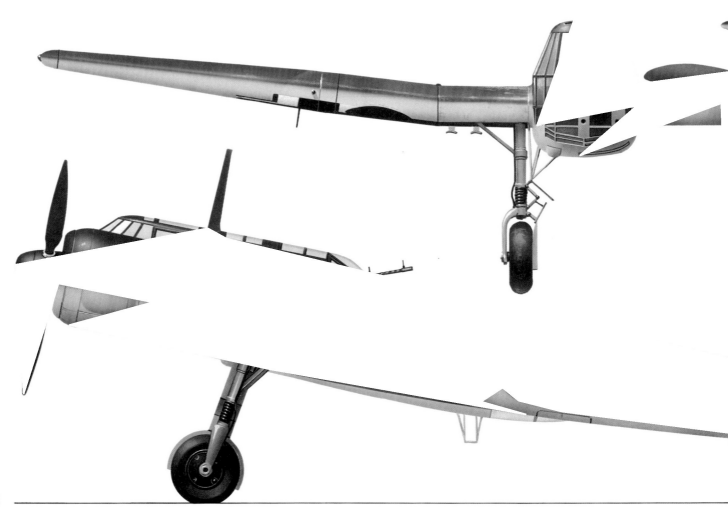

Iain Wyllie

Fieseler Storch

The Storch was the product of one man's ambition to develop an aircraft that could fly like no other. The Fi 156 that followed was a STOL design that had no equal. Born in the dark days of Germany in the late 1930s, it was not long before its military potential was noticed. In the hands of the Luftwaffe's best pilots its exploits, from the siege of Stalingrad to Mussolini's rescue, became legend.

All over northern Germany one finds gigantic nests atop the chimneys of country houses. They are made by storks, which, despite their great size, have to be able to take off and land vertically. It was appropriate that when Gerhard Fieseler won the contract to supply the Luftwaffe's multi-role army co-operation aircraft he should have called it Storch. It was perhaps the only Luftwaffe aircraft demonstrably better than any Allied counterpart.

Fieseler was a 22-victory pilot in World War I and probably the world's greatest inter-war aerobatic pilot. With chief designer Reinhold Mewes he specialised in what today are called STOL (short take-off and landing) aircraft. In most of his company's products (notably not including the V-1 flying bomb) he could come in over the airfield at 3000 m (9,845 ft) and then descend straight downwards to make a vertical soft landing, provided there was a slight breeze to make this feat possible.

In summer 1935 Fieseler, Mewes and technical director Erich Bachem (later creator of the Ba 349 Natter VTO fighter) designed the ultimate in practical STOL aircraft, the Fieseler Fi 156. It was no mere exercise, and was seen as fulfilling numerous roles both in civil life and for the recently disclosed Luftwaffe. It was a three-seat high-wing machine, powered by the excellent 179-kW (240-hp) Argus engine and with the wing liberally endowed with slats and flaps. A particular feature was the stalky landing gear arrangement, well suited to cushioning arrivals at unprecedented steep angles. The design was prepared in two versions, the Fi 156A with a fixed slat and

the Fi 156B with an automatic movable slat to avoid the speed penalty of the fixed slat in cruising flight. Surprisingly, the faster Fi 156B was never built.

Instead Fieseler manufactured three prototypes with fixed slats, the Fi 156 V1 to V3. The V1 (D-IKVN) flew on or about 24 May 1936, with a metal ground-adjustable propeller. The V2 (D-IDVS) had a wooden propeller, and the V3 (D-IGLI) had military equipment. Their performance was so impressive that the RLM (air ministry) ordered further prototypes and preparations for series production. Nevertheless, conforming with its policy of competition, the RLM wrote a specification around the Fi 156, by autumn 1936 named Storch, and issued it to industry. It resulted in the Messerschmitt Bf 163 similar to the Storch but with a variable-incidence wing, the Siebel Si 201 with a fully glazed two-seat nose cabin ahead of the pusher engine and single low-mounted tail boom, and the Focke-Wulf Fw 186 jump-start autogyro based on Cierva technology. The autogyro was not even considered, and by the time the rivals were flying the Storch was in production.

The first production version was the Fi 156A-1 utility and liaison machine. By mid-1937 the company had flown the V4 on skis, the military V5 and 10 Fi 156A-0 pre-production machines. One of the

The Storch may not have been the most sturdy of aircraft, but its performance was truly exceptional. It is no exaggeration to say that it could land within its own wingspan, testament enough to the design skills of Gerhard Fieseler and Reinhold Mewes.

Italian use of the Fieseler Storch was widespread, and the type will forever be remembered as the rescue ship for Mussolini during his imprisonment high up in a mountain hotel. This machine, complete with Italian fascist emblem, served with the Comando Aeronautica Albania (Regia Aeronautica) at Tirana in 1941.

latter, D-IJFN, put on a dazzling show at the Zurich meeting in July at which the DB-engined Dornier Do 17 and Messerschmitt Bf 109 also swept the board, marking Germany's emergence as a superior air power. The Storch repeatedly demonstrated full-load take-offs after a ground run of never more than 45 m (148 ft), and a fully controllable speed range of 51-174 km/h (32-108 mph).

It must be admitted that the Storch was large for its job, and the US Army Piper L-4 Grasshopper, its mass-produced equivalent, did most of the same tasks on 48 instead of 179 kW (65 instead of 240 hp). On the other hand, it could be argued that the aircraft bought by the RAF for the same duties was the Westland Lysander, which despite the best efforts of Westland could not come anywhere near the German aircraft's STOL qualities even with nearly 746 kW (1,000 hp). The truest test is perhaps an aircraft's influence on history. Immediately the Storch had emulators in at least 10 countries, US examples including the Ryan YO-51 Dragonfly, Vultee L-1 Vigilant and Bellanca O-50. As described below, a version was adopted by the USSR.

There was little unconventional about the design or construction. The fuselage, which was just half as long again as that of an L-4, was of welded steel tube with fabric covering. The strongly made cabin had a glazed area all round which was wider than the fuselage to give a clear view straight downwards. To the top of the cabin were attached the wooden wings, with fabric covering and braced to the bottom fuselage longerons by steel-tube V-struts. The wings could be folded backwards. Along the entire straight leading edge were fixed aluminium slats, while the entire trailing edge was formed by wooden slotted flaps, the outer sections serving as drooping ailerons with inboard balance tabs to reduce stick forces in roll. The flaps were not of Fieseler's *Rollflügel* pattern (resembling the Fowler) but simply large slotted flaps driven by rods in the wing root, jackscrews in the leading edge root and, via sprockets and chains, a handwheel on the left of the cockpit. Working the flaps was little effort, and they could go to 70°. Take-off was usually with 20° or none, but 40° could be used for really 'impossible' situations. The fin was metal and fabric, but the rest of the tail was wooden, with ply skin, the tailplane having variable incidence for trim.

The inverted V-8 engine was neatly installed, and its air cooling was to be a boon on the Eastern Front during World War II. It invariably started as soon as the electric starter was selected, and the access step projecting from the landing gear was seldom needed except to replenish oil. The standard propeller was a 2.6-m (102-in) Schwarz, with metal anti-erosion inserts in the outer leading edges. A 74-litre (16.28-Imp gal) tank was fitted in each wing, and a 205-litre (45-Imp gal) tank could be installed in place of the two passenger seats in tandem behind the pilot. The main legs and tailskid were all tall and had a long stroke, the main units having spiral springs with an oil dashpot to prevent bounce. Hydraulic brakes were hardly needed, and tyre pressure was low enough for almost any surface except fresh deep snow, though pilots soon learned to watch for ruts and large stones because the tyres were rather small. In a strong wind flaps had to be kept in on the ground or the Storch could be blown over.

Difficult target

It added up to a vehicle that could go almost anywhere and do a remarkable number of things. Tests against fighters appeared to confirm that, at around 55 km/h (34 mph), it was a very difficult target for fighters; there was almost trouble when Udet's camera-gun film showed not one picture of the elusive Storch! Another Fi 156A-0 was tested with three 110-lb (SC-50) bombs, with aim marks painted on the Plexiglas windows, while another did successful trials against a U-boat with inert 135-kg (298-lb) depth charges. Less unexpected were supply-dropping tests and trials with smoke apparatus.

Deliveries to the rapidly growing Luftwaffe began in late 1937, some of the first Fi 156A-1s going to the Legion Condor in Spain. Fieseler had to enlarge his factory at Kassel-Bettenhausen, and then to enlarge it again. He regretted not making the retractable-slat Fi 156B, but the Luftwaffe had no requirement for a higher cruising speed and there was no spare capacity for civil production (though there was plenty of demand). So the next version was the Fi 156C, which appeared in 1938 when output was about three per week. The main feature of the Fi 156C was provision for a 7.92-mm (0.312-in) MG15 firing through the raised rear part of the cabin. The gun was usually not installed on the Fi 156C-1, one or two of which were supplied to virtually every *Gruppe* in the Luftwaffe for general liaison duties. The Fi 156C-2 did have the gun, as well as a vertical recon-

Three Fi 156 prototypes were completed in 1936, this being the first of the trio. Fitted with a ground-adjustable-pitch airscrew, it took part in the highly successful flight test programme which in turn led to military interest. Evident in this view is the fixed slat along the entire leading edge of the wing – a key feature in the wing aerodynamics.

Throughout the war, nominal quantities of Storchs were supplied to various Axis forces, including Finland, which acquired two Fi 156C-1s in 1939, the second machine having a conventional undercarriage. This model featured a raised rear canopy for installation of a rear-firing machine-gun, though this was not a standard fit.

With a somewhat sarcastic code applied by American forces in Sicily, this Storch was flight-tested by Allied aircrew, who were highly impressed with the aircraft's handling characteristics. On the hinged wing trailing edge can be seen the slotted ailerons and slotted camber-changing flaps on the outer and inner sections respectively.

naissance camera, and was crewed by a pilot and observer/gunner, either of whom could work the radio. Optional fits included skis and attachments for a stretcher (litter).

By 1939 Fieseler was able to send a few Storchs to Finland and Switzerland. Presentation examples were given to the Italian Duce, Benito Mussolini (who had no idea how important a Storch would be later in his life) and, after a non-aggression pact in summer 1939, to Stalin. The latter was so impressed he instructed Oleg K. Antonov to produce a copy (no licence was sought). Antonov had no experience with steel-tube fuselages, and also no As 10C engines, but he very quickly produced an excellent copy in the OKA-38 Aist (stork), powered by the MV-6 engine derived from the 164-kW (220-hp) Renault 6-cylinder inline. The OKA-38 was adopted for production as the ShS (*Shtabnyi samolyet*, staff aircraft), but the factory was overrun by German troops before deliveries began in summer 1941.

On the front line

From the start of World War II the Storch went, literally, everywhere the German army went. Despite audacious missions in full view of the enemy it suffered amazingly few losses, the front-line life being (it was said) 10 times as long as that of the Bf 109 fighter. This is despite the fact the *Wustennotstaffeln* special rescue units were officially tasked with bringing back battle casualties and downed aircrew no matter where they were, and in North Africa the long-range Fi 156C-5 version often flew deep into trackless desert to get Luftwaffe aircrew. From late 1941 the Fi 156D-1 was produced in parallel with the Fi 156C, the new series having most of the right side hinged to facilitate rapid loading and unloading of stretchers. Yet another version which appeared in 1941 was the Fi 156E, with tandem-wheel tracked landing gears. This was not so much to reduce footprint pressure as to reduce damage and write-offs caused by taxiing over ruts and small obstructions, but though the Fi 156E appears to have performed as advertised, production was restricted to the 10 evaluation Fi 156E-0s.

Fieseler was increasingly required to produce Bf 109 and Focke-Wulf Fw 190 fighters, but nevertheless managed to deliver 484

In late 1943 the overriding need for Fw 190 production necessitated the transfer of Storch manufacture from Kassel to the Mraz factory at Chocen in Czechoslovakia. A total of 137 aircraft was produced in 1944, and production continued for several years after the war, this example finding its way on to the Czech civil register.

Storchs in 1942, while a further 121 came from a new production line at Puteaux in France, which had previously built Morane-Saulnier M.S.406 fighters before the French capitulation.

Subsequently all Storch production was transferred from the overburdened Kassel works, which delivered its last Fi 156 in October 1943. It sent the jigs and a few key workers to the Benes Mraz factory at Chocen, in what the Nazis called the Bohemia-Moravia Protectorate (Czechoslovakia). All subsequent Storch deliveries were to come from Puteaux or Chocen, and it is significant that, after the end of the war, both factories continued to build this useful aircraft even though ex-Luftwaffe machines were littering unlikely parts of the countryside. Total Luftwaffe acceptances were about 2,871, some of which were passed on to the forces of Bulgaria, Croatia, Finland, Hungary, Italy, Romania and Slovakia, all fighting on the Axis side on the Eastern Front.

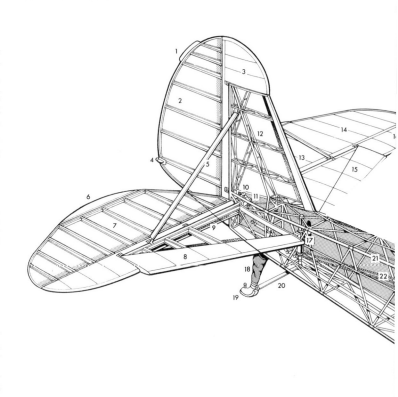

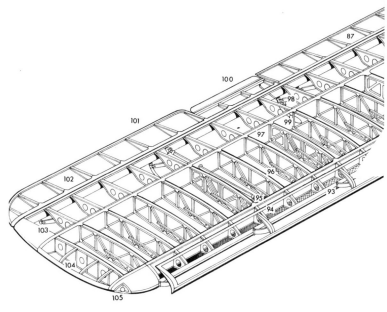

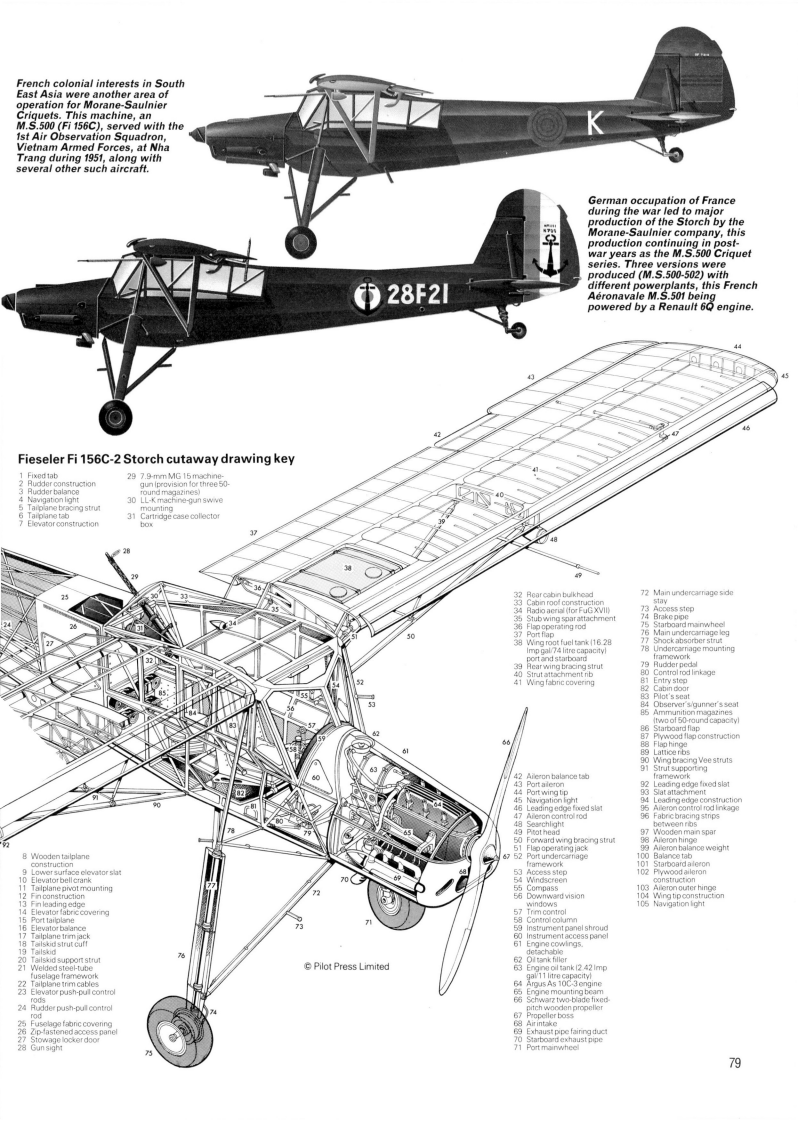

French colonial interests in South East Asia were another area of operation for Morane-Saulnier Criquets. This machine, an M.S.500 (Fi 156C), served with the 1st Air Observation Squadron, Vietnam Armed Forces, at Nha Trang during 1951, along with several other such aircraft.

German occupation of France during the war led to major production of the Storch by the Morane-Saulnier company, this production continuing in post-war years as the M.S.500 Criquet series. Three versions were produced (M.S.500-502) with different powerplants, this French Aéronavale M.S.501 being powered by a Renault 6Q engine.

Fieseler Fi 156C-2 Storch cutaway drawing key

1 Fixed tab
2 Rudder construction
3 Rudder balance
4 Navigation light
5 Tailplane bracing strut
6 Tailplane tab
7 Elevator construction
8 Wooden tailplane construction
9 Lower surface elevator slat
10 Elevator bell crank
11 Tailplane pivot mounting
12 Fin construction
13 Fin leading edge
14 Elevator fabric covering
15 Port tailplane
16 Elevator balance
17 Tailplane trim jack
18 Tailskid strut cuff
19 Tailskid
20 Tailskid support strut
21 Welded steel-tube fuselage framework
22 Tailplane trim cables
23 Elevator push-pull control rods
24 Rudder push-pull control rod
25 Fuselage fabric covering
26 Zip-fastened access panel
27 Stowage locker door
28 Gun sight

29 7.9-mm MG 15 machine-gun (provision for three 50-round magazines)
30 LL-K machine-gun swivel mounting
31 Cartridge case collector box
32 Rear cabin bulkhead
33 Cabin roof construction
34 Radio aerial (for FuG XVII)
35 Stub wing spar attachment
36 Flap operating rod
37 Port flap
38 Wing root fuel tank (16.28 Imp gal/74 litre capacity) port and starboard
39 Rear wing bracing strut
40 Strut attachment rib
41 Wing fabric covering
42 Aileron balance tab
43 Port aileron
44 Port wing tip
45 Navigation light
46 Leading edge fixed slat
47 Aileron control rod
48 Searchlight
49 Pitot head
50 Forward wing bracing strut
51 Flap operating jack
52 Port undercarriage framework
53 Access step
54 Windscreen
55 Compass
56 Downward vision windows
57 Trim control
58 Control column
59 Instrument panel shroud
60 Instrument access panel
61 Engine cowlings, detachable
62 Oil tank filler
63 Engine oil tank (2.42 Imp gal/11 litre capacity)
64 Argus As 10C-3 engine
65 Engine mounting beam
66 Schwarz two-blade fixed-pitch wooden propeller
67 Propeller boss
68 Air intake
69 Exhaust pipe fairing duct
70 Starboard exhaust pipe
71 Port mainwheel

72 Main undercarriage side stay
73 Access step
74 Brake pipe
75 Starboard mainwheel
76 Main undercarriage leg
77 Shock absorber strut
78 Undercarriage mounting framework
79 Rudder pedal
80 Control rod linkage
81 Entry step
82 Cabin door
83 Pilot's seat
84 Observer's/gunner's seat
85 Ammunition magazines (two of 50-round capacity)
86 Starboard flap
87 Plywood flap construction
88 Flap hinge
89 Lattice ribs
90 Wing bracing Vee struts
91 Strut supporting framework
92 Leading edge fixed slat
93 Slat attachment
94 Leading edge construction
95 Aileron control rod linkage
96 Fabric bracing strips between ribs
97 Wooden main spar
98 Aileron hinge
99 Aileron balance weight
100 Balance tab
101 Starboard aileron
102 Plywood aileron construction
103 Aileron outer hinge
104 Wing tip construction
105 Navigation light

© Pilot Press Limited

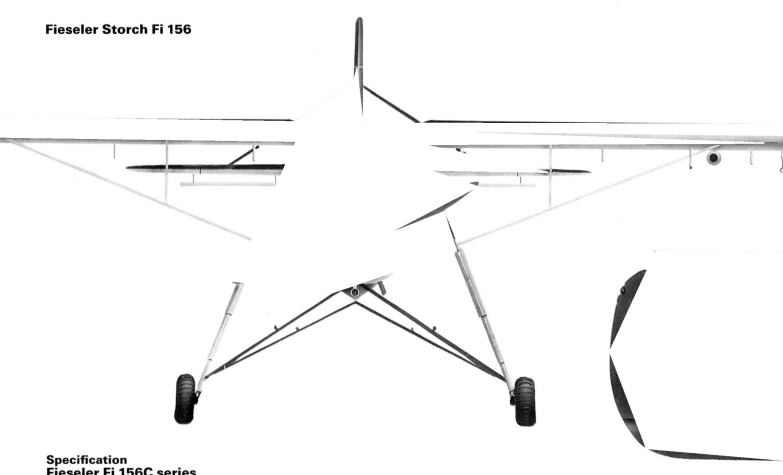

Specification
Fieseler Fi 156C series
Type: STOL liaison, observation and rescue aircraft
Powerplant: one 179-kW (240-hp) Argus As 10C-3 inverted V-8 air-cooled piston engine
Performance: maximum speed 175 km/h (109 mph); cruising speed 130 km/h (81 mph); range (standard wing fuel) 467 km (290 miles)
Weights: empty 930 kg (2,050 lb); normal loaded 1325 kg (2,920 lb)
Dimensions: span 14.25 m (46 ft 9 in); length 9.9 m (32 ft 5.76 in); height 3.0 m (10 ft 0 in); wing area 26.0 m^2 (279.86 sq ft)
Armament: provision for one 7.92-mm (0.312-in) MG15 machine-gun with four spare 75-round magazines.

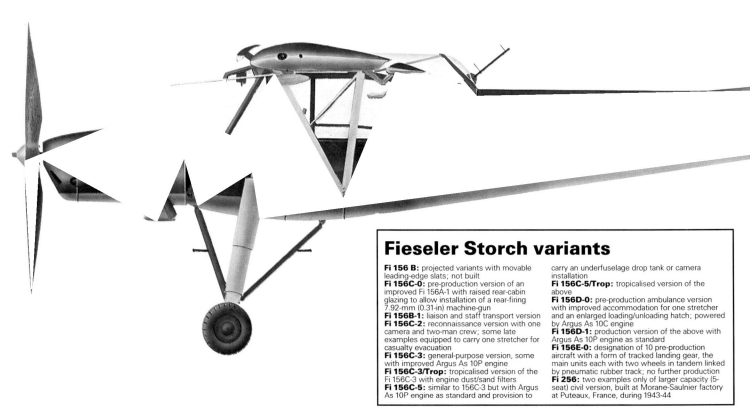

Fieseler Storch variants

Fi 156 B: projected variants with movable leading-edge slats; not built
Fi 156C-0: pre-production version of an improved Fi 156A-1 with raised rear-cabin glazing to allow installation of a rear-firing 7.92-mm (0.31-in) machine-gun
Fi 156B-1: liaison and staff transport version
Fi 156C-2: reconnaissance version with one camera and two-man crew; some late examples equipped to carry one stretcher for casualty evacuation
Fi 156C-3: general-purpose version, some with improved Argus As 10P engine
Fi 156C-3/Trop: tropicalised version of the Fi 156C-3 with engine dust/sand filters
Fi 156C-5: similar to 156C-3 but with Argus As 10P engine as standard and provision to

carry an underfuselage drop tank or camera installation
Fi 156C-5/Trop: tropicalised version of the above
Fi 156D-0: pre-production ambulance version with improved accommodation for one stretcher and an enlarged loading/unloading hatch; powered by Argus As 10C engine
Fi 156D-1: production version of the above with Argus As 10P engine as standard
Fi 156E-0: designation of 10 pre-production aircraft with a form of tracked landing gear, the main units each with two wheels in tandem linked by pneumatic rubber track; no further production
Fi 256: two examples only of larger capacity (5-seat) civil version, built at Morane-Saulnier factory at Puteaux, France, during 1943-44

Without doubt the Fieseler Storch was the prime example of an army co-operation and observation aircraft, and certainly the design by which other types operating in these roles were judged. This view of an Fi 156C-3 clearly illustrates the purposeful design of the undercarriage with the long compression legs incorporating long-stroke, oil-damping shock absorbers of high vertical descent rates. Such was the success of the Storch in its intended role that trials were conducted around supply-dropping, coastal patrol and light bombing roles, though only as secondary operations.

Fieseler Storch Fi 156

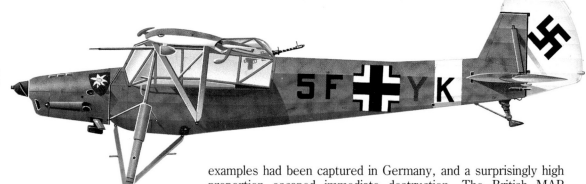

With its colour scheme identifying its desert theatre of operations during the conflict in North Africa, this Fi 156C-3/Trop was operated by 2.(H)/14 under Afrika Korps orders on tank-spotting duties. With excellent visibility and slow-flying characteristics, the Storch was ideal for such duties.

So far as is known the Storch did not fly night harassment missions with weapons on that front, as did thousands of Luftwaffe biplane trainers (many having the same As 10C engine), but the Storch nevertheless took part in many exciting actions. Certainly the most remarkable 'James Bond' type mission of the entire war (which received little publicity because it was by the losing side) took place on 12 September 1943. Italy had reached an armistice with the Allies, and the former Fascist dictator, Mussolini, had been taken prisoner. Most of the country was at once taken over by the German army, however, and Hitler ordered SS Haupsturm-führer Otto Skorzeny to find Mussolini and rescue him. Eventually Skorzeny located Mussolini as being held in the hotel on top of the pinnacle of the Gran Sasso in the Abruzzi mountains, reached only by cable-car. He organised a rescue using a Focke Achgelis Fa 223 Drache helicopter, but at the last moment this was unserviceable. Undeterred, Skorzeny went in a Storch, landed on the tiny terrace at the back of the hotel, got the former dictator and, severely overloaded, took off over the sheer edge.

Fleeing Berlin

Almost equal in excitement was one of the very last missions ever flown by a Storch of the Luftwaffe. On 23 April 1945 Hitler received a communication from Reichsmarschall Hermann Goering, previously his closest aide, which made him furious. He immediately dismissed Goering as C-in-C of the Luftwaffe (Goering having got out of Berlin to safer climes), and appointed in his stead Generaloberst Ritter von Greim. He sent a message from his bunker to Berlin-Gatow calling for von Greim, and Flugkapitän Hanna Reitsch brought him to the Führerbunker in a Storch, flying by night over the entire encircling Soviet armies and landing amidst piles of rubble and under enemy fire. Hitler formally invested von Greim, who was then flown out again by the brilliant woman test pilot. She was the last person to get out of beleaguered Berlin, and the return trip should on any rational basis have been impossible.

During the war at least 47 Storchs, nearly all of them Fi 156C-3/Trop or Fi 156C-5/Trop versions, were taken on charge by front-line RAF squadrons in the Mediterranean theatre. In the final few months of the war further examples came into the hands of Allied units in northern Europe. By May 1945 further undestroyed examples had been captured in Germany, and a surprisingly high proportion escaped immediate destruction. The British MAP (Ministry of Aircraft Production) carried out a formal evaluation of VX154, which numerically confirmed its outstanding qualities. Among more than 60 Storchs taken formally on RAF charge was VM472, the personal aircraft of Field Marshal Montgomery in preference to an Allied type. Another, brought to the UK by an air marshal, was reluctantly wrested from him and in 1946, in immaculate Ministry livery with serial VP546 (and British wheels), it was flown by Lieutenant Commander E. M. 'Winkle' Brown as a valued vehicle at Aero Flight, RAE Farnborough.

Peace and war again

Many hundreds of Storchs were built after the war in both France and liberated Czechoslovakia. The Puteaux factory had in fact built two prototypes of the Fi 256, which Fieseler had designed in 1941 as a civil successor. It looked like a Storch with a wider fuselage, but in fact hardly any parts were common. The wings had automatic slats, the fuselage was more streamlined, and the cabin seated two pairs of passengers behind the pilot instead of two single seats. The engine was an As 10P of 194 kW (260 hp). There was nothing wrong with the Fi 256, but the Luftwaffe declined to order it, and there was no obvious civil market.

Chocen-built aircraft after the war were known as the Mraz K.65 Cap. Production was terminated soon after the Communist take-over in 1948. The Puteaux designations were Morane-Saulnier M.S.500, 501 and 502: the M.S.500 resembled the standard Fieseler Fi 156C series; the M.S.501 looked like the Soviet Antonov OKA-38 in having a Renault 6Q inverted inline engine; and the most important version, made in substantial numbers, was the M.S.502 Criquet with a Salmson 9Abc radial. The radial seemed to suit the 'Cricket' admirably, and it had a long career with l'Armée de l'Air and l'Aéronavale. So, too, did the Argus-engined aircraft, and ex-French machines even served with the Vietnam forces throughout the 1950s. Another important user was the Swedish air force, whose S14 versions from Germany were supplemented by post-war French examples. Several Storchs, from various sources, got on the British civil register, and many examples, most of them built post-war, are still flying in several countries.

A common sight wherever German forces were operating, the Storch could perform in several valuable roles. Here an Fi 156D-1 in Tunisia illustrates the upward-hinging loading hatch on the lowered rear glazing, which permitted the carriage of one stretcher case in the rear fuselage after some arrangement of internal equipment.

Focke-Wulf Fw 189

Germany's aircraft manufacturers of the 1930s and 1940s were renowned for developing novel solutions to their problems. Few designs were as distinctive as Focke-Wulf's Fw 189. At first glance a fragile-looking aircraft, the Uhu distinguished itself in the toughest place possible: the Russian front.

In the mid-1930s aircraft technology was making rapid progress. The standard reconnaissance aircraft of the Luftwaffe was the He 46, a fabric-covered biplane resembling aircraft of World War I. Its replacement, first flown in autumn 1936, was the Hs 126, a stressed-skin monoplane. But even the 126 could be seen to be an interim type (though it gave good service in the early years of World War II). In February 1937 the air ministry in Berlin issued a specification for an even later aircraft with a crew of three, all-round vision and high performance.

It was a challenge, and produced one conventional response, the Arado Ar 198, and one unconventional one, the Focke-Wulf Fw 189. Whereas the Arado was a single-engined mid-wing monoplane, notable only for having extensive glazing on the underside of the fuselage as well as on top, the Fw 189 had an almost completely glazed central nacelle, twin engines and twin tail booms. Nor was this all. Hamburger Flugzeugbau decided to enter the contest with an even more radical aircraft, the extraordinary asymmetric BV 141, with a glazed nacelle on one side of the centreline and an unmanned 'fuselage' (with engine and tail) on the other!

The conservative officials favoured the Arado, thinking both the unconventional designs in some way inferior if not actually faulty. Gradually they began to see the advantages of the notion of a completely glazed crew nacelle, with if necessary an all-round field of fire for defensive guns. Moreover, Focke-Wulf's designers, led by Kurt Tank and (for the Fw 189) E. Kosel, pointed out that different kinds of nacelle could be fitted. They suggested a close-support version, a trainer and a single-seat armoured attack and anti-tank version, as

well as the army co-operation and reconnaissance model (which could also fly casualty evacuation, VIP transport and light cargo missions).

The odd BV 141 was destined never to go into production, though the first version flew well. Likewise, the Arado, initially the favourite of the air ministry staff, never got anywhere, but in this case it was because the prototype was a complete disappointment, on the scores of both handling and performance. In complete contrast, the Fw 189 proved to be an excellent aircraft in all respects. The V1 (first prototype) was flown by Dipl-Ing Tank in July 1938, and he was delighted with it. He called it Eule (Owl), though the Luftwaffe was to call the type the Uhu (Eagle Owl) and the official media dubbed it das Fliegende Auge (the Flying Eye).

In fact, apart from the twin-boom configuration, which never caused any of the feared problems, the Fw 189 was quite conventional. The all-metal stressed-skin structure had a smooth flush-riveted exterior. The wing comprised a rectangular centre-section and detachable panels bolted on just outboard of the tail booms and tapered on the leading edge only. The long-span ailerons and three sections of electrically operated split flap were all fabric covered. Likewise, while the rest of the tail was all-metal, the elevator and rudders were fabric covered. Each main landing gear had an

Supremely versatile and universally popular, the Uhu was essentially a low-altitude aircraft, befitting its tactical reconnaissance role. The ride was extremely smooth, while the extensive glazing gave good visibility although, surprisingly, forward vision was impaired by refraction from the sloping panels.

Fw 189A-1 of 1.
Aufklärungsstaffel (Heeres)/32,
based at Kemi in Finland in
June 1942. The brown/green
splinter camouflage was
common in this theatre.

Fw 189A-1 of 5.(H)/12 at Poltava,
Ukraine in the summer of 1942.
The unit operated under
Luftflotte 4.

H-shaped frame with twin shock absorbers in a levered suspension giving a long stroke, as in several Fw aircraft of the period. Oddly, in view of the company's predeliction for all-electric actuation, the gear was raised hydraulically, swinging back under the wing into a bay in the boom closed by twin doors. Linkage also pulled up the castoring tailwheel, which retracted sideways to the left to be stowed in the tailplane. On selecting landing gear down, at speeds below 160 km/h (99 mph), the main units were hydraulically extended but the tailwheel fell under its own weight, assisted by rubber pulleys.

The chosen engine, and nobody ever regretted it, was the Argus As 410A-1, an inverted-V with 12 aircooled cylinders. Very smooth at 3,100 rpm, and easy to start even in a Russian winter, this engine proved very reliable, though the 189 could be flown perfectly well on one. A single fuel tank of 110-litre (24-Imp gal) capacity was in each tailboom just behind the landing gear bay, the usual octane rating being 87. The prototype had simple fixed-pitch propellers, but from V3 every Fw 189 had two-blade Argus propellers with pitch controlled automatically by the prominent eight-vane cap free to rotate on the front of the spinner.

The central nacelle hardly changed from V1 to the last aircraft built (apart from two totally different versions described later). Basically a stressed-skin structure, almost the whole of it was covered with flat Plexiglas panels, some roof panels and those in the pointed tailcone being curved. Entry was from the wing on either side, through the huge space left by hingeing up the complete side and top windows on each side. The pilot sat well forward on the left, with pedals projecting on beams ahead of the floor. Almost all necessary controls were on the left, the R/T jack socket was at the rear of the roof centreline, and the flight instruments were in a row across the front of the cockpit slightly above eye level. The magnetic compass and rpm indicators were between the pilot's feet just ahead of the two-handed control yoke. On the right, slightly further back, was the seat for the navigator. He could face ahead and manage either the floor-

The first V1 prototype took to the air in July 1938 with Kurt Tank himself at the controls. The soundness of the design was such that production aircraft differed little from this machine. It was assigned the registration D-OPVN.

mounted camera(s), or take photos with a hand camera, or the GV 219d optical bombsight. Alternatively he could swivel his seat round and aim the dorsal gun(s). At the rear of the nacelle was a quilted mattress on which the rear gunner could lie. Oddly, this third crew member was called the flight mechanic, though there was little he could do apart from keep an eye out for interception from the rear. Management of the radio, which the third man might have performed, was yet one more duty for the overworked navigator.

From the start the mainstream Fw 189 was to be the A-series, as described. The V1 differed from production machines only in such details as the propellers, as described, and in having single-leg main gears. The V2, flown only a month later in August 1938, was armed with two MG 17 machine-guns in the wing roots, firing ahead and aimed by a ring/bead sight by the pilot, and three very similar MG 15s (fed by a saddle magazine instead of a belt), aimed through the nose, mid-upper position and tailcone. Four ETC 50/VIIId racks under the outer wings could carry 50-kg bombs or chemical containers for poison gas or smokescreens. Via further prototypes the pre-production Fw 189A-0 was completely defined by the beginning of 1939, but

The Fw 189 V4 served as a prototype for the production A-series aircraft, embodying minor changes such as revised cowlings. It later went on to various warfare trials, as seen here with 'Lost' chemical warfare equipment under the wings for the spraying of mustard gas.

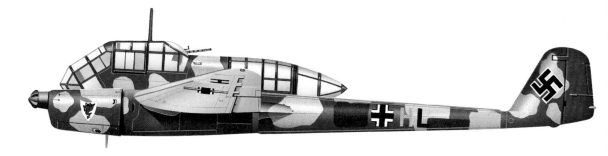

This Fw 189A-1 served with 1.(H)/32 at Petsamo in Northern Finland in December 1942. The disruptive meander camouflage was applied over the standard green summer camouflage.

Slovakia and Hungary were supplied with the Fw 189, this being an Fw 189A-2 of the latter's Hungarian 3/1 Short Range Reconnaissance Squadron (Ung.N.A. St). It was subordinated to Luftflotte 4 at Zamocz, eastern Poland in March 1944.

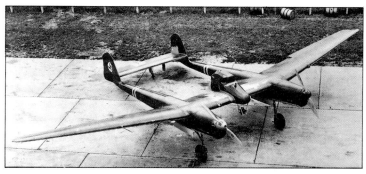

The Fw 189 V1 was rebuilt as the V1b to test the Fw 189C assault aircraft. Once again a new nacelle was fitted, this cramming a pilot and rear-facing gunner into a tiny, heavily-armoured cabin. Vision for both crew members was appalling, and the flying characteristics were altered distinctly for the worse.

rather to Tank's chagrin the Oberkommando der Luftwaffe expressed the view that there was no need for such an aircraft and that the Hs 126A-1 and B-1 were perfectly adequate. All the company could do was press ahead with other versions but, eventually, in spring 1940, permission was given to build 10 A-0s. At about the same time the inadequacies of the Hs 126 were becoming obvious in the campaign in the West, and Focke-Wulf was told to carry on beyond the A-0s with production A-1s for front-line service. This was reinforced by the excellent service evaluation by the Auflärungsstaffel, and, quite suddenly, from being unwanted, the twin-boom Uhu was a high-priority aircraft.

Focke-Wulf frantically tooled up to build the A-1 in series, but became increasingly overloaded, mainly because of the Fw 190 fighter.

As a second source the Aero factory at Prague Vysocany was swiftly tooled up, and in the course of 1941 the Czech plant delivered 151 Fw 189s compared with just 99 from the parent company at Bremen. It was obvious that the invasion of the Soviet Union, begun on 22 June 1941, was going to need all the Fw 189s that could be produced, so a major part of French industry was taken over by Focke-Wulf, and the Fw 189 production jigs were sent to France from Bremen. Breguet made outer wings at Bayonne, but most of the other parts were made by SNCASO, including the centre-section and nacelle at Bordeaux-Bacalan, booms and tail at Rochefort and other parts at Bordeaux-Bégles. Assembly and flight test was at Bordeaux-Mérignac. This was one of the few instances of a successful production programme in German-occupied France, output working up eventually to 20 per month.

The A-1 differed only in details (such as in having twin-leg main gears) from the fourth prototype. The nose gun was omitted, and armament comprised two MG 17s and two hand-aimed MG 15s. Four SC50 bombs were carried if necessary, and aimed either in dives or in level flight using the sight. Gas equipment was not used, but S 125 smokescreen containers were a common fit. The normal camera installations in the middle of the nacelle normally housed the ubiquitous Rb 20/30, but alternatives included the 15/18, 21/18 or 50/30, and a hand-held HK 12.5 or HK 19 was almost always carried. Other equipment included FuG 25 communications radio, G4 radio direction finding, and flare cartridges.

In mid-1941 production switched to the Fw 189A-2, in which the single MG 15s were replaced by the neater and fast-firing MG 81Z twin installations, each firing 3,600 rpm with belt feed. The rear cone had electric rotation to assist in aiming in all rearwards directions. Small numbers were also made of the A-3 dual-control trainer,

With a completely redesigned fuselage nacelle, the Fw 189B was intended as a five-seat trainer. Ten of the Fw 189B-1 production aircraft were delivered before Fw 189A production began. An Fw 189D floatplane trainer version was semi-completed.

Focke-Wulf Fw 189

This Fw 189A-1 served with
Nahaufklarüngsgruppe (NAGr)
1 from Dnepropetrovsk in the
Ukraine, March 1943. Note the
unit's red devil badge on the
engine cowling.

*Everything about the Fw 189 was slender, especially the wings and tail
booms. Despite this, it was an immensely strong aircraft, able to take
large amounts of battle damage. Flying low over the battlefield, this
was an important attribute of the type.*

supplemented by a few A-0 and A-1 aircraft brought up to A-3
standard. Though a few A-0s reached the 9.(H)/LG 2 training unit in
1940, the Fliegende Auge was hardly seen in front-line units until
1942. Then it became really important, progressively replacing the
Hs 126 in Luftwaffe and related units, and also serving with units of
the Slovakian and Hungarian air forces. It proved to be a reliable,
capable and very tough aircraft, on at least two occasions surviving
Soviet ramming attacks and frequently fighting off hostile fighters.

In late 1942 small numbers were delivered as A-4 close-support
and reconnaissance aircraft, with extra armour and with the forward-
firing MG 17s replaced by 20-mm MG FFs. The Bremen and Praguc
factories ceased production in 1943, but the French complex kept
going until January 1944. Including prototypes, output comprised six
in 1939, 38 in 1940, 250 in 1941, 327 in 1942, 226 in 1943 and 17 in
1944, making a grand total of 864. These numbers included a few for
the North African campaign with desert survival equipment and sand

*The cockpit of the Uhu resembled the compound eye of an insect, and
even the propaganda department of the RLM called the type 'das
Fliegende Auge'. The eight vanes on each propeller spinner regulated
the variable pitch mechanism.*

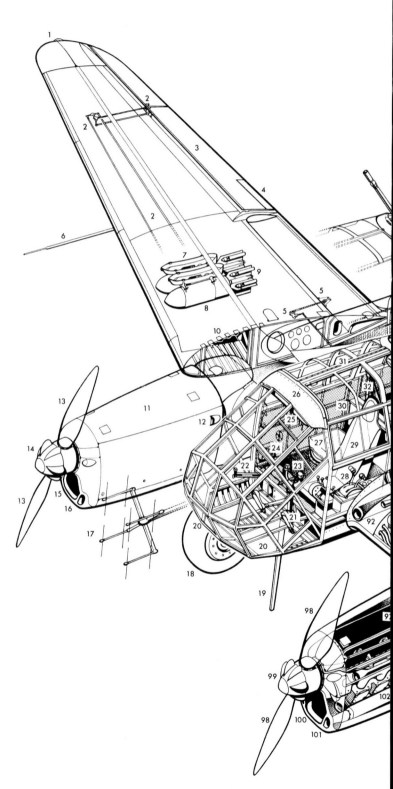

Focke-Wulf Fw 189A-2 cutaway drawing key

1 Starboard navigation light
2 Aileron control linkage (outer and inner)
3 Starboard aileron
4 Aileron tab
5 Starboard outer flap control linkage
6 Pitot tube
7 ETC 50/VIIId underwing rack fairings
8 Two 50-kg (110-lb) SC 50 bombs
9 Papier-maché 'screamers' attached to bomb fins
10 Wing centre/outer section join
11 Starboard engine nacelle
12 Air intake
13 Argus two-bladed controllable-pitch propeller
14 Pitch control vanes
15 Oil cooler intake
16 Engine air intake

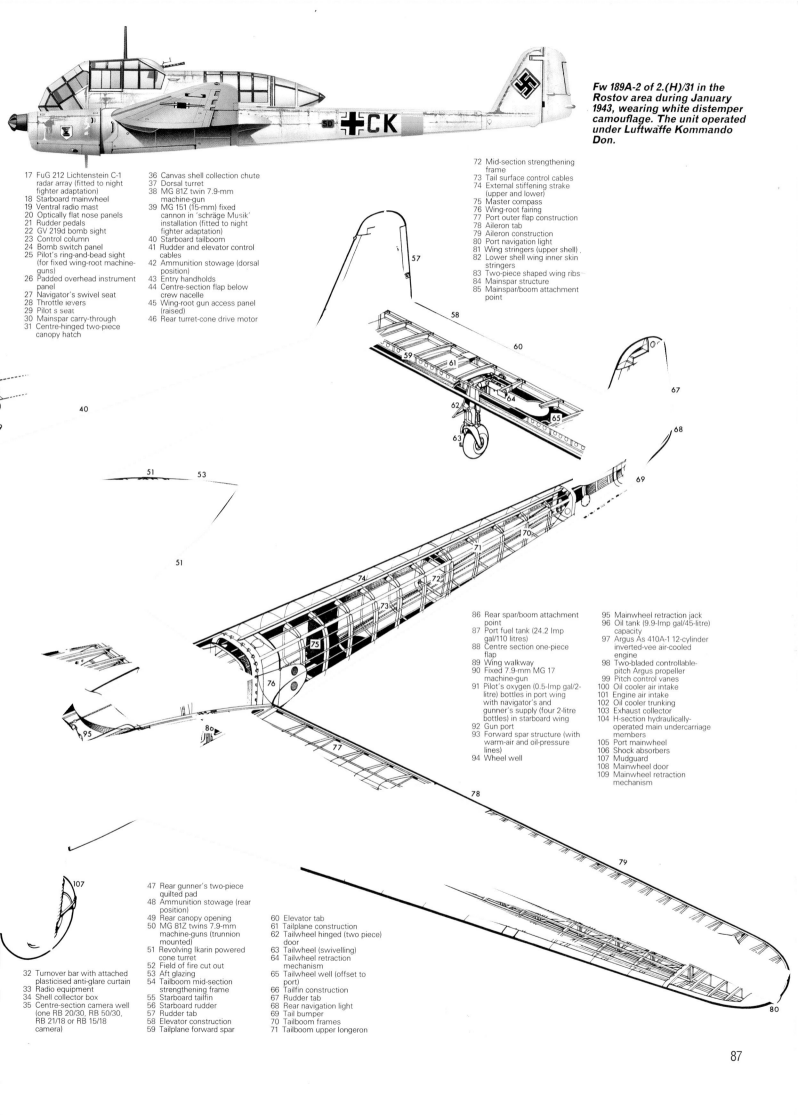

Fw 189A-2 of 2.(H)/31 in the Rostov area during January 1943, wearing white distemper camouflage. The unit operated under Luftwaffe Kommando Don.

17 FuG 212 Lichtenstein C-1 radar array (fitted to night fighter adaptation)
18 Starboard mainwheel
19 Ventral radio mast
20 Optically flat nose panels
21 Rudder pedals
22 GV 219d bomb sight
23 Control column
24 Bomb switch panel
25 Pilot's ring-and-bead sight (for fixed wing-root machine-guns)
26 Padded overhead instrument panel
27 Navigator's swivel seat
28 Throttle levers
29 Pilot's seat
30 Mainspar carry-through
31 Centre-hinged two-piece canopy hatch

36 Canvas shell collection chute
37 Dorsal turret
38 MG 81Z twin 7.9-mm machine-gun
39 MG 151 (15-mm) fixed cannon in 'schräge Musik' installation (fitted to night fighter adaptation)
40 Starboard tailboom
41 Rudder and elevator control cables
42 Ammunition stowage (dorsal position)
43 Entry handholds
44 Centre-section flap below crew nacelle
45 Wing-root gun access panel (raised)
46 Rear turret-cone drive motor

72 Mid-section strengthening frame
73 Tail surface control cables
74 External stiffening strake (upper and lower)
75 Master compass
76 Wing-root fairing
77 Port outer flap construction
78 Aileron tab
79 Aileron construction
80 Port navigation light
81 Wing stringers (upper shell)
82 Lower shell wing inner skin stringers
83 Two-piece shaped wing ribs
84 Mainspar structure
85 Mainspar/boom attachment point

86 Rear spar/boom attachment point
87 Port fuel tank (24.2 Imp gal/110 litres)
88 Centre section one-piece flap
89 Wing walkway
90 Fixed 7.9-mm MG 17 machine-gun
91 Pilot's oxygen (0.5-Imp gal/2-litre) bottles in port wing with navigator's and gunner's supply (four 2-litre bottles) in starboard wing
92 Gun port
93 Forward spar structure (with warm-air and oil-pressure lines)
94 Wheel well

95 Mainwheel retraction jack
96 Oil tank (9.9-Imp gal/45-litre) capacity
97 Argus As 410A-1 12-cylinder inverted-vee air-cooled engine
98 Two-bladed controllable-pitch Argus propeller
99 Pitch control vanes
100 Oil cooler air intake
101 Engine air intake
102 Oil cooler trunking
103 Exhaust collector
104 H-section hydraulically-operated main undercarriage members
105 Port mainwheel
106 Shock absorbers
107 Mudguard
108 Mainwheel door
109 Mainwheel retraction mechanism

32 Turnover bar with attached plasticised anti-glare curtain
33 Radio equipment
34 Shell collector box
35 Centre-section camera well (one RB 20/30, RB 50/30, RB 21/18 or RB 15/18 camera)

47 Rear gunner's two-piece quilted pad
48 Ammunition stowage (rear position)
49 Rear canopy opening
50 MG 81Z twins 7.9-mm machine-guns (trunnion mounted)
51 Revolving Ikarin powered cone turret
52 Field of fire cut out
53 Aft glazing
54 Tailboom mid-section strengthening frame
55 Starboard tailfin
56 Starboard rudder
57 Rudder tab
58 Elevator construction
59 Tailplane forward spar

60 Elevator tab
61 Tailplane construction
62 Tailwheel hinged (two piece) door
63 Tailwheel (swivelling)
64 Tailwheel retraction mechanism
65 Tailwheel well (offset to port)
66 Tailfin construction
67 Rudder tab
68 Rear navigation light
69 Tail bumper
70 Tailboom frames
71 Tailboom upper longeron

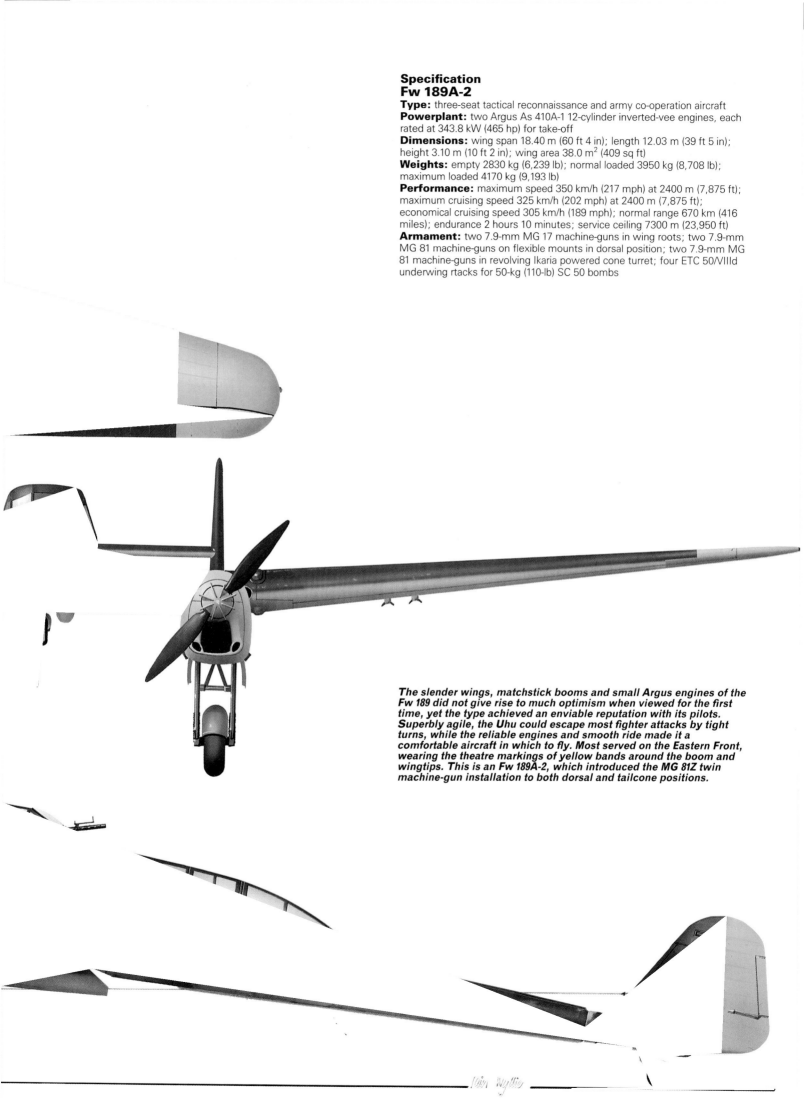

Specification
Fw 189A-2

Type: three-seat tactical reconnaissance and army co-operation aircraft

Powerplant: two Argus As 410A-1 12-cylinder inverted-vee engines, each rated at 343.8 kW (465 hp) for take-off

Dimensions: wing span 18.40 m (60 ft 4 in); length 12.03 m (39 ft 5 in); height 3.10 m (10 ft 2 in); wing area 38.0 m^2 (409 sq ft)

Weights: empty 2830 kg (6,239 lb); normal loaded 3950 kg (8,708 lb); maximum loaded 4170 kg (9,193 lb)

Performance: maximum speed 350 km/h (217 mph) at 2400 m (7,875 ft); maximum cruising speed 325 km/h (202 mph) at 2400 m (7,875 ft); economical cruising speed 305 km/h (189 mph); normal range 670 km (416 miles); endurance 2 hours 10 minutes; service ceiling 7300 m (23,950 ft)

Armament: two 7.9-mm MG 17 machine-guns in wing roots; two 7.9-mm MG 81 machine-guns on flexible mounts in dorsal position; two 7.9-mm MG 81 machine-guns in revolving Ikaria powered cone turret; four ETC 50/VIIId underwing rtacks for 50-kg (110-lb) SC 50 bombs

The slender wings, matchstick booms and small Argus engines of the Fw 189 did not give rise to much optimism when viewed for the first time, yet the type achieved an enviable reputation with its pilots. Superbly agile, the Uhu could escape most fighter attacks by tight turns, while the reliable engines and smooth ride made it a comfortable aircraft in which to fly. Most served on the Eastern Front, wearing the theatre markings of yellow bands around the boom and wingtips. This is an Fw 189A-2, which introduced the MG 81Z twin machine-gun installation to both dorsal and tailcone positions.

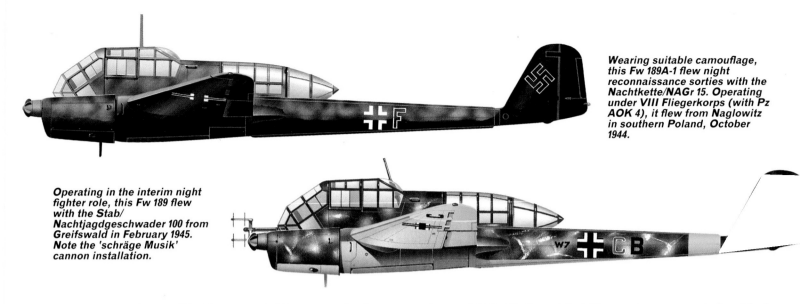

Wearing suitable camouflage, this Fw 189A-1 flew night reconnaissance sorties with the Nachtkette/NAGr 15. Operating under VIII Fliegerkorps (with Pz AOK 4), it flew from Naglowitz in southern Poland, October 1944.

Operating in the interim night fighter role, this Fw 189 flew with the Stab/Nachtjagdgeschwader 100 from Greifswald in February 1945. Note the 'schräge Musik' cannon installation.

filters, and two A-1s modified for use as staff transports for General-feldmarschall Kesselring and General Jeschonnek. In addition, at least 30 A-1s were modified as night fighters, serving with I/NJG 100 and with NJG 5. Conversion involved removing reconnaissance gear and various other items, adding FuG 212 Lichtenstein C-1 interception radar, with the usual quad array of dipole aerials ahead of the nose, and replacing the mid-upper MG 81Z guns by a fixed upward-firing MG 151/15 (occasionally an MG 15/20).

There were two main branches of the family that were terminated. The Fw 189B was to be a crew trainer, with accommodation for five, including dual pilot controls. The V5 prototype was accordingly completed in early 1939 with a conventional nacelle of stressed-skin construction, with just a normal glazed cockpit and further glazing for a cockpit at the rear. Obviously far more capable and economical than existing aircraft used for crew training, the Fw 189B appealed to the Luftwaffe at a time when the 189A did not, and in 1939-40 the Bremen works delivered three pre-production B-0s and 10 B-1s. There was to have been a twin-float seaplane version, the 189D, but this was cancelled.

The other main branch that did not go into production was the Fw 189C. This was to be an armoured close-support version, the nacelle taking the form of a cramped box just big enough for the pilot and an aft-facing rear gunner, the whole thing being made of thick armour with the exception of tiny inserts of thick armoured glass. In the

The V6 was also completed as an Fw 189C prototype, this being essentially similar to the V1b but incorporating variable pitch propellers and armament in the centre-section of the wing. This comprised two 20-mm MG FF cannon and four MG 17 machine-guns. A pair of MG 81s protected the rear.

winter of 1938-39 the original V1 prototype was rebuilt with the planned armoured nacelle, becoming the V1b, flown in spring 1939. The pilot could hardly see out, and far from being able to aim his MG 15 the gunner had hardly any vision at all. In any case the handling of the V1b was poor and performance unimpressive. On the other hand, the rival Henschel Hs 129 was even worse.

New engines, new ideas

In early 1940 Focke-Wulf flew the somewhat improved Fw 189 V6, with the revised engines and landing gear of the 189A-0, an improved armoured nacelle offering better visibility to both crew, and upgraded armament of two 20-mm MG FF and four MG 17 firing forwards and a twin MG 81Z firing aft. In the event, though the Hs 129 was from from satisfactory, it was picked for production mainly because of its smaller size and lower cost.

Though the As 410 was an excellent engine, Focke-Wulf kept investigating what might be done with more power. The Fw 189E was to be powered by the same French GR14M 4/5 radial of 522 kW (700 hp) as fitted to the production Hs 129B. SNCASO designed and carried out a single conversion, but this sole 189E crashed en route to evaluation in Germany in early 1943. Greater success attended the 189F, an A-2 powered by 447-kW (600-hp) As 411MA-1 engines as used on the Si 204D. This caused no problems, and the final 17 aircraft made at Bordeaux in 1944 were Fw 189F-1s. The F-2 was to have extra armour and electric landing-gear operation, but none was built. Also unbuilt, the 189G was to have had 708-kW (950-hp) As 402 engines and a strengthened structure.

DORNIER Do 217
Nighthawks of the Luftwaffe

The least known of the three big Luftwaffe bomber families of the war, the Do 17/215/217 in its later variants provided the basis for a powerful and well-armed night fighter, and for capable bomber, reconnaissance and anti-ship platforms.

One of the enduring puzzles of World War II is why the Do 217, an extremely capable bomber, should have remained apparently unknown to British intelligence despite the fact that the first prototype flew in a completely open place in August 1938. Subsequent prototypes cleared most of the surprising list of difficulties, and by December 1940 the Do 217E-1 bomber was in production. The surprise stemmed from the fact that the 217 was merely a heavier and more powerful version of the widely used Do 17Z.

To be frank the Do 17 was not the world's greatest tactical bomber, though it was nice to fly and had no limitations whatever (unlike the He 111 and Ju 88). The 217 was obviously potentially much more formidable, with BMW 801MA or ML engines of 1179 kW (1,580 hp) for take-off and a bombload of up to 2500 kg (5,511 lb). In practice the initial major version, the 217E-2, entered Luftwaffe service in 1941, long after the Battle of Britain had been lost. Dornier-Werke GmbH were never people to sit on their hands and wonder what had gone wrong. In June 1941 Claudius Dornier made a formal proposal for a Do 217 night-fighter, and it came at the right time.

Even at the time the existing 217 was recognised as not by any means an 'ultimate' aircraft. All versions were likely to weigh well over 13608 kg (30,000 lb) and probably more than 15876 kg (35,000 lb), and called for 1492-kW (2,000-hp) engines that were not available. On the other hand the basic 217 was a proven aircraft which many crews liked very much, and which could obviously – without changing the engines – be converted into a night-fighter. The original E-series internal fuel capacity of 2956 litres (650 Imp gals) was unchanged; it was enough for interception missions with the NJG wings and enough for intruder missions over England. The original E-series bomber had capacious bomb bays, and the night-fighter retained the rear bay to house (for example) eight SC 50X bombs of 50 kg (110 lb) each. In the forward bay was installed a tank of 1160 litres (255 Imp gals), giving a handsome margin over what aircrews might have expected.

The main, and obvious, change in the 217J night-fighter was the nose. Instead of a multi-pane Plexiglas nose for a bomb aimer, the J-1 had a 'solid' nose in which were installed four 20-mm MG FF cannon and four 7.92-mm MG 17 machine-guns. The E-2's aft defensive armament, comprising an MG131 dorsal turret and a hand-aimed MG131 in the ventral position, was retained unchanged. The J-1 was operational from February 1942. Crews liked its firepower and endurance, but found it a rather heavy brute which was sluggish when fast manoeuvres were called for (not often) and needed bigger airfields than most of those that were available. More serious was the

Apart from the obvious nose radar and armament, the Do 217J night-fighter differed little from the Do 217E bomber. Using this heavy aircraft as a fighter was not the ideal solution to Germany's night-fighter shortage, but it operated efficiently in concert with Messerschmitt Bf 110s.

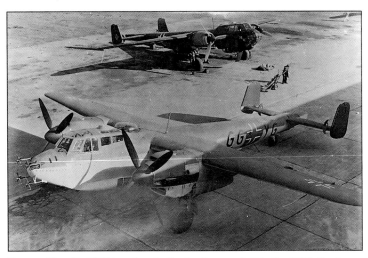

Seen with a **Do 217E** bomber in the background, this **Do 217N** displays the short slab-like wing and chunky **DB 603A** engine. During its career, most **Do 217N**s were fitted with four upward-firing **MG 151** cannon in schräge Musik installations, while some received the Lichtenstein **SN-2** radar.

Dornier Do 217N-2 R22 cutaway drawing key

1 Starboard navigation light	36 Pilot's seat	60 Wing strengthening plate
2 Wing skinning	37 Rudder pedals	61 Fuselage upper fuel tank
3 Control linkage	38 Folding seat	(231 Imp gal/1050 l
4 Starboard aileron	39 Upper pair of 20-mm MG 151	capacity)
5 Aileron trim tab	cannon (offset to starboard)	62 Port inner fuel tank (175 Imp
6 Starboard mainwheel	40 Compressed air bottles	gal/795 l capacity)
7 Mudguard	41 Lower pair of 20-mm MG 151	63 'Schräge Musik' gun
8 Mainwheel doors	cannon	muzzles
9 Engine nacelle fairing	42 Entry hatch	64 Radiator outlet gill
10 FuG 101 radio altimeter	43 Four cannon magazines (each	65 Aerial mast
11 FuG 25a (IFF)	of 200 rounds) – three to	66 Radiator
12 Entry ladder	starboard and one (deleted) to	67 Daimler-Benz DB 603A 12-
13 Entry hatch (open)	port	cylinder liquid-cooled engine
14 Radiator outlet gill	44 Folding map table	68 Propeller mechanism
15 Quick-release catches	45 Side armour	69 Propeller boss
16 Radiator intake	46 D/F blister (in jettisonable roof	70 Four-bladed propeller
17 Cartridge ejector chutes	panel)	71 Oil cooler intake
18 Flame damping exhaust	47 Wireless operator's ceiling	72 Armoured oil cooler
shroud	window	73 Engine bearer
19 Propeller boss	48 Wooden dorsal fairing	74 Flame-damping exhaust
20 Four-bladed VDM propeller	49 Radio equipment	shroud
21 Oil cooler intake	50 Wireless operator's seat	75 Supercharger air intake
22 Cannon muzzles	51 Aircraft self-destruct	76 Port oil tank (51.5 Imp
23 FuG 202 Lichtenstein BC radar	52 Fire extinguisher	gal/235 l capacity)
array	53 Flare cartridges	77 Port outer fuel tank (35 Imp
24 Machine-gun muzzles	54 Control run conduit	gal/160 l capacity)
25 Aerial tuner	55 Flanked off ventral gun	78 Balloon-cable cutter in
26 MG 17 machine-gun	position	leading edge
ammunition boxes	56 Wooden belly fairing	79 Leading-edge hot-air de-icing
27 Ammunition feed chute	57 Wooden formers	80 Hot air duct
28 Four 7.9-mm MG 17 machine-	58 Fuselage lower fuel tank (255	81 Landing light (swivelling)
guns	Imp gal/1016 0 l capacity)	82 Front spar
29 Gun cooling intakes	59 Longeron	83 Pitot head
30 Armoured windscreen		
31 Revi C12D gunsight		
32 Armourglass side panel		
33 Additional extent armour		
34 Control home		
35 Engine controls		

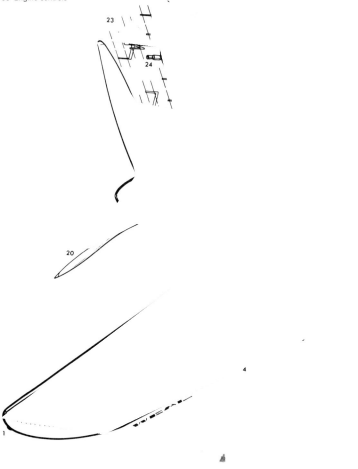

lack of airborne radar, though in 1941-42 most Luftwaffe night-fighter pilots were far from convinced that such new gimmicks were worth having.

Dornier has no record of the first flight of a 217J-2, with FuG 202 Lichtenstein BC radar, but it was probably in the spring of 1942. The J-2 was a definitive night-fighter, not an intruder, the bomb bays being eliminated. The J-2 was lighter than previous Do 217 versions, and despite the 'mattress' of radar antennas the flight performance was almost the same as before. Only small numbers were built, and few combat missions were flown before 1943.

This was because, despite the heavy armament, the 217J was never considered as anything but a stop-gap. Except for Rudolf Schoenert, none of the night-fighter "experten" even considered the 217, and Schoenert only had a soft spot for it because only this aircraft could accommodate his invention of oblique upward-firing guns – later called schräge Musik – with virtually no extra drag. Schoenert's original suggestion in 1941 was not proceeded with, but following tests with a Bf 110 and Do 17Z in 1942 the idea was resurrected. Schoenert managed to get three Do 217J-1s converted for tests at Wittmundhaven and Tarnewitz. Results were promising, and in winter 1942-43 the 2 Jagddivision had three more 217s converted at Diepensee with a more fully engineered installation of either four or

The nose of a **Do 217N-2** displays the main equipment of the night-fighter variants. Four **MG 17** machine-guns were mounted in the nose, with four **MG 151** 20-mm cannon underneath. The Matratzen aerial array was for the FuG 202 Lichtenstein **BC** or FuG 212 Lichtenstein **C**.

(one aircraft) six MG151/20s. In early 1943 these were tested with increasing success by Schoenert's 3/NJG 3. When Schoenert was given the command of II/NJG 5 (Bf 110s) he brought his own 217 with him. As a result, a standard Rüstsatze (factory modification) R22, for installing four MG151s at an angle of 70° into either the Do 217J or Ju 88C was introduced. These were the first schräge Musik kits to be officially approved for general use.

Thus, in the matter of armament, the 217 led all the other night-fighters in 1942-43, and it always had superior flight endurance. On the other hand its performance, as delivered by Dornier, was totally inadequate. None of the bomber's equipment had been removed

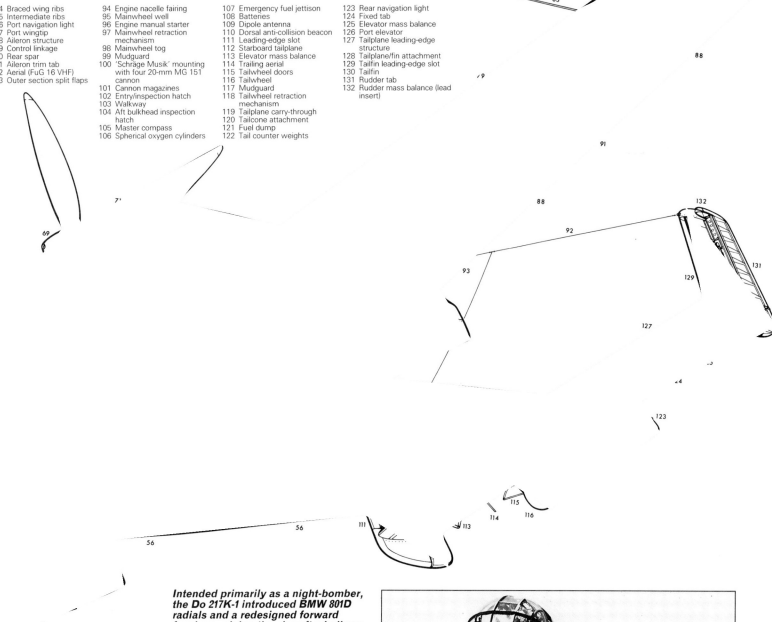

84 Braced wing ribs
85 Intermediate ribs
86 Port navigation light
87 Port wingtip
88 Aileron structure
89 Control linkage
90 Rear spar
91 Aileron trim tab
92 Aerial (FuG 16 VHF)
93 Outer section split flaps

94 Engine nacelle fairing
95 Mainwheel well
96 Engine manual starter
97 Mainwheel retraction
   mechanism
98 Mainwheel tog
99 Mudguard
100 'Schräge Musik' mounting
   with four 20-mm MG 151
   cannon
101 Cannon magazines
102 Entry/inspection hatch
103 Walkway
104 Aft bulkhead inspection
   hatch
105 Master compass
106 Spherical oxygen cylinders

107 Emergency fuel jettison
108 Batteries
109 Dipole antenna
110 Dorsal anti-collision beacon
111 Leading-edge slot
112 Starboard tailplane
113 Elevator mass balance
114 Trailing aerial
115 Tailwheel doors
116 Tailwheel
117 Mudguard
118 Tailwheel retraction
   mechanism
119 Tailplane carry-through
120 Tailcone attachment
121 Fuel dump
122 Tail counter weights

123 Rear navigation light
124 Fixed tab
125 Elevator mass balance
126 Port elevator
127 Tailplane leading-edge
   structure
128 Tailplane/fin attachment
129 Tailfin leading-edge slot
130 Tailfin
131 Rudder tab
132 Rudder mass balance (lead
   insert)

Intended primarily as a night-bomber, the Do 217K-1 introduced BMW 801D radials and a redesigned forward fuselage, giving the aircraft a bulbous look by eliminating the stepped cockpit. Note the twin MG 81 machine-guns mounted in the nose for defence.

(apart from the bombsight), so the operational Gruppen (all of which used the 217J in a mix with other types, usually the Bf 110) began removing as much as possible. Flame-dampers on the exhausts clearly had to stay, but the rear defensive guns, armour, dinghy, dive brakes and (in the J-1) bomb carriers and release mechanism were all removed. This had a considerable beneficial effect, maximum speed at optimum height of 5200 m (17,060 ft) rising from 430 to 510 km/h (267 to 317 mph) (still slower than the E-2 bomber) and time to climb to 5000 m (16,404 ft) being reduced from 35 to 24 minutes.

Meanwhile, from mid-1941 the Dornier works had been developing a series of different 217 versions. Several remained on the drawing board, but two families were destined by 1943 to supplant the original E and J sub-types as the standard production models. The first of these new series was the Do 217K, the first prototype of which (briefly fitted with a single-fin tail) made its maiden flight on 31 March 1942.

In all essentials the resulting production 217K-1, which began to come off production in about October 1942, was similar to the later E-series, and it was likewise intended for night bombing. The only significant changes were fitting BMW 801D engines, giving a maximum power of 1268 kW (1,700 hp), and a redesign of the forward fuselage. There had been nothing particularly wrong with the original cockpit of the Do 17Z/215/217E, but Dornier – influenced by Junkers' development of the Ju 88B/188 – developed a nose similar to

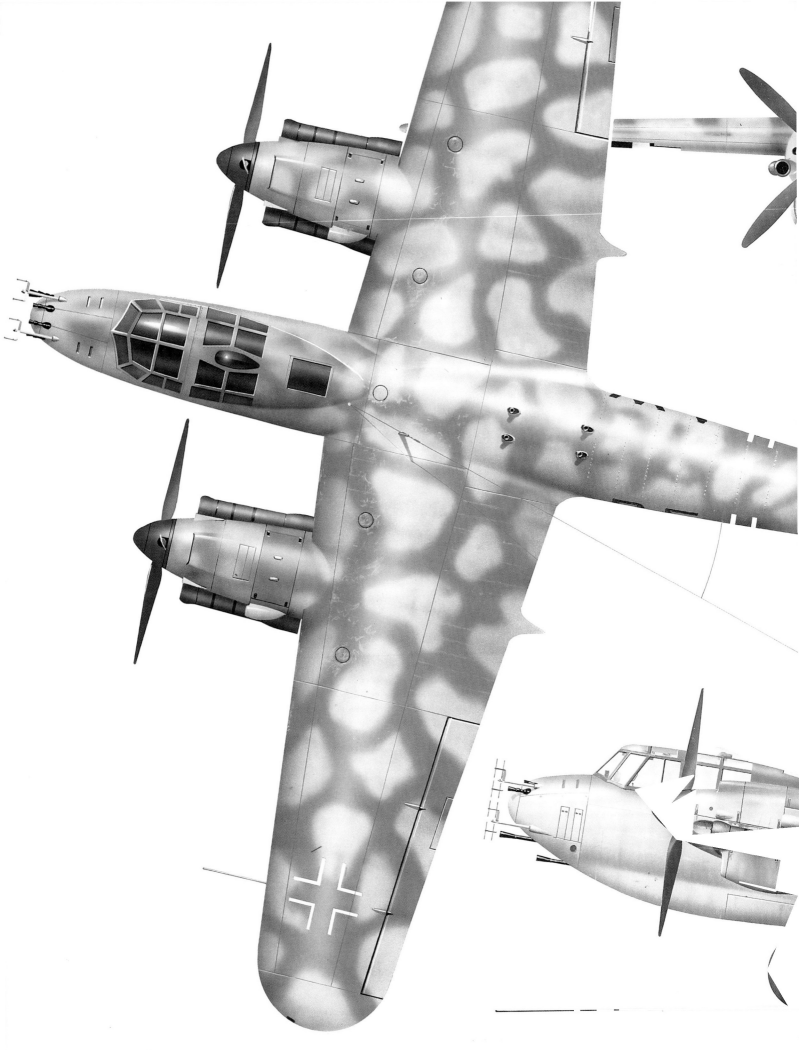

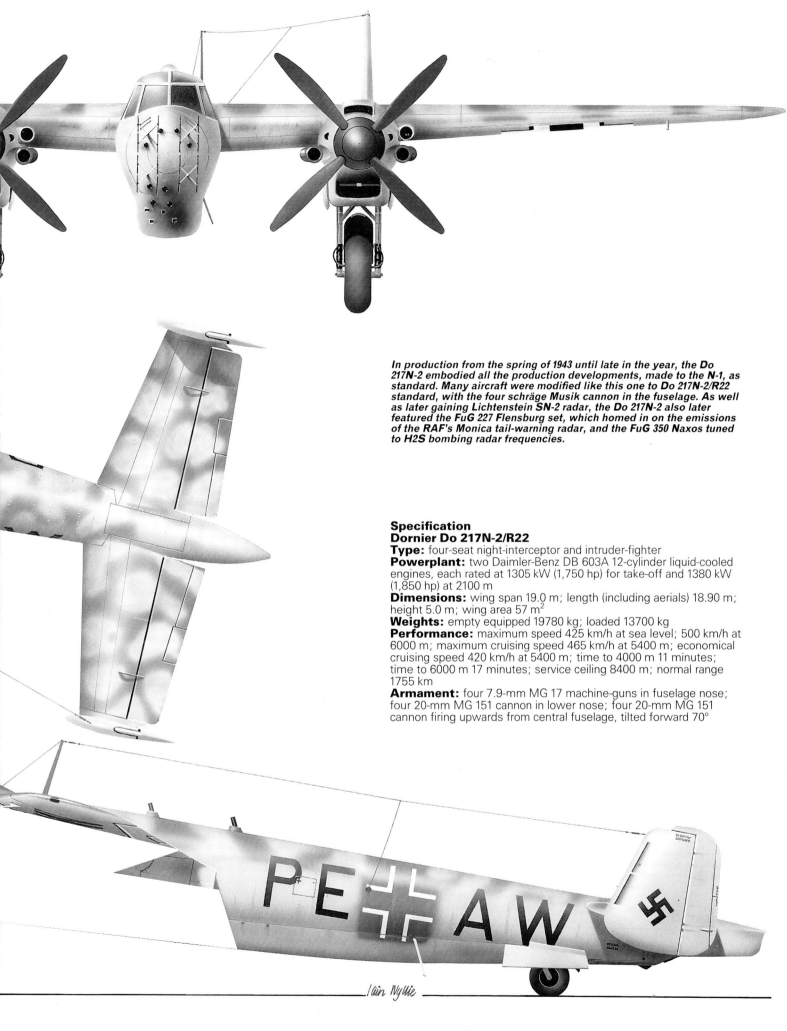

In production from the spring of 1943 until late in the year, the Do 217N-2 embodied all the production developments, made to the N-1, as standard. Many aircraft were modified like this one to Do 217N-2/R22 standard, with the four schräge Musik cannon in the fuselage. As well as later gaining Lichtenstein SN-2 radar, the Do 217N-2 also later featured the FuG 227 Flensburg set, which homed in on the emissions of the RAF's Monica tail-warning radar, and the FuG 350 Naxos tuned to H2S bombing radar frequencies.

Specification
Dornier Do 217N-2/R22
Type: four-seat night-interceptor and intruder-fighter
Powerplant: two Daimler-Benz DB 603A 12-cylinder liquid-cooled engines, each rated at 1305 kW (1,750 hp) for take-off and 1380 kW (1,850 hp) at 2100 m
Dimensions: wing span 19.0 m; length (including aerials) 18.90 m; height 5.0 m; wing area 57 m²
Weights: empty equipped 19780 kg; loaded 13700 kg
Performance: maximum speed 425 km/h at sea level; 500 km/h at 6000 m; maximum cruising speed 465 km/h at 5400 m; economical cruising speed 420 km/h at 5400 m; time to 4000 m 11 minutes; time to 6000 m 17 minutes; service ceiling 8400 m; normal range 1755 km
Armament: four 7.9-mm MG 17 machine-guns in fuselage nose; four 20-mm MG 151 cannon in lower nose; four 20-mm MG 151 cannon firing upwards from central fuselage, tilted forward 70°

Iain Wyllie

The Do 217K-2 was developed especially to carry the FX 1400 Fritz X stand-off missile, and featured extended wings (to 24.8 m) and pylons either side of the fuselage for missile carriage. Transmitters for the FuG 203a Kehl I guidance equipment were mounted on the wings. The aircraft served with III/KG 100.

that of the He 177 and FW 191, with the front glazed part continued up to the top of the fuselage. This had the slight drawback of making the pilot look ahead through distant Plexiglas on which he tended to mis-focus his eyes, especially when the panes reflected lighted parts of the cockpit. At first the K-1 had MG81Z twin 7.92-mm guns in the nose, two single MG81s firing to the sides/rear, an MG131 in the dorsal turret and another MG131 in the rear ventral position. Later two more MG81s were added firing to the sides. It was possible to fit the R19 installation of one or two MG81Z firing astern from the tailcone, but it was more common to have the R25 installation of a Perlon dive-bombing parachute. Not many K-1s were built, at least one being fitted with underwing racks for no fewer than four LT F5b torpedoes.

Running a few weeks later in timing, the Do 217K-2 was the heaviest of all production 217s, at 16850 kg (37,147 lb). It was specifically developed to carry the FX1400 radio-controlled heavy bomb, the He 111H having been found not really suitable for the task. The massive bombs, also known as Fritz X, were slung on special racks under the inner wings. An extra fuel tank of 1160 litres (255 Imp gals) capacity was fitted into the forward bomb bay. To carry the greatly increased weight the outer wings were extended in span from 19 to 24.8 m (62 ft 4 in to 81 ft 4 in), and handling and overall performance remained satisfactory. Almost all K-2s had the R19 fitting of twin MG81Z guns (four in all) in the tail, and some even had an MG81Z firing aft from the tail of each engine nacelle.

The K-2's greatest day was 9 September 1943. Maj Bernhard Jope's III/KG 100, based at Istres, made a concerted assault on the Italian fleet as it sailed to join the Allies. The greatest battleship,

Roma, took two direct hits, blew up and sank within minutes. Her sister, *Italia*, limped to Malta with 800 tons of water on board. Later the powerful bombs, each weighing 1570 kg (3,461 lb), crippled or sank many other ships. Some were launched by Do 217K-3s, which instead of having the FuG 203a Kehl I/FuG 230a Strassburg guidance link, had the FuG 203c or 203d Kehl IV with which the bomb aimer could guide either FX 1400 or the smaller Hs 293A winged bomb.

The other production Do 217 family were the M bombers and N night-fighters. Structurally these were similar to earlier versions; in fact the first 217M was merely a K-1 fitted with Daimler-Benz DB603A liquid-cooled engines, each of 1380 kW (1,850 maximum horsepower). The M-1 went into production almost straight away, being very similar to a K-1 except for having slightly better performance at high altitude. Not many were built, the need for night-fighters being more pressing, but one achieved notoriety on the night of 23 February 1944 when it made a perfect belly landing near Cambridge (soon flying in RAF markings), the crew having baled out over 100 km (62 miles) away near London!

Despite its later suffix letter the corresponding night-fighter, the Do 217N, flew as early as 31 July 1942, the DB603 engine installation having been designed in 1941. Production Do 217N-1s began to reach the Luftwaffe in January 1943. By this time critical feedback about the 217J had been going on for many months, and the NJG crews were disappointed to find the N-1 incorporated none of their mostly obvious recommendations. This was largely because the RLM, and Erhard Milch in particular, disallowed any modifications that would reduce output or increase costs. By mid-1943, however, Dornier had switched to the N-2, and also produced the U1 conversion set with which existing night-fighters could be modified. The chief changes were to remove the dorsal turret and lower rear gun gondola and add wooden fairings. The reduction in drag and removal of some two tonnes of weight raised flight performance to a useful level, maximum speed at medium heights exceeding 500 km/h (310 mph). With the devastating armament ·of four MG151s

To safeguard against non-delivery of the BMW engines, Dornier adapted the K-model to take the DB 603A engine as the Do 217M, both being similar in performance and produced in parallel. This example belly-landed in good condition during a 1944 attack on London and was subsequently repaired.

Few Do 217Ms were built as the need for night-fighters was greater in late 1943/44 than for bombers, and those initiated were largely completed as Do 217Ns. Various M variants were proposed, including a long-span missile carrier, but only the baseline M-1 was produced.

The Do 217J proved an adequate night-fighter, although lacking in speed and manoeuvrability. It was disliked for its high wing loading, this restricting its operations to only a few of the fields available. The forward-firing armament of four cannon and four machine-guns was hard-hitting.

and four MG17s firing ahead and four more MG151s firing at 70° upwards, the 217N-2 was a vast improvement over the J-1, and soon appeared with the FuG 220 Lichtenstein SN-2 radar. By 1944 217Js and Ns were scattered over a vast area of Germany and the occupied countries, as well as I/NJG 100 on the Eastern Front. On the other hand no Gruppe was ever solely equipped with the Do 217, and various problems militated against it ever becoming a top night-fighter as did the Bf 110G and Ju 88G. In the case of the best sub-type, the N-2, the main problem was an enduring series of troubles and shortages with the engines, so that aircraft were continually being cannibalised. For example as early as July 1943 all 14 Do 217Ns of II/NJG 3 were lying around with damaged engines, leaving the Gruppe to carry on with just seven Bf 110s. The point could also be made that the same DB 603 engines powered the He 219, and this was not only nearly 200 km/h (124 mph) faster but it was also a superior night-fighter in every way – but endlessly dogged by its own problems and production difficulties.

Total production of Do 217Js and Ns amounted to a mere 364, terminating in October 1943. From April 1943 until Italy's capitulation five months later small numbers of Do 217J-2s served with the 59° and 60° Gruppi of the Regia Aeronautica. They saw little action and suffered severe attrition from accidents and other problems.

Various related aircraft which never entered service were all intended for flight at high altitudes. First to be started, as an entry in the 1939-40 Bomber B requirement, was the Do 317. This was to be basically a 217 with DB604 engines, each with four banks totalling 24 cylinders and giving a maximum power of 1984 kW (2,660 hp) each, and with a four-seat pressure cabin in the nose. In 1940 this was dropped and some of its features used to assist development of the Do 217P, which had a similar pressure cabin but was powered by two DB603B engines supercharged by a large two-stage blower and intercooler in the rear fuselage, driven by a third engine, a DB605T. The first 217P flew in June 1942, and there were plans for a produc-

*Differing mainly in having **DB 603A** engines, the **Do 217N** also retained the aft bomb bay of its earlier predecessors, this having been dispensed with on the **Do 217K**. Some aircraft later had the **MG FF** cannon replaced by **MG 151s**. Still of 20-mm calibre, these offered a better trajectory and muzzle velocity.*

tion Do 217P-0 reconnaissance aircraft with almost the same extended outer wings as the K-2 (raising service ceiling to an estimated 16154 m /53,000 ft), but this was abandoned.

Meanwhile, in late 1941, the Do 317 was resurrected, and in early 1943 the first 317 began flight testing. This was planned in two versions. The 317A was a broadly conventional high-altitude bomber with DB603A engines, outwardly having much in common with the 217M apart from an odd tail with triangular vertical surfaces. The next-generation 317B was to have extended wings of 26 m (85 ft) span, huge DB610 double engines each of 2141 kW (2,870 hp), and defensive armament comprising a remotely controlled 20-mm MG151 in the tailcone and three twin-gun turrets, two of them remotely controlled. Eventually the 317 also ground to a halt, but five of the 317A series prototypes were modified as unpressurised launch aircraft for the Hs 293A radio-controlled missiles. Redesignated as Do 217Rs, they actually saw combat duty with III/KG 100 at Orléans-Bricy in 1944. At 17770 kg (39,021 lb) they were the heaviest of the whole 217/317 family actually to fly, though had they gone ahead, the 317A and 317B would have been much heavier still.

Heinkel He 219 Uhu

As the tide of the war turned, the German high command came to appreciate that its Nachtjager force needed better equipment. The He 219 had been on the drawing board since 1940, but official indifference and later Allied bombing progressively delayed its development. When the Uhu (Owl) did fly its performance was spectacular, even challenging the RAF's hitherto-unassailable Mosquitoes.

Britain's Sir Sydney Camm used to say "Follow the official specification and you are dead!" There have been countless occasions when superior combat aircraft have been created because the engineering team were able to get on with the job and do it in the best and most efficient way. Obvious examples are the de Havilland Mosquito and General Dynamics F-16. Another was the He 219. Designed as a versatile multi-role aircraft, it was finally developed purely for night-fighting and then criticised because it was so specialised.

Ernst Heinkel AG was one of the largest aircraft firms in Hitler's Germany, and it was certainly the most experienced in producing combat aircraft. In mid-1940 the Rostock-Marienehe head office had surplus design capacity, and this was put to use in creating a number of projects, one of which was Projekt 1064. This was a *Kampf-zerstörer*, literally a war-destroyer, but meaning a multi-role fighter, attack, reconnaissance and even torpedo aircraft. It incorporated many new features, including a tandem-seat pressurised cockpit in a rather serpent-like nose, a shoulder-high wing, giant underslung

engine nacelles housing twin-wheel main units of a tricycle landing gear, twin tail fins and remotely-controlled defensive gun barbettes.

It was just what the Luftwaffe really needed, but long-term planning at the ObdL (Luftwaffe high command) was conspicuously absent. Instead Projekt 1064 was looked at unfavourably because it used so many radical innovations. The 'American' idea of nosewheel gear was scorned, and Heinkel even had the temerity to pick the Daimler-Benz DB 603 engine, a big and powerful unit that, like the Heinkel project, had never been requested officially, and thus was itself under a cloud. Projekt 1064 was merely filed away and forgotten.

Fighting a lone battle to build up the Luftwaffe's vital night-fighter force was the harassed General der Nachtjagd, Josef Kammhuber.

Illustrated in this view of the pre-production He 219 V5 are several characteristic features including the stalky nosewheel member, this turning through 90° and retracting to lie flat beneath the cockpit. Also visible are the wing-root and belly-tray apertures for the six MG 151/15 guns, and radar aerial sockets.

He consistently failed in his efforts to get a truly advanced night-fighter designed for the job, but eventually he managed to gain an interview with Hitler. He left the room with 'special powers' enabling him to overrule his opponents, and as a result in October 1941 Projekt 1064 became the He 219, with a development contract. Kammhuber had been impressed by the potential of this design on a visit to Rostock, and considered it could be the night-fighter he was seeking. (At the same time Focke-Wulf received a contract for a night-fighter which became the Ta 154, dubbed Mosquito because of its wooden construction; it never entered service.)

Few changes were made to the Heinkel design, which retained its twin MG 131 barbettes above and below the rear fuselage and also the 2000-kg (4,409-lb) bombload. Forward-firing armament was to comprise two MG 151/15 cannon in the wing roots and a ventral installation of two MG 151/20s or a large 30-mm MK 103. The basic aircraft was a clean and efficient stressed-skin design, with powerful slotted flaps (often described incorrectly as Fowler-type). The engines had circular radiators giving the appearance of radials, and a retractable ladder was provided for access to the lofty cockpit, where pilot and radar observer sat back-to-back with an excellent all-round view. A 13-mm (0.51-in) MG 131 was provided for rear defence. In the centre fuselage were three tanks housing 2600 litres (572 Imp gal).

The He 219 V1 (first prototype) made its maiden flight on 15 November 1942, and demonstrated outstanding handling and performance. The only real problem was poor yaw/roll stability, rectified in the third aircraft by enlarging the tail and extending the rear fuselage. There then began a process of development and tinkering with the armament and equipment that became so complex that today it is impossible to unravel. Even during the war the RLM (air ministry) asked whether the profusion of types and designations could be simplified. The prototypes flew with a recorded 29 different variations of armament, while the plans for a manufacturing programme were thrown into disarray by repeated air raids on Rostock in March and April 1942, which twice destroyed virtually all the He 219 drawings. These attacks prompted Heinkel to plan for production at Vienna-Schwechat, fuselages being supplied from Mielec in Poland; but continued bitter opposition, led by Generalfeldmarschall Erhard Milch, repeatedly delayed any production of what any impartial observer must have concluded was an outstanding aircraft.

Competition and contracts

Back in August 1942 Kammhuber had urged Heinkel to think in terms of a complete operational *Gruppe* (wing) by 1 April 1943, but at that date the sum total of He 219s was five prototypes. In the first week of 1943 the third prototype He 219 was flown in mock combat against a Junkers Ju 188 (a type favoured as a night-fighter by Milch), leading to a highly biased RLM report which put in all the He 219's faults and omitted the enthusiastic comments of test pilots. It even suggested the Messerschmitt Bf 110 as an alternative to the new fighter. Nevertheless, later in that month Heinkel did receive the first production contract, for 127 aircraft.

On 25 March 1943 came a more detailed fly-off between an He 219 (probably the V4, with FuG 212 Lichtenstein C-1 radar), flown by the *Gruppenkommandeur* of I/NJG 1, Major Wernher Streib, and a Ju 88S and a Dornier Do 217N. The Dornier soon withdrew, but the Junkers was flown by a pilot as famous as Streib, Oberst Wiktor von

Lossberg of the technical staff. Brilliant as von Lossberg was, he had to concede defeat to the He 219, which by this time was becoming known as the Uhu (owl). The initial pre-series He 219A-0 was delivered from late May 1943 in He 219A-0R1 and R2 sub-types, respectively with the belly tray housing four MK 108s or four MK 103s. Both guns were of 30-mm calibre, but the MK 108 was a compact low-velocity weapon weighing 59 kg (130 lb) while the MK 103 was a massive gun weighing 145 kg (320 lb) and of tremendous power. Wing guns usually remained MG 151/20s. The pilot had a two-pronged control column, partly to ease the choice of either hand and partly to carry more switches and triggers. Guns were fired by the right hand, the top button firing the fuselage guns and the front trigger those in the wings. A further addition in at least one He 219A-0 was a compressed-air ejection seat for both occupants, the first in service in the world. There was an MF radio wire from the cockpit mast to each fin, but these were no real problem in emergency escape, and Heinkel was in fact looking ahead to the time when the He 219 would be jet-propelled. This also explained his original choice of nosewheel-type landing gear.

Five-kill debut

Initial deliveries went to I/NJG 1 at Venlo, on the Dutch frontier, where Streib determined to show what the type could do. It had C-1 radar, the intermediate set that followed FuG 202 and used the same group of small dipole aerials tuned to the 490 MHz frequency, but with two displays showing a direct view and a plan. The first combat mission was flown by Streib himself with backseater Fischer on the night of 11/12 June 1943 in He 219A-0 G9 + FB. The mission was an epic, for the Uhu shot down five RAF heavy bombers. On returning, however, Streib totally misjudged the approach because of a misted windscreen. Seeing the dim runway lights at the last moment he selected full flap at too high a speed; the circuits shorted and the flaps blew back under the air load. The aircraft hit the ground so hard it broke up, but both men walked away without a scratch.

On hearing this Milch said "Yes, but perhaps Streib would have shot down just as many had he been flying another type of aircraft." But over the next 10 days these immature machines, in just six

Photographed during evaluation in Britain after the war, this He 219A-5/R2 shows the aft cockpit canopy redesigned to eliminate the provision for an aft-firing MG 131 machine-gun – a feature discarded earlier by most He 219s in operational use.

further sorties, destroyed another 20 RAF bombers, including six Mosquitoes. No Mosquito had ever before been intercepted at night, and not even Milch could ignore this achievement. The main trouble was that, despite having an assembly line at Schwechat, another about to start deliveries at Marienehe and a third being set up at the vast plant at Oranienburg (on tapering off of He 111 production), Heinkel's huge network of plants simply could not deliver He 219s. This was partly because of the fantastic profusion of sub-variants, many of them launched to meet official criticisms. It was also because of shortages of critical parts, notably engines. Whereas the basic plan was for 100 aircraft to be delivered monthly, actual acceptances hardly ever exceeded 12 per month.

Deadly jazz

Subsequent sub-types are listed separately. Few attained production status, features that did become standard including longer nacelles housing extra fuel, removal of the rear gun (except on the three-seat He 219A-5/R4), installation of the powerful FuG 220 Lichtenstein SN-2 radar with huge *Hirschgeweih* (stag's antlers) dipole aerial array, FuG 220 tail-warning radar, the ejection seat and, not least, the *schräge Musik* (literally 'slanting music' or jazz) armament. This scheme dated from 1941, having been proposed by armament engineers at Tarnewitz and tested by an NJG *Experte*, Oberleutnant Rudolf Schoenert. The idea was that oblique upward-firing guns could be brought to bear accurately in a no-deflection shot by formating below and slightly behind the enemy bomber, using a special upward-looking sight. The scheme was made possible by the amazing fact that British heavy bombers not only had not one gun firing downwards but also not one window from which a formating night-fighter could be seen. The usual *schräge Musik* installation in the He 219 comprised two MK 108s each with 100 rounds, fixed aft of the fuselage tanks at an angle of 65°.

By mid-1944 the RLM officials who had time to think about the matter realised that the campaign against the Uhu had been misguided. Milch himself had gone, production being henceforth a series of massive dictates by civilian Albert Speer. One of these, the *Notprogramm* (emergency programme) of 1 November 1944, virtually halted all aircraft manufacture except that of jets and single-engine fighters. Thus the He 219 never did become the massive programme that should have been possible. The He 219 never equipped any unit

Heinkel He 219A-5 cutaway drawing key

1 FuG 212 Lichtenstein C-1 antenna
2 FuG 220 Lichtenstein SN-2 antenna
3 Armoured nose
4 Curved one-piece windscreen
5 Windscreen washer/wiper
6 Handhold
7 Inner armourglass windscreen
8 Revi 16B gunsight
9 Armoured visor (deleted on late production models)
10 Control column
11 Revi 16A-N overhead gunsight (*schräge Musik*)
12 Folding headrest
13 Pilot's compressed-air ejection seat
14 Port instrument console
15 Footholds
16 Crew entry ladder (hinged rearwards)
17 Nosewheel leg
18 Nosewheel doors
19 Compressed air bottles
20 Nosewheel retraction gear
21 Ejection seat mounting
22 Radar operator's ejection seat
23 Flare pistol port
24 Hinged headrest
25 Aerial mast
26 FuG 212 radar screen
27 FuG 220 radar screen
28 Fuselage frame (No. 9)
29 Port wing root cannon port
30 Forward fuel tank (244 Imp gal/1100 litres)
31 Fuel filler cap
32 Suppressed D/F aerial
33 Main spar connection joint
34 Flame damper tube
35 Liquid coolant tank
36 Airscrew shaft
37 Airscrew boss
38 VDM constant-speed airscrew
39 Daimler-Benz DB 603E engine
40 Supercharger
41 Oil tank
42 Airscrew de-icing tank
43 Main wing spar
44 Starboard wing heating unit
45 Intake
46 FuG 101 radio altimeter
47 Starboard navigation light
48 Starboard aileron
49 Wing construction
50 Aileron tab
51 Flap construction
52 Flap actuator
53 Underwing inspection panels
54 Nacelle fuel tank (86 Imp gal/390 litres)
55 Main undercarriage well
56 Inboard flap section
57 Mainwheel doors
58 Undercarriage pivot point
59 Firewall
60 Starter fuel tank
61 Centre fuel tank (110 Imp gal/500 litres)
62 Fuel filler cap
63 Fuselage frame (no. 17)
64 Wing/fuselage aft attachment point
65 Port 20-mm MG 151 cannon
66 Wing/fuselage main attachment point
67 Ammunition troughs (300 rpg; wing root and ventral port rear cannon)
68 Ammunition trough (300 rpg; ventral port forward cannon)
69 Airscrew de-icing tank
70 Oil tank
71 Engine accessories
72 Engine bearer
73 Daimler-Benz DB 603E engine

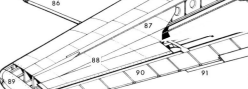

74 Liquid coolant tank
75 Controllable radiator gills
76 Airscrew boss
77 VDM constant-speed airscrew
78 Armoured-front annular radiator
79 Flame damper tube
80 Supercharger intake trunking
81 Port wing heating unit
82 Flap actuating jack
83 Aileron control quadrant
84 Landing light
85 Aileron tab control linkage
86 Pitot tube
87 Main wing spar
88 Wing skinning
89 Port navigation light
90 Port aileron
91 Fixed trim tab (port side only)
92 Auxiliary aileron tab
93 Twin mainwheel undercarriage
94 Mainwheel doors
95 Mainwheel leg
96 Starter fuel tank
97 Undercarriage retraction jack

106 Twin oblique-mounted 30-mm MK 108 cannon (*schräge Musik*)
107 Electrical supply cables (starboard fuselage wall)
108 Compressed air cylinders
109 Maintenance platform
110 Ventral antenna
111 FuG 25A (IFF) aerial
112 Service entry hatch
113 Walkway
114 Main electrical compartment
115 Crew escape dinghy
116 D/F loop (homing approach)
117 BLO 30/U fuselage heating and tailplane de-icing unit
118 Heating ducts
119 Fuselage frame (no. 31)
120 Tail unit control linkage
121 Intake
122 Tailplane construction
123 Aerials
124 Tailfin construction
125 Starboard rudder
126 Rudder tab
127 Rudder control hinge
128 Elevator construction
129 Elevator trim tab
130 Flettner auxiliary tab
131 FuG 220 tail-warning antenna
132 Trailing-aerial tube
133 Tail navigation light
134 Perspex tail cone

135 Tail bumper
136 Fuselage frame (no. 33)/tailplane attachment
137 Port elevator
138 Rudder tab hinge fairing
139 Port rudder
140 Built-in aerial (port tailfin leading-edge)
141 Tailfin skinning
142 Ventral weapons tray
143 Fuselage frame (no. 20)
144 Ventral maintenance hatch
145 Main junction boxes
146 Weapons access hatches
147 Ammunition feed chutes
148 Rear (inboard) 20-mm MG 151 cannon
149 Forward (outboard) 20-mm MG 151 cannon
150 Blast tubes
151 Gun sighting/correction hatch
152 Cannon ports

Heinkel He 219 variants

He 219 V1: first prototype, 1305.0-kW (1,750-hp) DB 603As, originally unarmed, later two MG 151/20 and pivoted MG 131; provision for two rear barbettes
He 219 V3: first with longer fuselage and larger tail; **V5** with C-1 radar; **V6** with six MG 151/15s and barbettes eliminated
He 219A-0: pre-production series, most with DB 603A, 14 armament schemes, at least one with ejection seats
He 219A-1: planned production with 1342.3-kW (1,800-hp) DB 603E; one only
He 219A-2: first production version, two-seater with DB 603As; basic armament two MK 108 and four MG 151/20, but following *Rüstsatz* kits offered variations: **R1** six MG 151/20; **R2** four MK 103 and two MG 151/20; **R3** four MK 108 and two MG 151/20; **R4** four MG 151/20 and two MK 108 oblique

He 219A-3: fighter-bomber with three crew and 1416.8-kW (1,900-hp) DB 603Gs; not built
He 219A-4: long-span reconnaissance-bomber with Jumo 222s; not built
He 219A-5: major production version, initially DB 603As, most 1342.3-kW (1,800-hp) DB 603Es, usual armament six MG 151/20 and two MK 108 oblique but many R-kits and other variations, **R4** adding third cockpit with raised canopy and pivoted MG 131
He 219A-6: lightweight 'anti-Mosquito' version, 11950 kg (26,345 lb) loaded, DB 603L two-stage engines with MW50 and GM 1 boost 650 km/h (404 mph) at up to 12000 m (39,370 ft)
He 219A-7: final production version 1416.8-kW (1,900-hp) DB 603Gs, all with two MK 108 oblique plus; **R1** two MK 108 wings plus or six forward-firing MK 108]; **R3** two MG 151/20 wings and two MG 151/20 plus two MK 108 ventral]; **R4** two MG 151/20 wings and two more ventral
He 319: unbuilt multi-role derivative
He 419: various derived projects culminating in **He 419B-1/R1**, six of which were flown (no picture); He 319 tail, very long-span wing of 59 m² (635 sq ft), two MG 151/20 wings and four MK 108 ventral 679 km/h (422 mph) to 13600 m (44,619 ft)
He 219B: series of developed long-span machines with extended fuselage, most DB 603As though planned for Jumo 222
He 219C: long-span wing of He 219B combined with totally new longer fuselage with four-seat pressure cabin at front and gunner in HDL 131V tail turret (four MG 131);
He 219C-1 night-fighter with two MK 108 under cockpit, two oblique behind cockpit and two MG 151/20 wings; **He 219C-2** fighter-bomber with two forward MK 103 and three SC 500-kg (1,102-lb) bombs under fuselage
Hü 211: high reconnaissance aircraft designed by Dr-Ing Hütter with the He 219 fuselage and tail married to 24.54-m (80-ft 6-in) wooden wing, tremendous range, speed and height but destroyed before completion

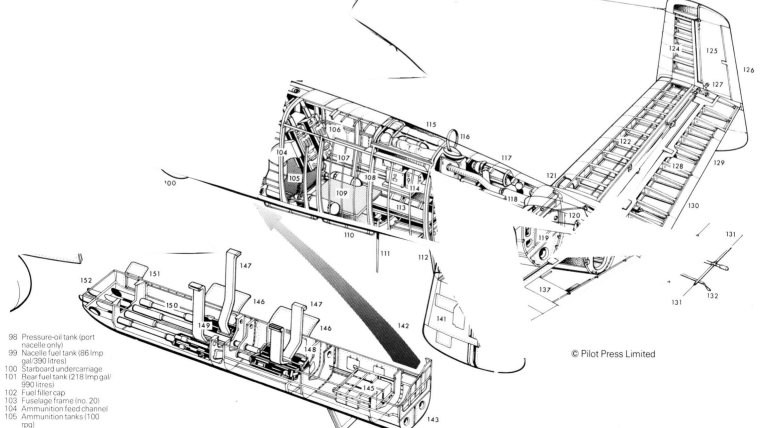

98 Pressure-oil tank (port nacelle only)
99 Nacelle fuel tank (86 Imp gal/390 litres)
100 Starboard undercarriage
101 Rear fuel tank (218 Imp gal/990 litres)
102 Fuel filler cap
103 Fuselage frame (no. 20)
104 Ammunition feed channel
105 Ammunition tanks (100 rpg)

© Pilot Press Limited

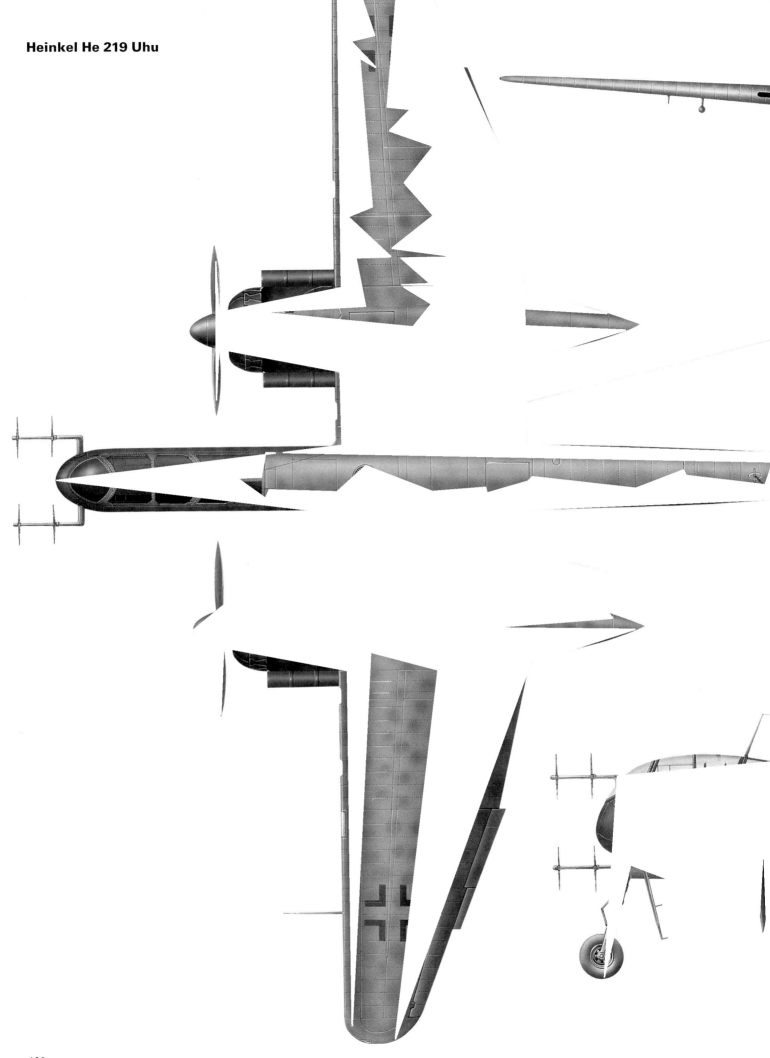

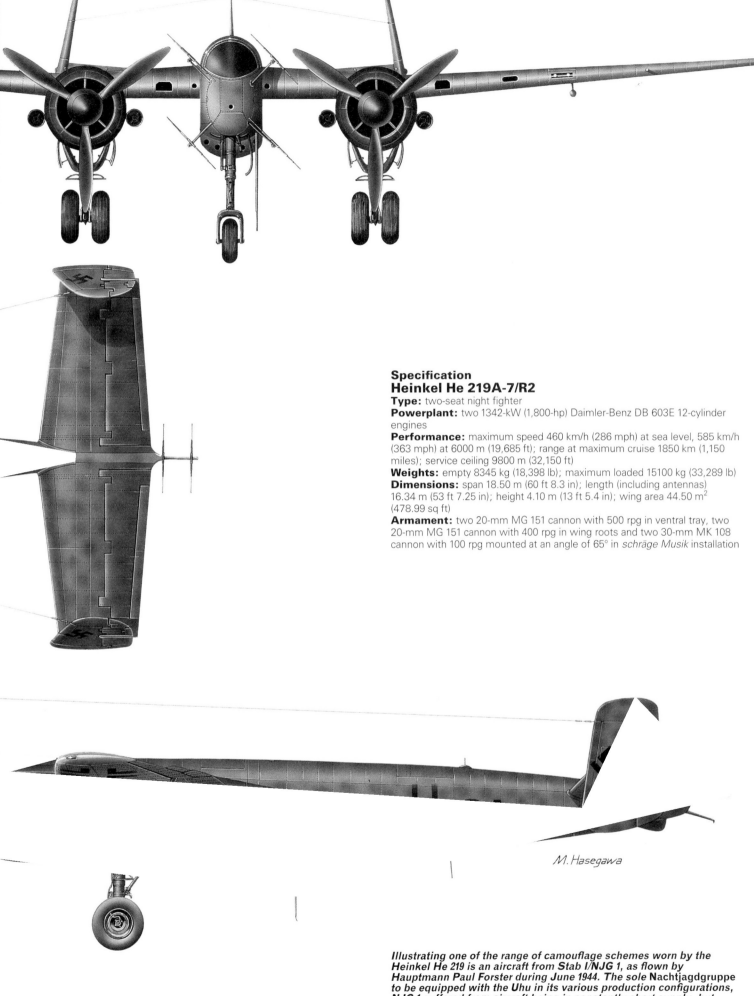

Specification
Heinkel He 219A-7/R2
Type: two-seat night fighter
Powerplant: two 1342-kW (1,800-hp) Daimler-Benz DB 603E 12-cylinder engines
Performance: maximum speed 460 km/h (286 mph) at sea level, 585 km/h (363 mph) at 6000 m (19,685 ft); range at maximum cruise 1850 km (1,150 miles); service ceiling 9800 m (32,150 ft)
Weights: empty 8345 kg (18,398 lb); maximum loaded 15100 kg (33,289 lb)
Dimensions: span 18.50 m (60 ft 8.3 in); length (including antennas) 16.34 m (53 ft 7.25 in); height 4.10 m (13 ft 5.4 in); wing area 44.50 m² (478.99 sq ft)
Armament: two 20-mm MG 151 cannon with 500 rpg in ventral tray, two 20-mm MG 151 cannon with 400 rpg in wing roots and two 30-mm MK 108 cannon with 100 rpg mounted at an angle of 65° in *schräge Musik* installation

M. Hasegawa

Illustrating one of the range of camouflage schemes worn by the Heinkel He 219 is an aircraft from Stab I/NJG 1, as flown by Hauptmann Paul Forster during June 1944. The sole Nachtjagdgruppe to be equipped with the Uhu in its various production configurations, NJG 1 suffered from aircraft being in constantly short supply, but nevertheless achieved good results against the RAF's night bombers until meeting its match in the form of the night-fighting Mosquito.

Heinkel He 219 Uhu

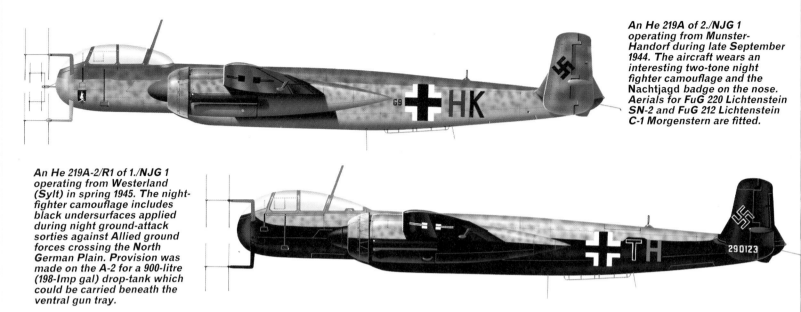

An He 219A of 2./NJG 1 operating from Munster-Handorf during late September 1944. The aircraft wears an interesting two-tone night fighter camouflage and the Nachtjagd badge on the nose. Aerials for FuG 220 Lichtenstein SN-2 and FuG 212 Lichtenstein C-1 Morgenstern are fitted.

An He 219A-2/R1 of 1./NJG 1 operating from Westerland (Sylt) in spring 1945. The night-fighter camouflage includes black undersurfaces applied during night ground-attack sorties against Allied ground forces crossing the North German Plain. Provision was made on the A-2 for a 900-litre (198-Imp gal) drop-tank which could be carried beneath the ventral gun tray.

except I/NJG 1 (ones and twos reached II/NJG 1, NJGr 10, Erg./JG 2 and NJSt Finnland and Norwegen, but the numbers were trivial). By June 1944 I/NJG 1 had 20 Uhus, almost all of the current production He 219A-2 and He 219A-5 types. By this time RAF Mosquitoes were making themselves felt not only as pathfinders and bombers but also as intruders, and the number of He 219s that failed to return from night sorties climbed significantly. Previous attrition had been very low, though I/NJG 1 lost three *Kommandeure* in succession in 1944, two of them having been killed in mid-air collisions. In January 1945 I/NJG 1's establishment was up to 64 aircraft, and total deliveries of all versions reached 268, plus about 20 development aircraft modified to acceptable operational standard by field units and a further six not on any official documents which were assembled and put into action by I/NJG 1 from replacement components and spares.

Operational assessments

So, how does one assess this controversial aircraft? There is no doubt it was a 1940 design of exceptional merit which could in a more ordered society have been developed for many roles with telling effect, as was the UK's Mosquito. The mass of sub-types merely diluted from the main production effort, and the consistent failure of Daimler-Benz and Junkers to deliver the hoped-for engines killed the advanced versions that would have kept the He 219 in front. As for the aircraft itself, opinions are divided.

According to Gebhard Aders (author of *Geschichte der deutschen Nachtjagd*) the He 219 "never achieved the values given in its manual. With almost full tanks and full armament the He 219 could not get above 8000 m (26,247 ft) . . . With Lichtenstein and flame dampers the maximum fell to about 500 km/h (311 mph) at this height . . ." On the other hand he states "The 219 was the only German night-fighter that could still climb on one engine, and even go round again for another landing attempt", a belief echoed by many former Uhu pilots. Yet that greatest of test pilots, Captain E. M. 'Winkle' Brown, who flew several captured He 219s, wrote in *Air International* that the type was "somewhat overrated . . . It suffered from what is perhaps the nastiest characteristic that any twin-engined aircraft can have: it was underpowered. This defect makes take-off a critical manoeuvre in the event of an engine failing, and a landing with one engine out can be equally critical. There certainly could be no overshooting with the He 219 in that condition."

This marginal performance is the more remarkable when it is remembered that the DB 603 was the largest of the inverted V-12 engines used by the Luftwaffe, with cubic capacity 65 per cent greater than that of the Merlin. The problem lay squarely in the growth of systems and equipment with which the Uhu was packed, so that a typical He 219A-7 version weighed more empty than any Ju 88 night-fighter, and more than a Mosquito fully loaded!

The final A-series He 219 was the A-7, the most important model to reach operational status. Utilising the improved DB 603G powerplant, this heavily-armoured high-altitude night fighter provided ejector seats for both crew members, improved avionics and increased armament. One reached I/NJG 1.

Messerschmitt Me 262

The Me 262 was not just a revolutionary engine in a conventional airframe. The design of its wings, tail unit and firepower was years ahead of its time – the aircraft was a winner all round. Moreover, unlike some of its predecessors, it was a joy to fly.

Young German gunners, huddled around their light 20-mm and 37-mm flak weapons, could be excused for a slight lack of attention to their task at their first sight of the Messerschmitt Me 262s on the snow-covered expanses of Rheine-Hopsten air base in the autumnal sleet of 1944. In every sense the sleek shark-like fuselage, mottled ochre and olive green, and beset with razor wings from which hung the huge turbojets, were a portent of the future. The noise, the high-pitched whine and howl, of the Jumo 004B-1 turbines, the swirls of snow, the hot paraffin-tainted blast: all were of a different time. But this was the present: beset by Allied air superiority on all sides, the skies over Westphalia were dangerous elements for operations of the Luftwaffe's dwindling strength. Black-helmeted pilots, crouched forward in the narrow cockpits of their Messerschmitt Me 262A-2a fighter-bombers, anxiously scanned the overcast for the first signs of the diving Hawker Tempests, North American P-51s or Supermarine Spitfires, as they coaxed throttles and jabbed brakes prior to take-off. Flak gunners trained their pieces along the approach paths, watched for the red Very lights that would bring them to instant action, and heard the thunder of the departing jets. With such machines, how could Germany lose the war in the air? Such a thought must have raced through minds. But the job of a flak gunner is humble, and he and his comrades could have had no insight into the extraordinary train of events and decisions that were instrumental in the denial in quantity of Germany's most potent air

weapon of World War II. In the heady days of 1941, when the Messerschmitt Me 262 series was born, no one person in the Third Reich could foresee the need, the desperate need, for an outstanding aircraft with which to wrest air supremacy from the hands of the enemy.

The Heinkel concern was already deeply involved in the development of a fighter powered by the new reaction-turbine engines when, on 4 January 1939, the Augsburg-based Messerschmitt AG received orders from the German air ministry (RLM, or Reichsluftfahrtministerium) to produce specifications for a similar type of aircraft. Two plans were drawn up by a team led by Dipl.Ing.Waldemar Voigt, one for a twin-boom configuration and the other for a pod-and-boom design. Neither of the two then existing turbojet designs was considered to be powerful enough for a single-engine fighter, and as a result Voigt was forced to turn to the design of a twin-engine aircraft.

Early development

Heinkel had already turned to twin engines with the development of the promising He 280 series powered by the six-stage axial-flow

*Messerschmitt Me 262B-1a/U1 under test with the **USAAF** coding of FE-610 (Foreign Evaluation) at Wright Field in 1946. The aircraft was captured by the British following possible service with the 10./NJG 11. The armament installed was two 30-mm MK 108A-3s and two 20-mm MG 151/20 cannon: AI radar was an FuG 218 (Neptun V).*

Messerschmitt Me 262

Messerschmitt Me 262A-1a fighter in the colours of the 9.Staffel Jagdgeschwader Nr 7, based at Parchim in early 1945 under 1.Jagddivision of I Jagdkorps in the defence of the Reich. After capture at the end of the war this particular aircraft, Nr 500491, was given the code FE-111 by the technical branch of the USAAF for evaluation. In the course of 1979 the aircraft was stripped down, refurbished and rebuilt in over 6,000 hours of work, and placed on display at the National Air and Space Museum, Washington DC, where it remains to this day. The illustration accentuates the Me 262's sleek lines: the airframe alone, in particular the wing design, was considered by the Allies to be far ahead of their own attainments in the field of high-speed flight.

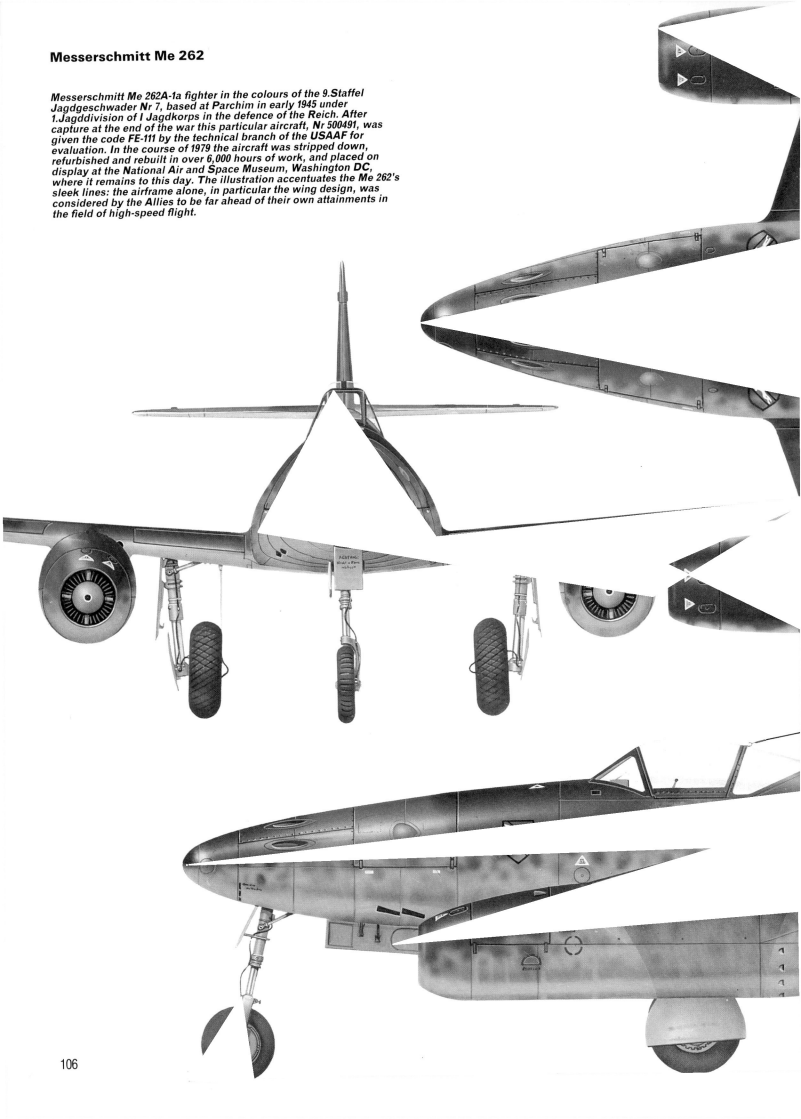

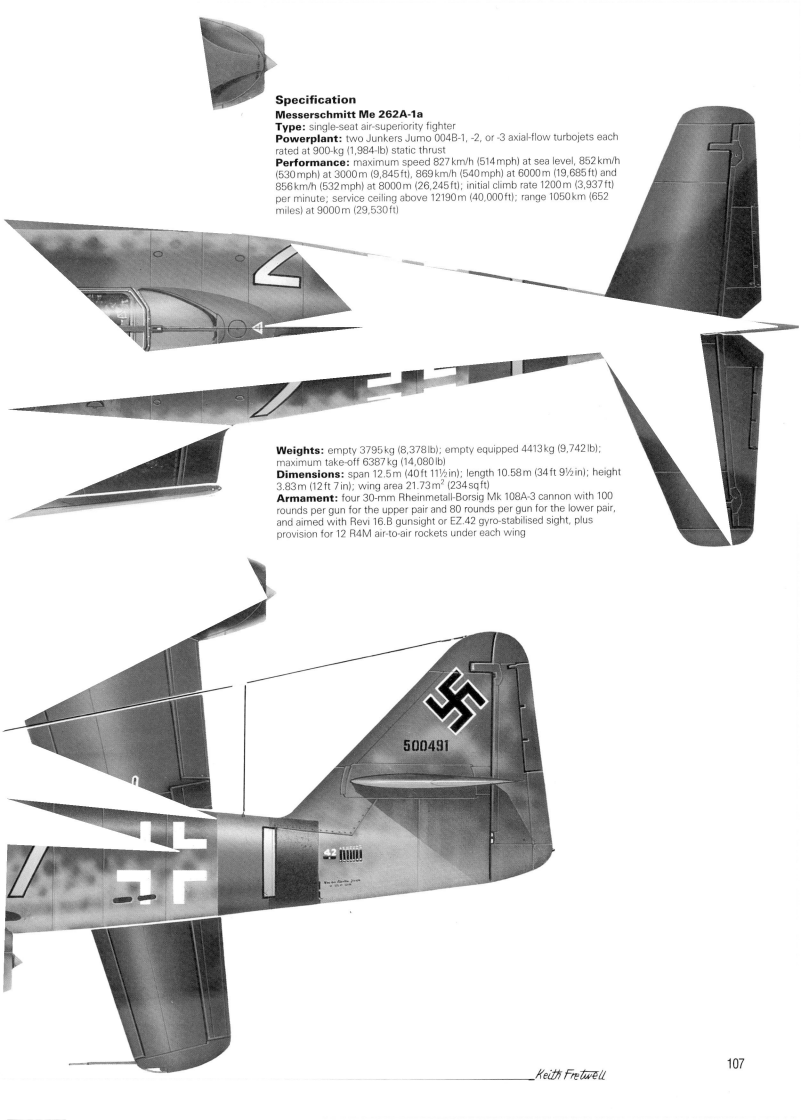

Specification
Messerschmitt Me 262A-1a

Type: single-seat air-superiority fighter

Powerplant: two Junkers Jumo 004B-1, -2, or -3 axial-flow turbojets each rated at 900-kg (1,984-lb) static thrust

Performance: maximum speed 827 km/h (514 mph) at sea level, 852 km/h (530 mph) at 3000 m (9,845 ft), 869 km/h (540 mph) at 6000 m (19,685 ft) and 856 km/h (532 mph) at 8000 m (26,245 ft); initial climb rate 1200 m (3,937 ft) per minute; service ceiling above 12190 m (40,000 ft); range 1050 km (652 miles) at 9000 m (29,530 ft)

Weights: empty 3795 kg (8,378 lb); empty equipped 4413 kg (9,742 lb); maximum take-off 6387 kg (14,080 lb)

Dimensions: span 12.5 m (40 ft 11½ in); length 10.58 m (34 ft 9½ in); height 3.83 m (12 ft 7 in); wing area 21.73 m² (234 sq ft)

Armament: four 30-mm Rheinmetall-Borsig Mk 108A-3 cannon with 100 rounds per gun for the upper pair and 80 rounds per gun for the lower pair, and aimed with Revi 16.B gunsight or EZ.42 gyro-stabilised sight, plus provision for 12 R4M air-to-air rockets under each wing

Keith Fretwell

In the quest for maximum rates of climb for point-defence work some Messerschmitt Me 262s were modified for development programmes with liquid-fuelled Walter rockets. Illustrated is the Me 262C-1a first flown by Gerd Linder on 27 February 1945. The type arrived too late to enter service, although Major Heinz Bär of III/EJG 2 claimed a P-47 in this Me 262C-1a in the spring of 1945.

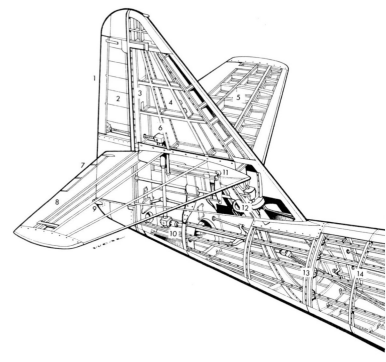

BMW P 3302 engines, and Germany's first definitive jet fighter, the Heinkel He 280 V2 prototype, lifted off from Rostock-Marienehe's runway at 15.18 on 30 March 1941 with Fritz Schäfer at the controls. And within six weeks of this maiden flight the UK too flew her first jet aircraft: powered by a Whittle-designed W1X centrifugal-type turbojet of 390-kg (860-lb) thrust, the Gloster E.28/39 took to the air on 15 May. Back at Augsburg work had proceeded slowly on the design of what at first bore none of the hallmarks that graced the Heinkel product, or gave any hint of the fineness of line that was a characteristic of Messerschmitt's piston-engine fighters. The design was termed the Messerschmitt P 1065 VI and, in the absence of its twin jet engines, was fitted with a 545-kW (730-hp) Junkers Jumo 210G driving a two-blade propeller. This ugly duckling was then renamed the Messerschmitt Me 262 V1, and was taken into the air for the first time on 18 April 1941. Test pilots Karl Baur and Fritz Wendel reported no vices on subsequent flight programmes: no urgency was attached to the flight development of the Me 262 V1 during that summer, for indeed little priority was deemed necessary. Of far greater import for the Messerschmitt concern were the improvements to the Bf 109 and Bf 110 combat types, and the development of their replacements.

The engines for the Me 262 V1 eventually arrived from Spandau in mid-November 1941: these were BMW 003s each of 550-kg (1,213-lb) static thrust. But on his first flight with the BMW 003s Wendel suffered a double flame-out shortly after take-off, and was forced to put PC+UA down with some damage. Fortunately, an alternative to the touchy BMWs was available. This was the Junkers Jumo 004 which had been developed by Dr Anselm Franz's team since its award of a contract as far back as July 1939 for a development specification. In their adherence to axial compressors, German engine designers showed much courage and foresight: this type of compressor was difficult to construct and balance, and was susceptible to vibration and could be damaged far more easily than the tough centrifugal type of compressor. But it became apparent that the acceleration rates, fuel efficiency, power output, and drag co-efficients of axial-flow turbojets far exceeded the figures produced by the tougher, and sometimes more reliable, centrifugal types. By August 1941 the Jumo 004 was giving 600-kg (1,323-lb) static thrust, and many of the earlier problems had been cured.

Jumo 004s were installed on the Messerschmitt Me 262 V3 (PC+UC), and this aircraft, bereft of the piston engine and still with tailwheel landing gear, left Leipheim's runway on the morning of 18 July 1942 in Wendel's experienced hands. It looked correct in every way, and it flew beautifully, and henceforth the fortunes of the Mes-

serschmitt Me 262 were to rise at the expense of its nearest rival, the Heinkel He 280, which suffered a series of setbacks until its eventual cancellation in March 1943.

In the Luftwaffe's interest

Service test pilots of the Erprobungsstelle (test establishment) at Rechlin showed interest in the Me 262 from its earliest days. It was largely at their instigation that Messerschmitt received contracts to produce a number of prototypes for weapons and engine tests. The experienced Major Wolfgang Späte had already reported his enthusiastic findings when the General der Jagdflieger, Adolf Galland, flew the Me 262 V4 on 22 May 1943, to become unequivocal in his

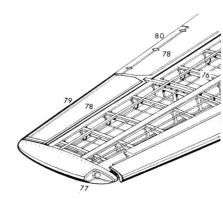

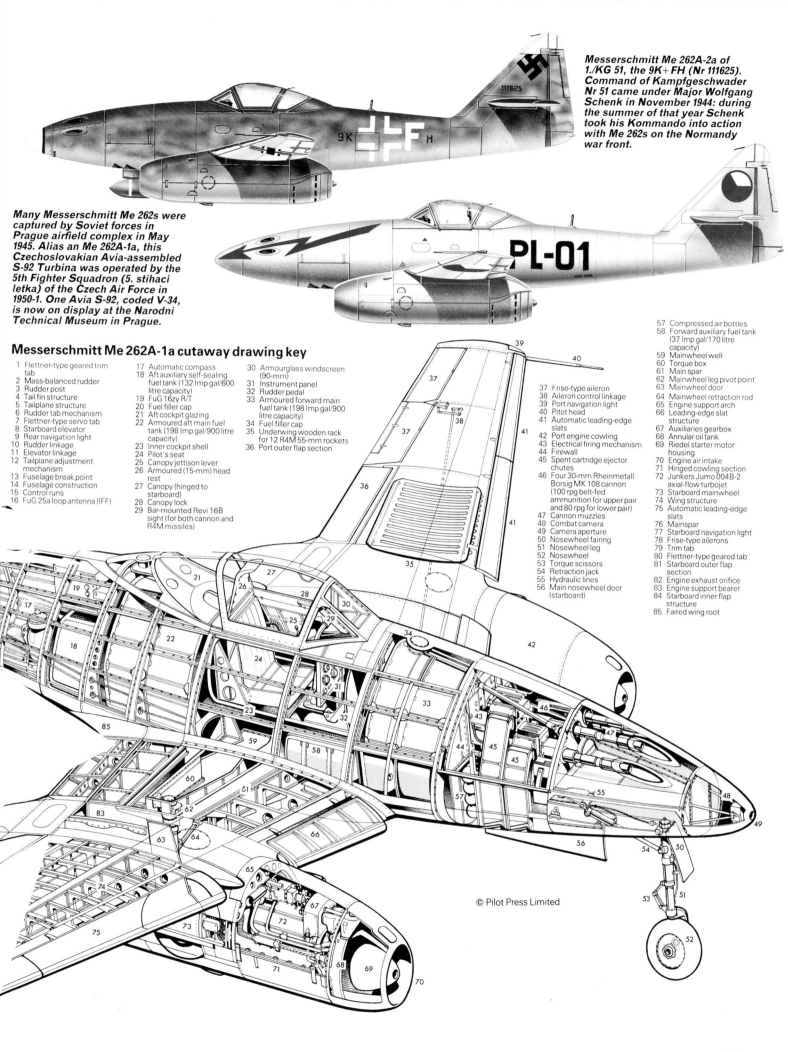

Messerschmitt Me 262A-2a of 1./KG 51, the 9K+FH (Nr 111625). Command of Kampfgeschwader Nr 51 came under Major Wolfgang Schenk in November 1944: during the summer of that year Schenk took his Kommando into action with Me 262s on the Normandy war front.

Many Messerschmitt Me 262s were captured by Soviet forces in Prague airfield complex in May 1945. Alias an Me 262A-1a, this Czechoslovakian Avia-assembled S-92 Turbina was operated by the 5th Fighter Squadron (5. stihaci letka) of the Czech Air Force in 1950-1. One Avia S-92, coded V-34, is now on display at the Narodni Technical Museum in Prague.

Messerschmitt Me 262A-1a cutaway drawing key

1 Flettner-type geared trim tab
2 Mass-balanced rudder
3 Rudder post
4 Tail fin structure
5 Tailplane structure
6 Rudder tab mechanism
7 Flettner-type servo tab
8 Starboard elevator
9 Rear navigation light
10 Rudder linkage
11 Elevator linkage
12 Tailplane adjustment mechanism
13 Fuselage break point
14 Fuselage construction
15 Control runs
16 FuG 25a loop antenna (IFF)
17 Automatic compass
18 Aft auxiliary self-sealing fuel tank (132 lmp gal/600 litre capacity)
19 FuG 16zy R/T
20 Fuel filler cap
21 Aft cockpit glazing
22 Armoured aft main fuel tank (198 lmp gal/900 litre capacity)
23 Inner cockpit shell
24 Pilot's seat
25 Canopy jettison lever
26 Armoured (15-mm) head rest
27 Canopy (hinged to starboard)
28 Canopy lock
29 Bar-mounted Revi 16B sight (for both cannon and R4M missiles)
30 Armourglass windscreen (90-mm)
31 Instrument panel
32 Rudder pedal
33 Armoured forward main fuel tank (198 lmp gal/900 litre capacity)
34 Fuel filler cap
35 Underwing wooden rack for 12 R4M 55-mm rockets
36 Port outer flap section
37 Frise-type aileron
38 Aileron control linkage
39 Port navigation light
40 Pitot head
41 Automatic leading-edge slats
42 Port engine cowling
43 Electrical firing mechanism
44 Firewall
45 Spent cartridge ejector chutes
46 Four 30-mm Rheinmetall Borsig MK 108 cannon (100 rpg belt-fed ammunition for upper pair and 80 rpg for lower pair)
47 Cannon muzzles
48 Combat camera
49 Camera aperture
50 Nosewheel fairing
51 Nosewheel leg
52 Nosewheel
53 Torque scissors
54 Retraction jack
55 Hydraulic lines
56 Main nosewheel door (starboard)
57 Compressed air bottles
58 Forward auxiliary fuel tank (37 lmp gal/170 litre capacity)
59 Mainwheel well
60 Torque box
61 Main spar
62 Mainwheel leg pivot point
63 Mainwheel door
64 Mainwheel retraction rod
65 Engine support arch
66 Leading-edge slat structure
67 Auxiliaries gearbox
68 Annular oil tank
69 Riedel starter motor housing
70 Engine air intake
71 Hinged cowling section
72 Junkers Jumo 004B-2 axial-flow turbojet
73 Starboard mainwheel
74 Wing structure
75 Automatic leading-edge slats
76 Mainspar
77 Starboard navigation light
78 Frise-type ailerons
79 Trim tab
80 Flettner-type geared tab
81 Starboard outer flap section
82 Engine exhaust orifice
83 Engine support bearer
84 Starboard inner flap structure
85 Faired wing root

© Pilot Press Limited

constant praise for this revolutionary aircraft. At a conference in Berlin on 25 May it was suggested that the piston-engine Messerschmitt Me 209A be cancelled, and that all efforts be directed to the production of the Me 262: three days later a production order for 100 was made. But other events now took a hand. On 17 August 1943 the US 8th Air Force's attack on Regensburg destroyed much of the embryonic Me 262 production lines, forcing Messerschmitt AG to move its jet development centres to Oberammergau, near the Bavarian Alps. The delay occasioned by the move was increased by a chronic shortage in the supply of skilled labour, and production slipped by many months.

In the meantime the Me 262 V5 introduced the tricycle landing gear that was to become standard, only on this prototype the nose-gear was fixed. The definitive Me 262 V6 (Jumo 004Bs) flew on 17 October 1943: the VI+AA featured a retractable tricycle landing gear, gun bays and blast ports, the electrically operated tailplane, and the beautiful high-speed wing with automatic leading-edge slats and trailing-edge flaps.

Can it carry bombs?

By the autumn of 1943 Germany was on the defensive in the USSR and Italy, and was being subjected to furious aerial assault by day and by night: not least of Hitler's concerns was when and where the Allies would strike in north-west Europe. During the amphibious invasions in North Africa, on Sicily, and recently of Italy at Salerno and Reggio, Allied air power had kept the Luftwaffe and the German naval forces at bay, and had thus prevented the loss of shipping that could have jeopardised the entire extent of these operations. Therefore nobody could have been surprised when many senior commanders, including Hitler himself, mooted the concept of the Messerschmitt Me 262 as a fighter-bomber as opposed to an interceptor: the idea was tactically sound. It was at Insterberg, in East Prussia, on 26 November 1943, that Hitler watched the dove-grey VI+AA being put through its party tricks by the able Gerd Linder. Present was Professor Willy Messerschmitt to answer the inevitable query from the fascinated Hitler: yes, indeed, the Me 262 could carry up to 1,000 kg (2,205 lb) of bombs with uncomplicated conversion work completed within two weeks per unit! So from this day the Messerschmitt Me 262 was destined to play a dual role: that of a fighter-bomber and that of a pure air-superiority fighter. Neither the role nor the aircraft could by now have had any influence on the outcome

Flight shot of an Me 262A-1a of III Gruppe of Ergänzungs-Jagdgeschwader Nr 2 (III/EJG 2). This powerful conversion unit, based at Lechfeld, flew many sorties against Allied aircraft in the spring of 1945, with Leutnant Bell downing a P-38 Lightning with this particular aircraft on 21 March 1945. The EJG 2 was formed on 2 November 1944.

of the war. It was too late to start a major production scheme: oil and aviation kerosene, precious alloys, and skilled airframe and engine specialists were at a premium. The Messerschmitt Me 262 had been recognised in its full potential, but too late in the war.

Service conversion of the Me 262 was placed under Hauptmann Werner Thierfelder's Erprobungskommando 262 at Lechfeld, to where the unit moved on 21 December 1943: pilots were drawn from 8. and 9./ZG 26. The EKdo 262 was given a batch of pre-production Me 262A-0 aircraft, and finally got into the swim of operations in the early summer of 1944. Thierfelder was killed in combat with 15th Air Force Mustangs over Bavaria on 18 July, and his place was taken by Hauptmann Neumeyer. The RAF brought back its first confirmation of the Me 262's existence on 25 July, when a de Havilland Mosquito of No. 544 (PR) Squadron was intercepted near Munich: Flight Lieutenant A. E. Wall and his navigator Flying Officer A. S. Lobban escaped with difficulty.

Equipped with Messerschmitt Me 262A-2a fighter-bombers, the Einsatzkommando Schenk (Major Wolfgang Schenk) was formed at

Third Messerschmitt Me 262 prototype. The Me 262 V3 was the first prototype to fly on turbojet power alone, the date being 18 July 1942. It was transferred to the German Aviation Experimental Establishment (DVL) in April 1944 for high-speed flight testing, and was written off on 12 September 1944 following damage in an air attack.

Messerschmitt Me 262

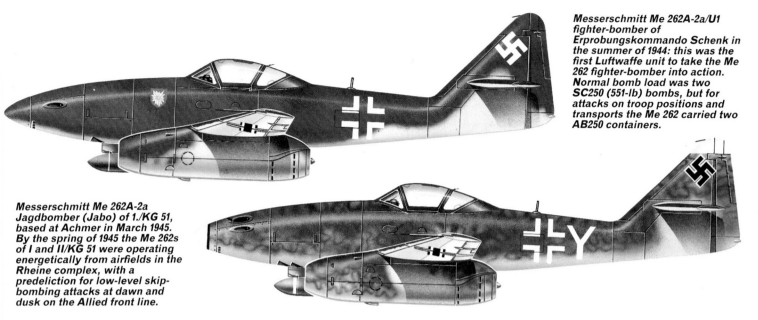

Messerschmitt Me 262A-2a/U1 fighter-bomber of Erprobungskommando Schenk in the summer of 1944: this was the first Luftwaffe unit to take the Me 262 fighter-bomber into action. Normal bomb load was two SC250 (551-lb) bombs, but for attacks on troop positions and transports the Me 262 carried two AB250 containers.

Messerschmitt Me 262A-2a Jagdbomber (Jabo) of 1./KG 51, based at Achmer in March 1945. By the spring of 1945 the Me 262s of I and II/KG 51 were operating energetically from airfields in the Rheine complex, with a predeliction for low-level skip-bombing attacks at dawn and dusk on the Allied front line.

Lechfeld in July, before posting to the Normandy invasion front: the unit was based at Châteaudun, Etampes and Creil, before pulling back to Juvincourt, near Reims, in late August. It was on 28 August 1944 that Allied fighter pilots downed the first Me 262 to be lost in combat: near Brussels, Major Joseph Myers and his wingman, Lieutenant M. D. Croy Jr, of the US 78th Fighter Group bounced Oberfeldwebel Lauer's Me 262 to force it down in a field. Operations by Einsatzkommando Schenk continued in a desultory manner until its incorporation into the I Gruppe of Kampfgeschwader 51, which began combat operations from Rheine-Hopsten under Major Unrau in October 1944. The value of the Me 262 as a reconnaissance aircraft was soon recognised, and a few went to the Einsatzkommando Braunegg, and to Nahaufklärungsgruppen 1 and 6.

Hitler's firm insistence on the Messerschmitt Me 262 being the property of the General der Kampfflieger (Marienfeld) denied Galland the opportunity of forming the first fighter unit until September 1944. One of Germany's finest fighter pilots, Major Walter Nowotny, formed the Kommando Nowotny based at Achmer and Hesepe near Osnabrück, to fly its first mission against Allied bombers and fighters on 3 October 1944. The Messerschmitt Me 262A-1a (two Jumo 004B-1 turbojets) formed the establishment of around 30. The armament was exceptionally potent and consisted of four Rheinmetall-Borsig MK 108A-3 30-mm cannon; the pilot was protected by 9-mm back armour, and a 90-mm armour-glass windscreen. With a maximum speed of 855km/h (531mph) at 8000m (26,245ft), the Me 262A-1a could outrun anything that the Allies had in their inventory, but proved to be vulnerable in the circuit pattern. Thus several Me 262s succumbed to bold Allied fighter attacks during the approach and shortly after take-off. Initially the Kommando Nowotny was given cover by III/JG 54 (Focke-Wulf Fw 190D-9s) from Varelbusch, but later some 120-140 Messerschmitt Bf 109G-10s and Bf 109K-4s and Focke-Wulfs were needed to protect I/KG 51's missions in the Rheine area in addition to very strong flak defences.

New bomber units

Kommando Nowotny disbanded shortly after the death of its leader on 8 November 1944. The potent jet, the presence of which thoroughly alarmed Allied intelligence in the west, continued to be used in penny packets on bombing attacks (with AB250 containers) on Allied front lines, reconnaissance missions, and an occasional foray against enemy fighters. In mid-November Oberst Johannes Steinhoff formed the nucleus of Jagdgeschwader 7 at Brandenburg-Briest: the III Gruppe was formed from the survivors of Kommando Nowotny, while the I/JG 7 was later formed at Parchim. Four additional bomber units were formed on 30 January 1945: these were KG(J)6, KG(J)27, KG(J)54 and KG(J)55. Of these only I/KG(J) 54 at Giebelstadt, II/KG(J) 54 at Kitzingen and III/KG(J) 6 at Prague-Ruzyne played any part in operations, usually at reasonably high loss. The only occasions on which Jagdgeschwader 7 made any impact were during the battles of 18-21 March 1945 when, using Oranienburg and Parchim, a daily average of some 40 or more sorties were put up against American bombers. A new unguided air-to-air weapon, the R4M rocket, was used for the first time on Me 262A-1a fighters during these encounters. Final day operations fell to Generalleutnant Adolf Galland's Jagdverband 44 (JV 44) at München-Riem, to the aforementioned units, and to the night-fighting Messerschmitt Me 262B-1a/U1 aircraft of 10./NJG 11 at Burg.

Over the period March 1944 to 20 April 1945 the Luftwaffe took delivery of 1,433 Me 262s, but for the Allies the impact of this fine aircraft was largely psychological. On inspection after the war's end the fact was acknowledged that in design of airframe and engine the Messerschmitt Me 262 was years ahead of aircraft of other nations, and its secrets permitted the Russians and the Anglo-Americans to accelerate development of jet fighter and bomber aircraft to the magic of Mach 1.0 and beyond over the ensuing years.

Messerschmitt Me 262 variants

Me 262 V1: first prototype (PC+UA) with single Junkers Jumo 210G piston engine; later fitted with two BMW 003 turbojets
Me 262 V2: test airframe for fitment of two BMW 003 turbojets
Me 262 V3: test airframe (PC+UC) with two Junkers Jumo 004 turbojets; first prototype to be flown by service test pilots; fourth prototype
Me 262 V4 (PC+UD) of similar configuration
Me 262 V5: fitted with two Jumo 004s, this PC+UE differed in having a fixed nosewheel, whereas previous prototypes had conventional tail wheels
Me 262 V6: definitive prototype (VI+AA) with lighter Jumo 004B-1 turbojets, and retractable tricycle landing gear, the **Me 262 V7** (VI+AB) was similar but with re-designed cockpit canopy and cockpit pressurisation; many subsequent *Versuchs* prototypes evolved for testing of engines, radio, radar, and weapons' systems
Me 262A-0: pre-production airframes based on the Me 262 V7 configuration; 23 units produced, and passed to test-centre at Rechlin and to service trials detachment (EKdo 262) in late April 1944
Me 262A-1a: standard interceptor fighter configuration with Jumo 004B-1 turbojets, four Rheinmetall-Borsig MK 108A-330-mm cannon, Revi 16.B gunsight, and FuG 16zY radio; the **Me 262A-1a/U1** designation covered three trials units with two MG 151, two MK 103 and two MK 108 cannon
Me 262A-2a: standard fighter-bomber configuration; similar to Me 262A-1a but with two Schloss 503A-1 bomb racks for two 250-kg (551-lb) bombs, and armament normally reduced to two 30-mm MK 108 cannon; the **Me 262A-2a/U2** was a trials development with Lotfe 7H bomb-sight, glazed nose, and accommodation for prone bomb-aimer
Me 262A-3a: trials models intended for close-support role
Me 262A-5a: reconnaissance-fighter with either twin nose-mounted Rb 50/30 oblique cameras, or single Rb 20/30 or Rb 75/30 ; adapted to the reconnaissance role the **Me 262A-1a/U3** was used by a number of units
Me 262B-1a: conversion trainer with dual flight controls under redesigned canopy; deletion of rear main fuel tank necessitated carriage of two 300-litre (66-Imp gal) drop-tanks on Schloss 503A-1 Wikingschiff racks
Me 262B-1a/U1: interim two-seat night-fighter with FuG 218 *Neptun V* airborne interception radar and FuG 350 ZC (*Naxos*) passive homer; fewer than a dozen in service by 1945
Me 262dB-2a: definitive night-fighter with lengthened fuselage to contain additional fuel tanks; two produce
Me 262C-1a: point-defence interceptor-fighter with twin Jumo 004B-1s supplemented by tail-mounted Walter R II-211/3 (HWK 509) bi-fuel rocket motor to give outstanding rates of climb; one trials aircraft produced
Me 262C-2b: point-defence interceptor; twin BMW 003R power units, each consisting of a BMW 003A turbojet and a BMW 718 bi-fuel rocket, fitted in place of conventional motors; one produced

Index